Selected Course Outlines and
Reading Lists from American
Colleges and Universities

Women's History

VOL. I – AMERICAN HISTORY

edited by Louise L. Stevenson

FRANKLIN AND MARSHALL COLLEGE

New Enlarged and Updated Edition

Markus Wiener Publishers
Princeton

New enlarged and updated edition, 1998

For information write to:
  Markus Wiener Publishers
  231 Nassau Street, Princeton, NJ 08542

Library of Congress Cataloging-in-Publication Data

Women's history/edited by Louise L. Stevenson—4th Updated and
  enlarged edition.
    (Selected course outlines and reading lists from American
  universities and colleges)
    Includes bibliographical references.
    Contents: v. I. American History
    ISBN 1-55876-176-4 (paper)
    1. Women—United States—History—Outlines, syllabi, etc.
  I. Stevenson Louise L.   II. Series: Selected reading lists and course
  outlines from American colleges and universities.
  HQ1410.W683   1998   98-34398
  305.4'0973—dc21   CIP

Printed in the United States of America

Table of Contents

Foreword

Several years ago wise heads predicted that no more editions of this syllabi collection would be necessary. Graduate students and scholars presumably would research syllabi in women's history on the internet. The preference for a syllabus guide in old-fashioned book form soon made itself known. Popular demand called forth this new edition.

Part of the excitement of assembling this collection every few years arises from its witness to new subjects of scholarly interest. While former editions are testament to the central position of race and class in women's history, this edition documents new understandings now available from consideration of gender and sexuality.

My thanks to everyone who contributed syllabi and reading guides for this edition. Your generosity and cooperation are vital ingredients of this project.

Louise L. Stevenson
Editor

1. One-Semester Graduate and Undergraduate Courses

History 333/Women's Studies 333--Topics in the History of American Women
Susan Porter Benson--Fall 1996

The last three decades have witnessed a remarkable flowering of women's history in the United States. Both the sheer quantity of material available and the scope of research have expanded enormously. Women's historians have grappled with difficult empirical and theoretical problems as they have studied people who: 'ives are often excluded from traditional historical sources and defined out of conventional historical paradigms. Lively debates in the field revolve around such key questions as: how can women's history be a truly multicultural undertaking? How can women's history simultaneously study women in their own right and produce a gendered history of the entire society? How can women's history best use the insights of recent literary theory? This semester we will sample recent U.S. women's history by examining works, often diverse and sometimes contradictory, on some of the central topics in the field.

Office Hours:
I will hold office hours in 230 Wood Hall from 10:00 to 12:00 on Thursdays (telephone 486-3650). I am available in my Women's Studies office, 426 Beach Hall, most of the day on Monday, Wednesday (except 9/4, 9/25, 10/16, and 11/6), and Thursday, and I would be happy to see you there. You may see me there by appointment or just drop in, but it's best to call first to see if I'm available. My Beach Hall office extension is 486-1131; that line has voice mail, and **all** telephone messages should be left there rather than in Wood Hall.

Class Format:
Attendance at all class sessions is required.

Class sessions will revolve around discussions of the reading and the issues it raises. One student will present each book to the seminar; students will present either one or two books (see below). The presentation should run about ten, and not over fifteen, minutes. I reserve the right to cut you off when fifteen minutes have passed. Because these presentations will set the tone for the discussion of the topics at hand, they will require careful preparation. Different books will demand different sorts of treatment, but some general guidelines apply in all cases:
1. Include a brief, schematic summary of the book's content, enough to give those who haven't read the book a basis for participating in the discussion.
2. Consider the author's point of view or theoretical basis as well as the types of evidence marshalled in support of the book's argument.
3. Offer a critique of the book, pointing to its strengths and weaknesses and offering an overall assessment of its contribution to women's and gender history.
4. Relate the book to the week's topic, evaluating its contribution to an understanding of the theme under consideration. You may also want to relate the book to previous weeks' discussions and/or to suggest issues on which the seminar discussion can focus.
5. Present the book in a lively way that will provoke discussion; avoid the stultifying manner of academic book reviews.

<u>Written Work:</u>
1. **Book review**: Each student must prepare a written analysis of one or two books on
   which she/he does <u>not</u> report to the class, loosely following the guidelines for the
   class reports. This paper should be no longer than three double-spaced typewritten
   pages.
   Each student will choose one of the following options:
   1. One class report and two book reviews.
   2. Two class reports and one book review. (This option will be available only after
   each student has chosen one book.)
      Students who choose this option will, after one of the class reports, write a
      critique of her/his own report and of the direction of the subsequent
      discussion. The critique should consider, among others, the following
      questions:
          a. Which points received too much attention?
          b. Which points were neglected?
          c. How might the discussion have proceeded more productively?
          d. What questions arose, either explicitly or implicitly, that deserve
          future attention in the course?
          e. How might the class report have been done differently so as to have
          been more effective and productive of discussion?
      The critique should be no longer than three double-spaced typed pages. It will
      not be revised. **Critiques are due at the next class session.**
2. **Review essay**: Each student must write a paper integrating all of the assigned reading
   for one week; this should <u>not</u> be a week in which the student gives a class report or
   writes a book review. Again, you can begin with the guidelines for the class reports,
   but in this paper you must integrate the diverse perspectives in the readings into a
   coherent discussion of the theoretical and empirical themes and problems they raise.
   This paper should not be longer than five double-spaced typed pages.

Procedures for both book reviews and review essays: The papers will be due <u>before</u> the
beginning of the class for which the reading is assigned. I will read and comment on
each paper and meet with you to discuss it. You will then revise and resubmit the
paper within a week after we meet. Submit the rough draft along with the revised
paper. Ideally, you should do the book review before the review essay.

3. **Each student must write either a bibliographic essay or a paper based on a limited
   selection of primary sources.**
   A. **Bibliographic essay:** The essay should survey a slice of the secondary literature
   in U.S. women's history, organizing it in a way that allows the reader to
   understand the variety of work and the controversies surrounding it. You
   should both supply critical analysis of individual works, pointing to their
   strong and weak aspects, and work toward a summary understanding of the
   development and current state of historical writing on your topic. Finally, you
   should point out what seem to you to be the most fruitful possibilities for
   further inquiry in the field. Think of this essay as the review-of-the-literature
   stage of a larger research project.

Procedures for bibliographic essays: You must consult with me before choosing a topic. A prospectus of a paragraph or two in length is due on October 1. The prospectus should briefly discuss your topic and its relation to your overall program of study and should include a tentative bibliography. Because this paper is meant to be an exercise rather than a full-scale bibliographic essay, you should limit your bibliography to five books or the equivalent (rule of thumb: 4 articles = 1 book). Books assigned for the course count toward this total if you did not read them for class; otherwise, they do not count although you should of course include them in your essay. Except in unusual circumstances which you should clear with me in advance, you may not include review essays in your bibliography. This paper, which should be about ten double-spaced typewritten pages, is due in my Wood Hall office by noon on Tuesday, December 17.

Primary source-based paper: This paper will analyze a small section of primary source material in the light of the theoretical, methodological, and empirical discussions in the course. This should not be thought of as a full-scale research paper, but rather as a pilot study that allows you to try your hand at analyzing a limited body of evidence. The paper should develop a clear, evidence-based argument and place that argument in the larger context of U.S. women's history as presented in this course.

Procedures for the primary source-based paper: You must consult with me on the choice of both a general topic and a suitable body of primary material. It is impossible to set a general standard for what constitutes a "suitable body" of material, and each student who chooses this option will have to work closely with me to define the universe of evidence. You should choose an aspect of a topic that has to some degree been covered in class in order to limit the amount of secondary reading you will need to do. A prospectus describing your topic, the sources you will use, and the relation of the project to your overall program of study is due October 1. This paper, which should be about ten double-spaced typewritten pages, is due in my Wood Hall office by noon on Tuesday, December 17.

WARNING: I shall not accept any bibliographic essay or primary source-based paper for which I have not approved a prospectus.

Grading:
The approximate weights for each component of the class work are:

Class reports (without critique)	5%
Class reports with critique **or** book reviews--10% each	20%
Review essay	20%
Bibliographic essay	40%
Class participation	15%

Reading:
Assigned books are on sale at the Co-op. All articles and books are on reserve at Babbidge Library; in most cases, Babbidge catalogs articles in books by the name of the book's editor rather than the article author. Articles are on reserve in 328 Wood Hall and in the Women's Studies Library, 410 Beach Hall; articles in both these venues are filed by article author.

Schedule:
As you prepare for each class, consider the relevance of previous weeks' reading to the week's topic.

9/3--Introduction to and Organization of the Course

9/10--Women's History, Women's Theory, Women's Culture
All read either A. or B.
A.
Joan Kelly, "The Social Relation of the Sexes: Methodological Implications of Women's History," Women, History, and Theory, pp. 1-18
Sonya Rose, Kathleen Canning, Anna Clark, Mariana Valverde, and Marcia R. Sawyer, "Women's History/Gender History: Is Feminist History Losing its Critical Edge?" Journal of Women's History 5 #1 (Spring 1993), 89-128
B.
Joan Wallach Scott, Gender and the Politics of History, Chapters 1 & 2
Nancy Hewitt, "Beyond the Search for Sisterhood: American Women's History in the 1980s," Social History 10 (October 1985), 299-321, reprinted in Ellen DuBois and Vicki Ruiz, eds., Unequal Sisters: A Multicultural Reader in U.S. Women's History
Elsa Barkley Brown, "African-American women's quilting: A framework for conceptualizing and teaching African-American women's history," Signs 14 #4 (Summer 1989), 921-929
All read either C. or D.
C.
Carroll Smith-Rosenberg, "The Female World of Love and Ritual," Signs 1 #1 (Autumn 1975), 1-29
Sharon Harley, "For the Good of Family and Race: Gender, Work, and Domestic Roles in the Black Community, 1880-1930," Signs 15 #2 (Winter 1990), 336-349
Christina Simmons, "Companionate Marriage and the Lesbian Threat," Frontiers 4 #3 (Fall 1979), 54-59
Judith Walzer Leavitt, "Under the Shadow of Maternity: American Women's Responses to Death and Debility Fears in Nineteenth-Century Childbirth," Feminist Studies 12 #1 (Spring 1986), 129-154
D.
Linda Kerber, "Separate Spheres, Female Worlds, Woman's Place: The Rhetoric of Women's History," Journal of American History 75 #1 (June 1988), 9-39
E. Anthony Rotundo, "Romantic Friendship: Male Intimacy and Middle-Class Youth in the Northern United States, 1800-1900," Journal of Social History 23 #1 (Fall 1989), 1-25
Continued on next page

Estelle B. Freedman, "Separatism as Strategy: Female Institution Building and American Feminism, 1870-1930," Feminist Studies 5 #3 (Fall 1979), 512-529

Marylynne Diggs, "Romantic Friends or a 'Different Race of Creatures'? The Representation of Lesbian Pathology in Nineteenth-Century America," Feminist Studies 21 # 2 (Summer 1995), 317-340

Optional:

Cecile Dauphin, Anette Farge, Genevieve Fraisse, Christiane Klapisch-Zuber, Rose-Marie Lagrave, Michelle Perrot, Pierette Pfzerat, Yannick Ripa, Pauline Schmitt-Pantel, Daniele Voldman, "Women's Culture and Women's Power: An Attempt at Historiography," and comments by Karen Offen, Nell Irvin Painter, Hilda L. Smith, and Lois W. Banner, Journal of Women's History 1 #1 (Spring 1989), 63-107 **or**

Ellen DuBois, Mari Jo Buhle, Temma Kaplan, Gerda Lerner, and Carroll Smith-Rosenberg, "Politics and Culture in Women's History," Feminist Studies 6 #1 (Spring 1980), 28-64

9/17--Life on the Land

Read one of the following:

Joan Jensen, Loosening the Bonds: Mid-Atlantic Farm Women, 1750-1850

Sarah Deutsch, No Separate Refuge: Culture, Class, and Gender on an Anglo-Hispanic Frontier in the American Southwest, 1880-1940

Plus one of the following:

Susan A. Mann, "Slavery, Sharecropping, and Sexual Inequality," Signs 14 #4 (Summer 1989), 774-798

Lucy Eldersveld Murphy, "Autonomy and the Economic Roles of Indian Women of the Fox-Wisconsin River Region, 1763-1832," in Nancy Shoemaker, ed., Negotiators of Change: Historical Perspectives on Native American Women, pp. 72-89

9/24--Women and Industrialization

Read one of the following:

Thomas Dublin, Women at Work: The Transformation of Work and Community in Lowell

Christine Stansell, City of Women: Sex and Class in New York, 1789-1860

Plus one of the following:

Mary H. Blewett, "The Sexual Division of Labor and the Artisan Tradition in Early Industrial Capitalism: The Case of New England Shoemaking, 1780-1860," in Carol Groneman and Mary Beth Norton, eds., "To Toil the Livelong Day": America's Women at Work, 1780-1930, pp. 35-46

Mary H. Blewett, "Manhood and the Market: The Politics of Gender and Class among the Textile Workers of Fall River, Massachusetts, 1870-1880," in Ava Baron, ed., Work Engendered: Toward a New History of American Labor, pp. 92-113

10/1--The Home
Read one of the following:
Jeanne Boydston, Home and Work: Housework, Wages, and the Ideology of Labor in the
  Early Republic
Phyllis Palmer, Domesticity and Dirt: Housewives and Domestic Servants in the United
  States, 1920-1945
Plus one of the following:
Elizabeth Clark-Lewis, "'This Work Had a End': African-American Domestic Workers in
  Washington, D.C., 1910-1940," in Carol Groneman and Mary Beth Norton, "To Toil
  the Livelong Day": America's Women at Work, 1780-1930, pp., 196-212
Darlene Clark Hine, "The Housewives' League of Detroit: Black Women and Economic
  Nationalism," in Nancy A. Hewitt and Suzanne Lebsock, eds., Visible Women: New
  Essays on American Activism, pp. 223-241

10/8--Gendered Discourses
Read one of the following:
Cornelia Hughes Dayton, Women Before the Bar: Gender, Law, and Society in Connecticut,
  1639-1789
Ruth Milkman, Gender at Work: The Dynamics of Job Segregation by Sex during World
  War II
Plus:
Kathleen Canning, "Feminist History after the Linguistic Turn: Historicizing Discourse and
  Experience," Signs 19 #2 (Winter 1994), 368-404

10/15--Race and Gender
Read one of the following:
Glenda Elizabeth Gilmore, Gender and Jim Crow: Women and the Politics of White
  Supremacy in North Carolina, 1896-1920
Rickie Solinger, Wake Up Little Susie: Single Pregnancy and Race Before Roe v. Wade
Plus one of the following:
Evelyn Nakano Glenn, "From Servitude to Service Work: Historical Continuities in the
  Racial Division of Paid Reproductive Labor," Signs 18 #1 (Autumn 1992), 1-43
Evelyn Brooks Higginbotham, "African-American Women's History and the Metalanguage of
  Race," Signs 17 #2 (Winter 1992), 251-274

10/22--Women, Gender, and Family
Read one of the following:
Linda Gordon, Heroes of Their Own Lives: The Politics and History of Family Violence
Elaine Tyler May, Homeward Bound: American Families in the Cold War Era
Plus:
Exchange between Joan W. Scott and Linda Gordon, Signs 15 #4 (Summer 1990), 848-860
Joanne Meyerowitz, "Beyond the Feminine Mystique: A Reassessment of Postwar Popular
  Culture, 1946-1958" in Joanne Meyerowitz, ed., Not June Cleaver: Women and
  Gender in Postwar America, 1945-1960, pp. 229-262

8

10/29--Women and Community
Read one of the following:
Elizabeth Lapovsky Kennedy and Madeline D. Davis, Boots of Leather, Slippers of Gold: The History of a Lesbian Community
Ardis Cameron, Radicals of the Worst Sort: Laboring Women in Lawrence, Massachusetts, 1860-1912
Plus:
Sarah Deutsch, "Reconceiving the City: Women, Space, and Power in Boston, 1870-1910," Gender and History 6 #2 (August 1994), 202-223

11/5--Immigrant Women
Read one of the following:
Judy Yung, Unbound Feet: A Social History of Chinese Women in San Francisco
Vicki Ruiz, Cannery Women, Cannery Lives: Mexican Women, Unionization, and the California Food Processing Industry, 1930-1950
Plus:
Judith E. Smith, "The Bonds of Kinship," Chapter Three of Family Connections: A History of Italian and Jewish Immigrant Lives in Providence, Rhode Island, 1900-1940, pp. 83-123

11/12--Women and Reform
Read one of the following:
Lori D. Ginzberg, Women and the Work of Benevolence: Morality, Politics, and Class in the Nineteenth Century
Evelyn Brooks Higginbotham, Righteous Discontent: The Women's Movement in the Black Baptist Church, 1880-1920
Plus one of the following:
Paula Baker, "The Domestication of Politics: Women and American Political Society, 1780-1920," American Historical Review 89 #3 (June 1984), 620-647
Linda Gordon, "Black and White Visions of Welfare: Women's Welfare Activism, 1890-1945," Journal of American History 78 #2 (September 1991), 559-590

11/19--Feminism and Labor Militancy
Read one of the following:
Meredith Tax, The Rising of the Women: Feminist Solidarity and Class Conflict, 1880-1917
Nancy Cott, The Grounding of Modern Feminism
Plus one of the following:
Rosalyn Terborg-Penn, "Discontented Black Feminists: Prelude and Postscript to the Passage of the Nineteenth Amendment," in Lois Scharf and Joan M. Jensen, eds., Decades of Discontent: The Women's Movement, 1920-1940, pp. 261-278
Jacquelyn Dowd Hall, "Disorderly Women: Gender and Labor Militancy in the Appalachian South," Journal of American History 73 #2 (September 1986), 354-382

12/3--Popular Culture
Read one of the following:
Kathy Peiss, Cheap Amusements: Working Women and Leisure in Turn-of-the-Century New
York
Susan J. Douglas, Where the Girls Are: Growing Up Female with the Mass Media
Plus:
Hazel V. Carby, "Policing the Black Woman's Body in an Urban Context," Critical Inquiry
18 (Summer 1992), 738-755

12/10--Writing Women's Biography
Read one of the following:
Laurel Thatcher Ulrich, A Midwife's Tale: The Life of Martha Ballard, Based on Her
Diary, 1785-1812
Jacquelyn Dowd Hall, Revolt Against Chivalry: Jessie Daniel Ames and the Women's
Campaign Against Lynching
Plus one of the following:
Jacquelyn Dowd Hall, "Second Thoughts: On Writing a Feminist Biography," Feminist
Studies 13 #1 (Spring 1987), 19-37
Susan Geiger, "What's So Feminist About Doing Women's Oral History?" Journal of
Women's History 2 #1 (Spring 1990), 169-182
Nell Irvin Painter, "Sojourner Truth in Life and Memory: Writing the Biography of an
American Exotic," Gender & History 2 #1 (Spring 1990), 3-16

12/17--Bibliographic essay or primary source-based paper due in my Wood Hall office at
noon.

HIST300/WOMS300
Women in American History
Fall, 1997

Professor: Anne Boylan   Office: 206 Munroe Hall (831-2188)
       Office Hours: Mondays & Wednesdays 10:15-12:00
                  (and other times by appointment)
       E-mail: anne.boylan@mvs.udel.edu

REQUIRED BOOKS: (available at the Bookstore)
           Kerber & DeHart, Women's America (core text)
           Jacobs, Incidents in the Life of a Slave Girl
           Uchida, Desert Exile
           Moody, Coming of Age in Mississippi

RECOMMENDED: Hoffecker, Beneath Thy Guiding Hand: A History of
                Women at the University of Delaware
           (this book is required for students in section 80)

IMPORTANT REFERENCE WORKS:
All students should acquaint themselves with these works, which
can be found in the Library Reference Room:
(NAW)   Notable American Women, 1607-1950 (3 volumes) &
           Notable American Women: The Modern Period, 1950-1975
(BWA)   Black Women in America: An Historical Encyclopedia (2
           volumes)
Names of some of the women whose biographies can be found in
these works are listed on the syllabus below.

COURSE REQUIREMENTS:
       1) Attendance: Students are expected to attend class and to
participate in class discussion. More than five unexcused
absences will be cause for reduction of a student's grade. In
accordance with University policy, any student who misses the
first three classes of the semester may be dropped.
       2) Exams: There will be two take-home essay exams, a midterm
and a final, based on lectures and readings. Questions and
guidelines will be handed out in class. Exam dates are listed on
the syllabus.
       3) Quizzes: There will be three quizzes, based primarily on
course readings (including lecture handouts). Quiz dates are
listed on the syllabus.
       4) Book analysis: Each student will write a 4-5 page
analytical essay based on one of the course readings (excluding
the core text and Hoffecker book). Guidelines will be handed out
in class. Students in Section 80 will have the opportunity to
read and analyze an additional book and write a comparative
analysis.
       5) "Field Trip": Each student will take a "field trip"
outside of class by attending an event related to women's history
or women's issues and writing a two-paragraph summary and
reaction to the event. See handouts for suggested activities.

       Students are expected to be familiar with the policy on

11

academic honesty found in the Student Handbook. If you are in doubt about any course requirement, please consult me before attempting to complete it.

GRADING: (These are merely guidelines; I also give credit for participation in class discussion and for intangibles such as improvement.) Each exam counts 30%; the quizzes together count 20%; the book analysis counts 20%.

SYLLABUS
Below is a week-by-week listing of lecture topics and assignments; it is not written in stone, however, and may change if either interest or necessity dictates a change.

Sept. 3-5
Course introduction; background to colonization
Assignment: Women's America, pp. 3-37
NAW: Pocahontas, Mary Rowlandson

Sept. 8-12
Colonization & colonial families
Assignment: Women's America, pp. 37-46, 47-50, 65-67, 564-67
NAW: Mary Brant, Mary Musgrove, Catherine Tekakwitha

Sept. 15-19
Women in Public
Assignment: Women's America, pp. 50-64, 68-84
NAW, BWA: Anne Bradstreet, Margaret Brent, Coincoin, Jane Colden, Anne Hutchinson, Mary Katharine Goddard, Sarah Kemble Knight, Deborah Moody, Margaret Winthrop, Maria Van Rensselaer

Sept. 22-26
The American Revolution & after
Assignment: Women's America, pp. 85-95, 168-83
NAW, BWA: Abigail Adams, Sarah Allen, Sarah Franklin Bache, Margaret Corbin, Deborah Franklin, Judith Sargent Murray, Betsy Ross, Tituba, Deborah Sampson, Phillis Wheatley

**Quiz #1   Friday September 26

Sept. 29-
Oct. 3
Free Women in Industrializing America
Assignment: Women's America, pp. 97-99, 117-168, 184-200
NAW, BWA: Sarah Bagley, Catharine Beecher, Joanna Graham Bethune Elizabeth Blackwell, Sarah J. Hale, Mary Edmonia Lewis, Henrietta Regulus Ray, Lydia H. Sigourney, Emma Hart Willard

Oct. 6-10
Enslaved women
Assignment: Women's America, pp. 101-117
Jacobs, Incidents in the Life of a Slave Girl (all)
NAW, BWA: Sarah Mapps Douglass, Mary Ann Shadd Cary, Sarah Grimke, Harriet Jacobs, Elizabeth Keckley, Lucy Larcom, Susie King Taylor, Angelina Grimke Weld, Sojourner Truth

**First Book Analysis due Monday, October 13

Oct.   Antislavery & Women's Rights
13-17   Assignment: Women's America, pp. 201-219, 567-572
            NAW, BWA: Abigail Scott Duniway, Abby Kelley Foster,
            Lucretia Mott, Henrietta Ray, Harriet Tubman, Elizabeth
            Cady Stanton, Charlotte Forten Grimke

University Holiday, Monday October 20
**Mid-term Take-Home Exam due Wednesday October 22; 9:05 a.m.

Oct.   Women's Work, 1880-1920
22-24   Assignment: Women's America, pp. 220-225, 227-230, 240-
                        264, 276-285
            NAW, BWA: Frances E. W. Harper, Leonora O'Reilly,
            Florence Kelley, Sarah Emma Edmonds, Charlotte Ray,
            Maggie Lena Walker

Oct.   Women's Institutions & Organizations, 1860-1920
27-31   Assignment: Women's America, pp. 231-239, 265-275, 285-
                        294
            NAW, BWA: Jane Addams, Nannie Burroughs, Anna Julia
            Cooper, Fanny Jackson Coppin, Alice Hamilton, Lugenia
            Burns Hope, Florence Kelley, Mary Gove Nichols, Ellen
            Richards, Josephine St. Pierre Ruffin, M. Carey Thomas,
            Lillian Wald, Maggie Lena Walker, Ida B. Wells-Barnett,
            Frances Willard, Fannie Barrier Williams

Nov.   Feminism and Suffrage, 1880-1920
3-7   Assignment: Women's America, pp. 295-343, 572-582
            NAW, BWA: Margaret Anderson, Alva Belmont, Lucy Burns,
            Carrie Chapman Catt, Alice Dunbar-Nelson, Charlotte
            Perkins Gilman, Emma Goldman, Mary Church Terrell
            Anna Howard Shaw, Madam C. J. Walker, Ida B. Wells-
            Barnett

**Quiz #2 Monday November 10

Nov.   After Suffrage
10-14   Assignment: Women's America, pp. 351-393, 407-431, 582-
                        583
            NAW, BWA: Jessie Daniel Ames, Marian Anderson, Mary
            McLeod Bethune, Irene Castle, Crystal Eastman,
            Josephine Herbst, Zora Neale Hurston, Frances Perkins,
            Eleanor Roosevelt, Margaret Sanger

Nov.   Wartime and Postwar America
17-21   Assignment: Women's America, pp. 440-477, 562-563
                        Uchida, Desert Exile (all)
            NAW, BWA: Blanche Ames, Mary Anderson, Mary Dewson,
            Crystal Fauset, Lena Levine, Rose Pesotta, Rose
            Schneiderman, Mary Van Kleeck, Mary Heaton Vorse

**Second Book Analysis due Monday November 24

Nov.   The "Feminine Mystique"
24-26   Assignment: Women's America, pp. 478-493, 507-16, 583-
                                            586
                         Comi..g of Age in Mississippi (all)
            BWA: Pauli Murray
(Thanksgiving Holiday Friday)

**Third Book Analysis due Wednesday, December 3

Dec.   The Revival of Feminism
1-5   Assignment: Women's America, pp. 516-532, 587-598
            NAW, BWA: Rubye Doris Smith Robinson

**Quiz #3 Monday, December 8

Dec.   Recent Women's History
8-10   Assignment: Women's America, pp. 533-560

December 16 ** Final Exam due at 1:00 p.m in 209 Ewing

HIST611-011
Seminar: U.S. Women's History
Fall, 1996

Anne M. Boylan   Office: 320 Ewing   Phone: 831-2188
                Office Hours: Mon., Wed., 10-11:45
                              (other times by appointment)
                E-mail: anne.boylan@mvs.udel.edu
                History Department FAX #: 831-1538

This course focuses on analysis and discussion of historiographical and theoretical issues in women's history. The course
is constructed around a series of topics, arranged in a rough
chronology. If you have not had an undergraduate survey course
in women's history, I would urge you to read a general text in
the field, such as Sara Evans, Born for Liberty or Nancy Woloch,
Women and the American Experience.

REQUIRED BOOKS: The following required books are available in
the bookstore; all required readings (including articles) are on
2-hour reserve in the library.
    Eleanor Flexner, Century of Struggle
    Carol Karlsen, The Devil in the Shape of a Woman
    Linda Kerber, Women of the Republic
    Laurel Thatcher Ulrich, A Midwife's Tale
    Suzanne Lebsock, The Free Women of Petersburg
    Lori Ginzberg, Women and the Work of Benevolence
    Christine Stansell, City of Women
    Elizabeth Fox-Genovese, Within the Plantation Household
    Joanne Meyerowitz, Women Adrift
    Peggy Pascoe, Relations of Rescue
    Robyn Muncy, Creating a Female Dominion in American Reform
    Evelyn Brooks Higginbotham, Righteous Discontent
    Jacquelyn Dowd Hall, Revolt Against Chivalry
    Nancy F. Cott, The Grounding of Modern Feminism
    Ruth Milkman, Women at Work

OPTIONAL: I have ordered some copies of the following books,
from which we will be reading some articles; purchase is
optional.
    Ellen DuBois and Vicki Ruiz, eds., Unequal Sisters
    Joanne Meyerowitz, ed., Not June Cleaver
    Linda Kerber, et al., eds., U.S. History as Women's History

COURSE REQUIREMENTS:

    Grades in the seminar will rest on two bases: active,
intelligent participation in seminar discussion (34%); and
completion of written assignments (66%). At the end of the
semester, each student will receive a written discussion
evaluation and a discussion grade. Review essays will be graded
and returned, ordinarily within a week of receipt. Reaction
essays will be returned but not graded.

Reading: Your primary responsibility is to read each week's core reading and come to class prepared to discuss it. I realize that students have varying comfort levels when it comes to talking in front of a group and will take into account quality as well as quantity of class participation. We will work on encouraging maximum participation. I recommend that you keep reading notes, with questions, on the assignments. The syllabus also lists "recommended" readings; these include some of the key works on the week's topic. Students preparing for qualifying exams should be familiar with as many of the recommended readings as possible.

Written Assignments: Each student will write three 6-8 page review essays. In addition, each student will prepare two 3-page "reaction essays" during weeks in which she/he is not writing a review essay.

Review Essays: Each of you will choose three dates on which to submit essays. These should be analytical and evaluative, focusing on the book assigned for the week, but (as much as possible) referring also to other assigned readings. They should not merely summarize the readings. Your essays should identify the thesis and main points in the readings, highlight the key historiographical issues they raise, analyze the persuasiveness of the evidence presented, identify their contribution to the topic in question, and provide a thoughtful assessment of them. If you need guidance in writing your essays, be sure to see me, or consult with me by electronic mail.

(In general, it is a good idea to become a regular reader of book reviews and review essays in such journals as the JAH, AHR, Reviews in American History, Journal of Social History, Journal of Women's History, Signs, and American Quarterly.)

Reaction Essays: These are to be shorter, much more informal pieces, in which you provide some reaction to or questions about the week's readings. You should submit these essays to me by noon Wednesday, keeping a copy for yourself. There is no prescribed content or format for these essays. I want you to use them to raise questions about the readings, or to mention things in them you found particularly interesting, thought-provoking, or bothersome -- in other words, to formulate some reaction to them. These essays will not be graded.

SYLLABUS

SEPTEMBER 4: Introductory class
Core reading:
--Joan W. Scott, "History and Difference," Daedalus, 116 (Fall, 1987), 93-118; reprinted as "American Women Historians, 1884-1984," in Gender and the Politics of History

SEPTEMBER 11: Women's History: The Development of the Field
Core reading:
--Eleanor Flexner, Century of Struggle
--Nancy A. Hewitt, "Beyond the Search for Sisterhood: American Women's History in the 1980s," Unequal Sisters, pp. 1-14
--Joanne Meyerowitz, "American Women's History: The Fall of Women's Culture," Canadian Review of American Studies (1992)

Recommended:
-Evelyn Brooks Higginbotham, "African American Women's History and the Metalanguage of Race," Signs, 17 (Winter 1992)
-Karen Offen, ed. Writing Women's History
-Julia Cherry Spruill, Women's Life and Work in the Southern Colonies
-Elisabeth Anthony Dexter, Colonial Women of Affairs
-Mary Sumner Benson, Women in Eighteenth-Century America
-Mary Ritter Beard, Woman as a Force in History

SEPTEMBER 18: Women in Pre-Industrial America, I
Core reading:
--Carol Karlsen, The Devil in the Shape of a Woman
--Joan Scott, "Gender: A Useful Category of Historical Analysis," in Gender and the Politics of History, pp. 28-50

Recommended:
-Mary Beth Norton, Founding Mothers and Fathers: Gendered Power in the Forming of American Society
-Mary Beth Norton, "The Myth of the Golden Age," in Women of America: A History, ed. Norton and Carol Berkin, pp. 37-47
-Lois Green Carr and Lorena Walsh, "The Planter's Wife: The Experience of White Women in 17th Century Maryland," William and Mary Quarterly, 34 (1977), 542-571
-Paul Boyer and Steven Nissenbaum, Salem Possessed
-Carol Devens, Countering Colonization: Native American Women and Great Lakes Missions, 1630-1900
Cornelia Hughes Dayton, Women Before the Bar: Gender, Law and Society in Connecticut, 1639-1789

SEPTEMBER 25: Women in Pre-Industrial America, II
Core reading:
--Linda K. Kerber, Women of the Republic OR
--Laurel Thatcher Ulrich, A Midwife's Tale
--Nancy Shoemaker, "The Rise or Fall of Iroquois Women," Journal of Women's History, 2 (1991): 39-57

Recommended:
-Mary Beth Norton, Liberty's Daughters
-Ruth Bloch, "The Gendered Meanings of Virtue in Revolutionary America," Signs, 13 (1987)
-Ronald Hoffman and Peter Albert, eds., Women in the Age of the American Revolution
-Susan Juster, Disorderly Women: Sexual Politics and

Evangelicalism in Revolutionary New England
    -Laurel Thatcher Ulrich, Good Wives
    -Joan Gunderson, "Independence, Citizenship, and the
American Revolution," Signs, 13 (1987)

OCTOBER 2: Antebellum America and "Women's Sphere"
Core reading:
    --Gerda Lerner, "The Lady and the Mill Girl: Changes in the
Status of Women in the Age of Jackson," in The Majority Finds its
Past, pp. 15-30
    --Carroll Smith-Rosenberg, "The Female World of Love and
Ritual: Relations Between Women in Nineteenth-Century America,"
in Disorderly Conduct, pp. 53-76
    --Suzanne Lebsock, The Free Women of Petersburg

Recommended:
    -Nancy F. Cott, The Bonds of Womanhood
    -Mary P. Ryan, Cradle of the Middle CLass
    -Kathryn Kish Sklar, Catharine Beecher
    -Carroll Smith-Rosenberg, Disorderly Conduct
    -Jeanne Boydston, Home and Work
    -Karen V. Hansen, "'No Kisses is Like Youres': An Erotic
Friendship between Two African-American Women during the Mid-
Nineteenth Century," Gender & History, 7 (August 1995): 153-82

OCTOBER 9: Working-Class Women and Domesticity
Core reading:
    --Christine Stansell, City of Women
    --Linda K. Kerber, "Separate Spheres, Female Worlds, Woman's
Place: The Rhetoric of Women's History," Journal of American
History, 75 (1988), 3-39

Recommended:
    -Thomas Dublin, Women at Work
    _Thomas Dublin, Transforming Women's Work
    -Mary Blewett, Men, Women, and Work
    -Joan M. Jensen, Loosening the Bonds: Mid-Atlantic Farm
Women, 1750-1850
    -Nancy Gray Osterud, Bonds of Community

OCTOBER 16: Slavery
Core reading:
    --Elizabeth Fox-Genovese, Within the Plantation Household
    --Deborah Gray White, "Female Slaves: Sex Roles and Status
in the Antebellum Plantation South," in Unequal Sisters, pp. 20-
32

Recommended:
    -Deborah Gray White, Arn't I a Woman? Female Slaves in the
Plantation South
    -Jacqueline Jones, Labor of Love, Labor of Sorrow, chap. 1

-Drew Gilpin Faust, _Mothers of Invention: Women of the Slaveholding South in the American Civil War_
-Brenda Stevenson, _Life in Black andWhite: Family and Community in the Slave South_
-Jean Fagan Yellin, ed., _Incidents in the Life of a Slave Girl_

OCTOBER 23: Benevolence and Reform
Core reading:
--Lori D. Ginzberg, _Women and the Work of Benevolence_

Recommended:
-Nancy A. Hewitt, _Women's Activism and Social Change_
-Mary P. Ryan, _Women in Public_
-Anne Firor Scott, _Natural Allies_
-Barbara Leslie Epstein, _The Politics of Domesticity_
-Barbara Meil Hobson, _Uneasy Virtue: The Politics of Prostitution and the American Reform Tradition_
-Anne M. Boylan, "Benevolence and Antislavery Activity among African American Women in New York and Boston, 1820-1840," in _The Abolitionist Sisterhood: Women's Political Culture in Antebellum America_, ed. Jean Fagan Yellin and John C. Van Horne

OCTOBER 30: Working Women and Women's Work
Core reading:
--Joanne Meyerowitz, _Women Adrift_
--Kathy Peiss, "'Charity Girls' and City Pleasures: Historical Notes on Working-Class Sexuality, 1880-1920," in _Unequal Sisters_, pp. 157-166
--Joan Jensen, "Native American Women and Agriculture: A Seneca Case Study," in _Unequal Sisters_

Recommended:
-Angel Kwolek-Folland, _Engendering Business: Men and Women in the Corporate Office, 1870-1930_
-Sharon Hartman Strom, _Beyond the Typewriter_
-Tamara K. Hareven, _Family Time and Industrial Time_
-Susan Porter Benson, _Counter Cultures_
-Lynn Weiner, _From Working Girl to Working Mother_
-George J. Sanchez, "'Go After the Women': Americanization and the Mexican Immigrant Woman, 1915-1929," in _Unequal Sisters_
-Ava Baron, ed., _Work Engendered_

NOVEMBER 6: Voluntarism and Professionalism
Core reading:
--Estelle B. Freedman, "Separatism as Strategy: Female Institution-Building and American Feminism, 1870-1930," _Feminist Studies_, 5 (1979)
--Peggy Pascoe, _Relations of Rescue_ **AND**
--Robyn Muncy, _Creating a Female Dominion in American Reform_
--Kathryn Kish Sklar, "Two Political Cultures in the

Progressive Era: The National Consumers' League and the American Association for Labor Legislation," in U.S. History as Women's History

Recommended:
    -Dolores Janiewski, "Giving Women a Future: Alice Fletcher, the 'Woman Question,' and 'Indian Reform,'" in Visible Women, ed. Nancy A. Hewitt and Suzanne Lebsock
    -Elsa Barkley Brown, "Womanist Consciousness: Maggie Lena Walker and the Independent Order of St. Luke," in Unequal Sisters
    -Seth Koven and Sonya Michel, "Womanly Duties: Maternalist Politics and the Origins of Welfare States in France, Germany, Great Britain and the United States, 1880-1920," American Historical Review (October 1990)
    -Seth Koven and Sonya Michel, eds., Mothers of a New World
    -Theda Skocpol, Protecting Soldiers and Mothers
    -Kathryn Kish Sklar, Florence Kelley and the Nation's Work
    -Linda Gordon, ed. Women, the State, and Welfare

NOVEMBER 13: Sexuality and Race
Core reading:
    --Jacquelyn Dowd Hall, Revolt Against Chivalry
    --Gail Bederman, "Civilization, the Decline of Middle-Class Manliness, and Ida B. Wells's Anti-Lynching Campaign," in Manliness and Civilization

Recommended:
    -Estelle B. Freedman and John D'Emilio, Intimate Matters
    -Gail Bederman, Manliness and Civilization
    -George Chauncey, Gay New York
    -Ann Snitow, ed., Powers of Desire
    -Paula Giddings, When and Where I Enter
    -Mary E. Frederickson, "'Each One is Dependent on the Other'" in Visible Women, ed., Nancy A. Hewitt and Suzanne Lebsock
    -Darlene Clark Hine, "Rape and the Inner Lives of Black Women in the Middle West: Preliminary Thoughts on the Culture of Dissemblance," in Unequal Sisters

NOVEMBER 20: Religion and Reform
Core reading:
    --Evelyn Brooks Higginbotham, Righteous Discontent
    --Deborah Gray White, "The Cost of Club Work, the Price of Black Feminism," in Visible Women, ed. Nancy A. Hewitt and Suzanne Lebsock

Recommended:
    -Stephanie Shaw, What a Woman Ought to Be and Do
    -Adrienne Lash Jones, Jane Edna Hunter
    -Cynthia Neverson-Morton, Afro-American Women of the South and the Advancement of the Race, 1895-1925
    -Dorothy Salem, To Better Our World: Black Women in Organized Reform, 1890-1920

NOVEMBER 27: NO CLASS

DECEMBER 4: Feminism
Core reading:
    --Nancy F. Cott, The Grounding of Modern Feminism
    --Suzanne Lebsock, "Women Suffrage and White Supremacy: A
Virginia Case Study," in Visible Women, ed. Nancy A. Hewitt and
Suzanne Lebsock
    --Estelle B. Freedman, "Separatism Revisited: Women's
Institutions, Social Reform, and the Career of Miriam Van
Waters," in U.S. History as Women's History

Recomended:
    -Ellen DuBois, Feminism and Suffrage
    -Rosalyn Terborg-Penn, "Discontented Black Feminists:
Prelude and Postscript to the Passage of the 19th
Amendment," in Decades of Discontent, ed. Joan Jensen
    -Carroll Smith-Rosenberg, "The New Woman and the Androgyne,"
in Disorderly Conduct, pp. 245-296
    -J. Stanley Lemons, The Woman Citizen
    -Clarke A. Chambers, Seedtime for Reform

DECEMBER 11: Wartime and Postwar Work
Core reading:
    --Ruth Milkman, Women at Work
    --Joanne Meyerowitz, "Beyond the Feminine Mystique: A
Reassessment of Postwar Mass Culture, 1946-1958," in Not June
Cleaver
    --Susan Lynn, "Gender and Progressive Politics: A Bridge to
Social Activism of the 1960s," in Not June Cleaver
    --Daniel Horowitz, "Rethinking Betty Friedan and The
Feminine Mystique: Labor Union Radicalism and Feminism in Cold
War America," American Quarterly, 48 (March 1996): 1-42

Recommended:
    -Susan Lynn, Progressive Women in Conservative Times
    -Amy Swerdlow, Women Strike for Peace
    -Cynthia Harrison, On Account of Sex
    -Ka.... anderson, Wartime Women

(This list focuses primarily on books, though it includes some
notable articles. Only a few biographies are listed.)

I. REFERENCE WORKS: HISTORIOGRAPHY; THEORY

Gretchen Bataille, ed., Native American Women: A Biographical
    Dictionary
Evelyn Brooks Higginbotham, "African American Women's History
    and the Metalanguage of Race," Signs, 17 (1992)
Judith Butler and Joan Scott, eds., Feminists Theorize the
    Political
Kathleen Canning, "Feminist History after the Linguistic Turn:
    Historicizing Discourse and Experience," Signs, 19 (1994)
Nancy F. Cott, ed., The History of Women in the United States:
    Historical Articles on Women's Lives and Activities, 20 vols
Ellen DuBois, et al., "Politics and Culture in Women's
    History," FS, 6 (Spring, 1980)
Gayle Veronica Fischer, "The 75th Anniversary of Women's Suffrage
    in the United States: A Bibliographic Essay," JWH, 7 (Fall,
    1995): 172-199
Linda Gordon, "On 'Difference,'" Genders (1991)
Rayna Green, "Review Essay: Native American Women," Signs, 6
    (1980)
Jacquelyn Dowd Hall, "Women's History Goes to Trial: EEOC v Sears
    Roebuck and Company," Signs, 11 (1986)
Jacquelyn Dowd Hall and Anne Firor Scott, "Women in the
    South," in Interpreting Southern History:
    Historiographical Essays in Honor of S. W. Higginbotham,
    ed. John B. Boles and Evelyn Thomas Nolen
Nancy Hewitt, "Beyond the Search for Sisterhood: American
    Women's History in the 1980s," Social History, 10 (1985)
Andrea Hinding, Clarke Chambers, et al., Women's History
    Sources: A Guide to Archives and Manuscript Collections
    in the United States (2 vols.)
Darlene Clark Hine, "Lifting the Veil, Shattering the Silence:
    Black Women's History in Slavery and Freedom," in The
    State of Afro-American History: Past, Present, and
    Future, ed. Darlene Clark Hine
_____, ed., Black Women in America: An Historical
    Encyclopedia (2 vols.)
_____, Black Women in United States History:
    From Colonial Times to the Present (16 vols.)Edward T.
James, Janet Wilson James, and Paul Boyer, eds., Notable
    American Women: A Biographical Directory, 1607-
    1950 (3 vols.); vol. 4, 1950-75, ed. Barbara Sicherman
Joan M. Jensen and Darlis Miller, "The Gentle Tamers Revisited:
    New Approaches to the History of Women in the American
    West," Pacific Historical Review, 49 (1980)
Joan Kelly-Gadol, "The Social Relations of the Sexes:
    Methodological Implications of Women's History," Signs, 1
    (1975)

22

Linda K. Kerber, "Separate Spheres, Female Worlds, Woman's
   Place: The Rhetoric of Women's History," JAH, 75 (1988)
Albert Krichmar, ed., The Women's Rights Movement in the
   United States, 1848-1970
Joanne Meyerowitz, "American Women's History: The Fall of Women's
   Culture," Canadian Review of American Studies (1992)
Ruth Milkman, "Women's History and the Sears Case," FS 12 (1986)
Page Putnam Miller, Reclaiming the Past: Landmarks of Women's
   History
Eva Moseley, "Women in Archives: Documenting the History of
   Women in America," American Archivist, 36 (1973)
Karen Offen, ed., Writing Women's History
Denise Riley, "Am I That Name?" Feminism and the Category
   "Woman" in History
Darlene R. Roth, "Review Essay: Growing Like Topsy: Research
   Guides to Women's History," JAH, 70 (1983)
Dorothy C. Salem, ed., African American Women: A Biographical
   Dictionary
Lynn Scherr, Susan B. Anthony Slept Here (historic sites)
Joan W. Scott, Gender and the Politics of History, especially:
   "Gender: A Useful Category of Historical Analysis"
Ann-Louise Shapiro, ed., Feminists Revision History
Barbara Sicherman, E. William Monter, Joan W. Scott, and
   Kathryn Kish Sklar, Recent United States Scholarship on
   the History of Women
Martha Jane Soltow and Mary K. Wery, ed., American Women and
   the Labor Movement, 1825-1974: An Annotated Bibliography
Patricia E. Sweeney, ed., Biographies of American Women: An
   Annotated Bibliography
Deborah Gray White, "Mining the Forgotten: Manuscript Sources
   for Black Women's History," JAH, 74 (1987)
Journal of Women's History; bibliographies on women's history

II. USEFUL TEXTS AND DOCUMENTARY COLLECTIONS

Rosalyn Baxandall, Linda Gordon, and Susan Reverby, America's
   Working Women: A Documentary History -- 1600 to the
   Present
Carol Berkin and Mary Beth Norton, eds., Women of America: A
   History
W. Elliott Brownlee and Mary H. Brownlee, eds., Women in the
   American Economy: A Documentary History
Nancy F. Cott, ed., Root of Bitterness: Documents in the
   Social History of American Women
Nancy F. Cott and Elizabeth Pleck, eds., A Heritage of Her
   Own:Toward a New Social History of American Women
Virginia Drachman, ed., Women Lawyers and the Origins of
   Professional Identity in America: The Letters of the Equity
   Club, 1887-1890
Ellen Carol DuBois and Vicki L. Ruiz, Unequal Sisters: A
   Multicultural Reader in U.S. Women's History
Sara M. Evans, Born for Liberty: A History of Women in America
Eleanor Flexner, Century of Struggle: The Women's Rights

Movement in the United States
Jean Friedman, William G. Shade, Mary Jane Capozolli, Our
American Sisters: Women in American Life and Thought
Claudia Goldin, Understanding the Gender Gap: An Economic
History of American Women
Linda Kerber and Jane DeHart Mathews, Women's America:
Refocusing the Past
_____, Alice Kessler-Harris, and Kathryn Kish Sklar, eds.,
U.S. History as Women's History: New Feminist Essays
Aileen S. Kraditor, ed., Up From the Pedestal: Selected
Writings in the History of American Feminism
Gerda Lerner, ed., Black Women in White America: A Documentary
History
_____, ed., The Female Experience
_____, The Majority Finds its Past
Julie Matthaei, An Economic History of American Women
Ruth Barnes Moynihan, et al., Second to None: A Documentary
History of American Women
_____, So Much to Be Done: Women Settlers on the
Mining and Ranching Frontier
Mary Beth Norton, ed., Main Problems in American Women's
History
Alice S. Rossi, ed., The Feminist Papers: From Adams to de
Beauvoir
Mary P. Ryan, Womanhood in America
Anne Firor Scott, Making the Invisible Woman Visible
Susan Ware, Modern American Women: A Documentary History
Nancy Woloch, Women and the American Experience
_____, Early American Women: A Documentary History, 1600-
1900

III. SURVEYS AND COLLECTIONS ON SPECIFIC SUBJECTS

Harriet Hyman Alonso, Peace as a Woman's Issue: A History of the
U.S. Movement for World Peace and Women's Rights
Karen Anderson, Changing Woman: A History of Racial Ethnic Women
in Modern America
Lois W. Banner, American Beauty
Ava Baron, ed., Work Engendered: Toward a New History of
American Labor
Maureen Beecher and Lavinia Anderson, Sisters in Spirit:
Mormon Women in Historical & Cultural Perspective
Virginia Bernhard, et al., eds., Southern Women: Histories and
Identities
Milton Cantor and Bruce Laurie, eds., Sex, Class and the
Woman Worker
Alice H. Cook, et al., The Most Difficult Revolution: Women and
Trade Unions
Ruth Schwartz Cowan, More Work for Mother: The Ironies of
Household Technology from the Open Hearth to the Microwave
Margaret Creighton and Lisa Norling, Iron Men, Wooden Women:
Gender and Seafaring, 1700-1920
Carl Degler, At Odds: Women and the Family in America from the

Revolution to the Present
John D'Emilio and Estelle B. Freedman, Intimate Matters: A
    History of Sexuality in America
Josephine Donovan, Feminist Theory: The Intellectual Traditions
    of American Feminism
Paula Giddings, When and Where I Enter: The Impact of Black
    Women on Race and Sex in America
Linda Gordon, ed., Women, the Family, and the State
Carol Groneman and Mary Beth Norton, "To Toil the Livelong Day"
    America's Women at Work, 1780-1980
Tamara K. Hareven, ed., Family and Kin in Urban Communities,
    1700-1930
_____, ed., Transitions: The Family and the Life
    Course in Historical Perspective
Darlene Clark Hine, et al., eds., "We Specialze in the Wholly
    Impossible": A Reader in Black Women's History
Joan Hoff, Law, Gender, and Injustice: A Legal History of U.S.
    Women
Karen Kennelly, American Catholic Women: A Historical Exploration
Alice Kessler-Harris, Out to Work: A History of Wage-Earning
    Women in the United States
_____, A Woman's Wage: Historical Meanings &
    Social Consequences
Janet Wilson James, ed., Women in American Religion
Elizabeth Jameson and Susan Armitage, eds., Writing the Range:
    Race, Class, and Culture in the Women's West
Jacqueline Jones, Labor of Love, Labor of Sorrow: Black Women,
    Work, and the Family from Slavery to the Present
Judith Walzer Leavitt, ed., Women and Health in America
_____, Brought to Bed: Childbearing in
    America, 1750-1950
Gerda Lerner, The Creation of Feminist Consciousness, 700 A.D.-
    1870
James C. Mohr, Abortion in America: The Origins and Evolution
    of National Policy
Regina Morantz-Sanchez, Sympathy and Science: Women Physicians
    in American Medicine
Patricia Morton, ed., Discovering the Women in Slavery: Emancipa-
    ting Perspectives on the American Past
Vera Norwood, Made from this Earth: American Women and Nature
Kathy Peiss and Christina Simmons, eds., Passion and Power:
    Sexuality in History
James C. Reed, From Private Vice to Public Virtue: The Birth
    Control Movement and American Society since 1830
Rosemary Radford Reuther and Rosemary Skinner Keller, eds.
    Women and Religion in America
Margaret Rossiter, Women Scientists in America: Struggles and
    Strategies to 1940
_____, Women Scientists in America: Before Affirmative
    Action, 1940-1972
Ellen Rothman, Hands and Hearts: A History of Courtship in
    America
Anne Firor Scott, Natural Allies: Women's Associations in
    American History

Nancy Shoemaker, ed., Negotiators of Change: Essays on Native
    American Women's History
Barbara Miller Solomon, In The Company of Educated Women: A
    History of Women and Higher Education in America
Ann Snitow, et al., eds., Powers of Desire
Susan Strasser, Never Done: A History of American Housework
Rosalyn Terborg-Penn and Sharon Harley, eds., The Afro-
    American Woman: Struggles and Images
Robert V. Wells, Revolutions in Americans' Lives: A
    Demographic Perspective on the History of Americans
Linda Witt, Karen M. Paget, & Glenna Matthews, Running as a
    Woman: Gender and Power in American Politics
Judy Yung, Unbound Feet: A Social History of Chinese Women in
    San Francisco

IV. COLONIAL AND REVOLUTIONARY PERIODS

Mary Sumner Benson, Women in Eighteenth-Century America: A
    Study of Opinion and Social Usage
Ruth H. Bloch, "The Gendered Meanings of Virtue in
    Revolutionary America," Signs, 13 (1987)
Richard Buel and Joy Day Buel, The Way of Duty: A Woman and
    Her Family in Revolutionary America
Lois Green Carr and Lorena Walsh, "The Planter's Wife: The
    Experiences of White Women in Seventeenth-Century
    Maryland," WMQ, 34 (1977)
Nancy F. Cott, "Divorce and the Changing Status of Women in
    Eighteenth-Century Massachusetts," WMQ, 33 (1976)
Cornelia Hughes Dayton, Women before the Bar: Gender, Law, and
    Society in Connecticut, 1639-1789
John Demos, A Little Commonwealth: Family Life in Plymouth
    Colony
Elisabeth Anthony Dexter, Colonial Women of Affairs
_____, Career Women of America, 1776-1840
Joan R. Gunderson and Gwen Victor Gampel, "Married Women's
    Legal Status in Eighteenth-Century New York and Virginia,"
    WMQ, 39 (1982)
Ramon Gutierrez, When Jesus Came, the Corn Mothers Went Away:
    Power and Sexuality in New Mexico, 1500-1846
Ronald Hoffman and Peter Albert, eds., Women in the Age of the
    American Revolution
Susan Juster, Disorderly Women: Sexual Politics & Evangelicalism
    in Revolutionary New England
Carol Karlsen, The Devil in the Shape of a Woman: Witchcraft
    in Colonial New England
Linda K. Kerber, et al., "Beyond Roles, Beyond Spheres:
    Thinking about Gender in the Early Republic," WMQ, 46
    (1989)
Linda K. Kerber, Women of the Republic: Intellect and Ideology
    in Revolutionary America
Lyle Koehler, A Search For Power: The "Weaker Sex" in
    Seventeenth Century New England
Allen Kulikoff, "The Beginnings of the Afro-American Family in

Maryland, " in The American Family in Social-Historical
Perspective, ed. Michael Gordon
Gary B. Nash, Forging Freedom: The Formation of Philadelphia's
Black Community, 1720-1840
Mary Beth Norton, Liberty's Daughters: The Revolutionary
Experience of American Women
_____, Founding Mothers and Fathers: Gendered Power in
the Shaping of American Society
_____, "The Evolution of White Women's Experience
in Early America," AHR, 89 (1984)
_____, "Gender and Defamation in 17th-Century
Maryland," WMQ, 44 (1987)
Marylynn Salmon, Women and the Law of Property in Early
America
Carroll Smith-Rosenberg, "Domesticating 'Virtue': Coquettes and
Revolutionaries in Young America," in Literature and the
Body, ed. Elaine Scarry
Julia Cherry Spruill, Women's Life and Work in the Southern
Colonies
Laurel Thatcher Ulrich, Good Wives: Image and Reality in the
Lives of Women in Northern New England, 1650-1750
_____, A Midwife's Tale: The Life of Martha
Ballard, Based on Her Diary, 1785-1812
Lisa Wilson, Life After Death: Widows in Pennsylvania, 1750-1850

V. NINETEENTH CENTURY

Elaine Abelson, When Ladies Go A-Thieving: Middle-Class Shop-
lifters in the Victorian Department Store
Paula Baker, "The Domestication of Politics: Women and
American Political Society, 1780-1920," AHR, 89 (1984)
_____, The Moral Frameworks of Public Life: Gender, Politics
and the State in Rural New York, 1870-1930
Peter Bardaglio, Reconstructing the Household: Families, Sex,
and the Law in the 19th-Century South
Norma Basch, In the Eyes of the Law: Women, Marriage, and
Property in Nineteenth-Century New York
Karen Blair, The Clubwoman as Feminist: True Womanhood
Redefined
Carol Bleser, ed., In Love and in Sorrow: Women, Family, and
Marriage in the Victorian South, 1830-1860
Mary Blewett, Men, Women, and Work: Gender, Class and Protest
in the New England Shoe Industry, 1780-1910
Ruth Bordin, Frances Willard: A Biography
_____, Woman and Temperance: The Quest for Power and
Liberty
Jeanne Boydston, Home and Work: Housework, Wages, and the
Ideology of Labor in the Early Republic
Janet Farrell Brodie, Contraception and Abortion in Nineteenth-
Century America
Steven Buechler, The Transformation of the Woman Suffrage
Movement: The Case of Illinois, 1850-1920
Mari Jo Buhle and Paul Buhle, eds., The Concise History of

Women Suffrage
Mari Jo Buhle, Women and American Socialism, 1870-1920
Lee Chambers-Schiller, Liberty, A Better Husband: Single Women
    in America: The Generations of 1780-1840
Nancy F. Cott, The Bonds of Womanhood: "Woman's Sphere" in New
    England, 1780-1835
_____, "Passionlessness: An Interpretation of
    Victorian Sexual Ideology, 1790-1850," Signs, 4 (1978-79)
Margery Davies, Woman's Place is at the Typewriter: Office Work
    and Office Workers, 1870-1930
Hasia R. Diner, Erin's Daughters in America: Irish Immigrant
    Women in the Nineteenth Century
Thomas Dublin, Women at Work: The Transformation of Work and
    Community in Lowell, Massachusetts, 1826-1860
_____, Transforming Women's Work: New England Lives in
    the Industrial Revolution
Ellen Carol DuBois, Feminism and Suffrage: The Emergence of
    an Independent Women's Movement, 1848-1869
_____, ed., Elizabeth Cady Stanton/Susan B.
    Anthony: Correspondence, Writings, Speeches
Faye E. Dudden, Serving Women: Household Service in Nineteenth
    Century America
_____, Women in the American Theatre: Actresses and
    Audiences, 1790-1870
Barbara Leslie Epstein, The Politics of Domesticity: Women,
    Evangelism, and Temperance in Nineteenth-Century America
Mary Ewens, The Role of the Nun in 19th-Century America
John Mack Faragher, Women and Men on the Overland Trail
Christie Anne Farnham, The Education of the Southern Belle:
    Higher Education and Student Socialization in the Antebellum
    South
Drew Gilpin Faust, "'Trying to do a Man's Business': Slavery,
    Violence and Gender in the American Civil War," G&H (1992)
_____, Mothers of Invention: Women of the Slave-
    holding South in the American Civil War
Roberta Frankfort, Collegiate Women: Domesticity and Career in
    Turn of the Century America
Elizabeth Fox-Genovese, Within the Plantation Household: Black
    and White Women of the Old South
Estelle B. Freedman, Their Sisters' Keepers: Women's Prison
    Reform in America, 1830-1930
_____, "Separatism as Strategy: Female
    Institution Building and American Feminism, 1870-1930,"
    FS, 5 (1979)
Miriam Formanek-Brunell, Made to Play House: Dolls and the Com-
    mercialization of American Girlhood, 1830-1930
Lori D. Ginzberg, Women and the Work of Benevolence: Morality,
    Politics and Class in the 19th Century U.S.
Linda Gordon, Woman's Body, Woman's Right: A Social History
    of Birth Control in America
Harvey Green, The Light of the Home: An Intimate View of the
    Lives of Women in Victorian America
Elisabeth Griffith, In Her Own Right: The Life of Elizabeth
    Cady Stanton

28

Timothy Guilfoyle, City of Eros: New York City, Prostitution, and
    the Commercialization of Sex, 1790-1920
Karen V. Hansen, A Very Social Time: Crafting Community in
    Antebellum New England
Blanche Glassman Hersh, The Slavery of Sex: Feminist-
    Abolitionists
Nancy A. Hewitt, Women's Activism and Social Change: Rochester,
    New York, 1822-1872
Marjorie Wood Hill, Their Sisters' Keepers: Prostitution in New
    York City
Barbara Miel Hobson, Uneasy Virtue: The Politics of
    Prostitution and the American Reform Tradition
Sylvia D. Hoffert, When Hens Crow: The Woman's Rights Movement
    in Antebellum America
Julie Roy Jeffrey, Frontier Women: The Trans-Mississippi West
    _____, Converting the West: A Biography of Narcissa
    Whitman
Joan M. Jensen, Loosening the Bonds: Mid-Atlantic Farm Women,
    1750-1850
Polly Welts Kaufman, Women Teachers on the Frontier
Mary Kelley, Private Woman, Public Stage: Literary Domesticity
    in Nineteenth-Century America
S. J. Kleinberg, The Shadow of the Mills: Working-Class Families
    in Pittsburgh, 1870-1907
Aileen S. Kraditor, Ideas of the Woman Suffrage Movement, 1890-
    1920
William Leach, True Love and Perfect Union: The Feminist
    Reform of Sex and Society
Suzanne Lebsock, The Free Women of Petersburg: Status and
    Culture in a Southern Town, 1784-1860
Elizabeth D. Leonard, Yankee Women: Gender Battles in the Civil
    War
Gerda Lerner, The Grimke Sisters from South Carolina
Susan Levine, Labor's True Woman: Carpet Weavers,
    Industrialization, and Labor Reform in the Gilded Age
Karen Lystra, Searching the Heart: Men, Women, and Romantic
    Love in Nineteenth-Century America
Ann Patton Malone, Sweet Chariot: Slave Family and Household
    Structure in Nineteenth-Century Louisiana
Theodora Penny Martin, The Sound of our own Voices: Women's
    Study Clubs, 1860-1910
Kathleen McCarthy, Women's Culture: American Philanthropy and Art
    1830-1939
Stephanie McCurry, Masters of Small Worlds: Yeoman Households,
    Gender Relations & the Political Culture of the Antebellum
    South Carolina Low Country
Judith A. McGaw, "No Passive Victims, No Separate Spheres: A
    Feminist Perspective on Technology's History," In
    Context: History and the History of Techology, ed.
    Stephen Cunliffe
Sally G. McMillen, Motherhood in the Old South: Pregnancy,
    Childbirth, and Infant Rearing
Marilyn Ferris Motz, True Sisterhod: Michigan Women and their
    Kin, 1820-1920

Cynthia Neverdon-Morton, Afro-American Women of the South and the Advancement of the Race
William O'Neill, Everyone Was Brave: The Rise and Fall of Feminism in America
Nancy Grey Osterud, Bonds of Community: The Lives of Farm Women in Nineteenth Century America
Peggy Pascoe, Relations of Rescue: The Search for Female Moral Authority in the American West, 1874-1939
Theda Perdue, "Cherokee Women and the Trail of Tears," JWH (1989)
George C. Rable, Civil Wars: Women and the Crisis of Southern Nationalism
Cynthia Eagle Russett, Sexual Science: The Victorian Construction of Womanhood
Mary P. Ryan, Cradle of the Middle Class: The Family in Oneida County, New York, 1790-1865
_____, Women in Public: Between Banners and Ballots, 1825-1885
Anne Firor Scott, The Southern Lady: From Pedestal to Politics
Kathryn Kish Sklar, Catharine Beecher: A Study in American Domesticity
_____, Florence Kelley and the Nation's Work: The Rise of Women's Political Culture, 1830-1900
Carroll Smith-Rosenberg, Disorderly Conduct: Visions of Gender in Victorian America
Amy Gilman Srebnick, The Mysterious Death of Mary Rogers: Sex and Culture in 19th-century New York
Christine Stansell, City of Women: Sex and Class in New York, 1789-1860
Dorothy Sterling, ed., We are Your Sisters: Black Women in the Nineteenth Century
Madeline Stern, We the Women: Career Firsts of 19th-Century America
Brenda Stevenson, Life in Black and White: Family and Community in the Slave South
Carole Turbin, Working Women of Collar City: Gender, Class and Community in Troy, 1864-86
Barbara Welter, Dimity Convictions: The American Woman in the Nineteenth Century
Deborah Gray White, Arn't I a Woman? Female Slaves in the Plantation South
LeeAnn Whites, The Civil War as a Crisis in Gender: Augusta, Georgia, 1860-1890
Jean Fagan Yellin, Women and Sisters: The Antislavery Feminists in American Culture
_____ and John Van Horne, eds., The Abolitionist Sisterhood: Women's Political Culture in Antebellum America

VI. TWENTIETH CENTURY

Ruth Alexander, The "Girl Problem": Female Sexual Delinquency in New York, 1900-1930

Karen Anderson, Wartime Women: Sex Roles, Family Relations,
    and the Status of Women During World War II
Beth L. Bailey, From Front Porch to Back Seat: Courtship
    in Twentieth Century America
_____ and David Farber, The First Strange Place: Race
    and Sex in World War II Hawaii
Gail Bederman, Manliness and Civilization: A Cultural History of
    Gender and Race in the U.S., 1880-1917
Susan Porter Benson, Counter Cultures: Saleswomen, Managers,
    and Customers in American Department Stores, 1890-1940
Julia Kirk Blackwelder, Women of the Depression: Caste and
    Culture in San Antonio, 1929-1939
Kathleen Blee, Women of the Klan
Susan Cahn, Coming on Strong: Gender and Sexuality in 20th-
    Century Women's Sport
Ardis Cameron, Radicals of the Worst Wort: Laboring Women in
    Lawrence, Massachusetts, 1860-1912
Jane Jerome Camhi, Women Against Women: American Anti-Suffragism,
    1880-1920
William Chafe, The American Woman: Her Changing Social,
    Economic, and Political Roles, 1920-1970
Elizabeth Clark-Lewis, Living In, Living Out: African-American
    Domestics in Washington, D.C., 1910-1940
Miriam Cohen, Workshop to Office: Two Generations of Italian
    Women in New York City, 1900-1950
Blanche Wiesen Cook, Eleanor Roosevelt, 2 vols.
Patricia Cooper, Once a Cigar Maker: Men, Women, and Work
    Culture in American Cigar Factories, 1900-1919
Nancy F. Cott, The Grounding of Modern Feminism
Vicki L. Crawford, et al., eds., Women in the Civil Rights
    Movement: Trailblazers and Torchbearers, 1941-1965
Sarah Deutsch, No Separate Refuge: Cluture, Class, and Gender
    on an Anglo-Hispanic Frontier in the American Southwest,
    1880-1940
Ileen A. DeVault, Sons and Daughters of Labor: Class and Clerical
    Work in Turn-of-the-Century Pittsburgh
Sara M. Evans, Personal Politics: The Roots of Women's
    Liberation in the Civil Rights Movement and the New Left
Lillian Faderman, Odd Girls and Twilight Lovers: Lesbian Life in
    20th-Century America
Paula Fass, The Damned and the Beautiful: American Youth in
    the 1920s
Elizabeth Faue, Community of Suffering and Struggle: Women,
    Men, and the Labor Movement in Minneapolis, 1915-1945
Peter G. Filene, Him/Her/Self: Sex Roles in Modern America
Lisa Fine, The Souls of the Skyscrapers: Female Clerical
    Workers in Chicago, 1870-1930
Ellen Fitzpatrick, Endless Crusade: Women Social Scientists
    and Progressive Reform
Noralee Frankel and Nancy S. Dye, eds., Gender, Class, Race &
    Reform in the Progressive Era
Estelle Freedman, Maternal Justice: Miriam Van Waters and the
    Female Reform Tradition, 1887-1974
Nancy Gabin, Feminism in the Labor Movement: Women and the

United Auto Workers, 1935-1975
Evelyn Nakano Glenn, Issei, Nisei, War Bride: Three
    Generations of Japanese American Women in Domestic
    Service
Susan Glenn, Daughters of the Shtetl: Life and Labor in the
    Immigrant Generation
Linda Gordon, Heroes of their Own Lives: The Politics and
    History of Family Violence
_____, Pitied but not Entitled: Single Mothers and the
    History of Welfare
Lynn Gordon, Gender and Higher Education in the Progressive
    Era
Maurine Weiner Greenwald, Women, War, and Work: The Impact of
    World War I on Women Workers in the United States
Jacquelyn Dowd Hall, Revolt Against Chivalry: Jessie Daniel
    Ames and the Women's Campaign Against Lynching
_____, "Disorderly Women: Gender and Labor
    Militancy in the Appalachian South," JAH, 73 (1986)
Cynthia Harrison, On Account of Sex: The Politics of Women's
    Issues, 1945-1968
Evelyn Brooks Higginbotham, Righteous Discontent: The Women's
    Movement in the Black Baptist Church, 1880-1920
Margaret R. Higonnet, ed., Behind the Lines: Gender and the
    Two World Wars
Darlene Clark Hine, Black Women in White: Racial Conflict and
    Cooperation in the Nursing Profession, 1890-1950
Thomas J. Jablonsky, The Home, Heaven, and Mother Party: Female
    Anti-Suffragists in the US, 1868-1920
Dolores Janiewski, Sisterhood Denied: Race, Gender, and Class
    in a New South Community
Glen Jeansonne, Women of the Far Right: The Mothers' Movement and
    World War II
Kathleen Jellison, Entitled to Power: Farm Women and Technology,
    1913-1963
David M. Katzman, Seven Days a Week: Women and Domestic
    Service in Industrializing America
David Kennedy, Birth Control in America: The Career of
    Margaret Sanger
Elizabeth Lapovsky Kennedy and Madeline D. Davis, Boots of
    Leather, Slippers of Gold: The History of a Lesbian
    Community
Alisa Klaus, Every Child a Lion: The Origins of Maternal and
    Infant Health Policy in the United States and France,
    1890-1920
Joyce L. Kornbluh and Mary Frederickson, eds., Sisterhood and
    Solidarity: Workers' Education for Women, 1914-1984
Seth Koven and Sonya Michel, eds., Mothers of a New World:
    Maternalist Politics and the Origins of the Welfare State
Regina G. Kunzel, Fallen Women, Problem Girls: Unmarried Mothers
    and the Professionalization of Social Work, 1890-1945
Angel Kwolek-Folland, Engendering Business: Men and Women in the
    Corporate Office, 1870-1930
Molly Ladd-Taylor, Mother-Work: Women, Child Welfare, and the
    State, 1890-1930

Gretchen Lemke-Santangelo, Abiding Courage: African American Migrant Women and the East Bay Community

J. Stanley _____, The Woman Citizen: Social Feminism in 1920s

Louise Lamphere, From Working Mothers to Working Daughters

Judy Barrett Litoff, ed., We're in this War, Too: World War II Letters from American Women in Uniform

Elizabeth Lunbeck, The Psychiatric Persuasion: Knowledge, Gender, and Power in Modern America

Susan Lynn, Progressive Women in Conservative Times: Racial Justice, Peace, and Feminism, 1945 to the 1960s

Elaine Tyler May, Homeward Bound: American Families in the Cold War Era

_____, Great Expectations: Marriage and Divorce in Post-Victorian America

Donald G. Mathews and Jane DeHart, Sex, Gender, and the Politics of ERA: A State and the Nation

Carole R. McCann, Birth Control Politics in the United States, 1916-1945

Barbara Melosh, The Physician's Hand: Work, Culture, and Conflict in American Nursing

_____, ed., Gender and American History Since 1890

Joanne J. Meyerowitz, Women Adrift: Independent Wage Earners in Chicago, 1880-1930

_____, ed., Not June Cleaver: Women and Gender in Postwar America

Ruth Milkman, Gender at Work: The Dynamics of Job Segregation by Sex during World War II

Gwendolyn Mink, The Wages of Motherhood: Inequality in the Welfare State, 1917-1942

Marian J. Morton, And Sin No More: Social Policy and Unwed Mothers in Cleveland, 1855-1990

Robyn Muncy, Creating a Female Dominion in American Reform, 1890-1930

Vera Norwood, Made from this Earth: American Women and Nature

Mary E. Odem, Delinquent Daughters: Protecting and Policing Adolescent Female Sexuality in the US, 1885-1920

Annelise Orlick, Common Sense and a Little Fire: Women and Working-Class Politics in the US, 1900-1965

Phyllis Palmer, Domesticity and Dirt: Housewives and Domestic Servants in the United States, 1920-1945

Kathy Peiss, Cheap Amusements: Working Women and Leisure in Turn-of-the-Century New York

Kenneth D. Rose, American Women and the Repeal of Prohibition

Ruth Rosen, The Lost Sisterhood: Prostitution in America, 1900-18

Rosalind Rosenberg, Beyond Separate Spheres: Intellectual Roots of Modern Feminism

_____, Divided Lives: American Women in the 20th Century

Sheila Rothman, Woman's Proper Place: A History of Changing Ideals and Practices, 1870 to the Present

Vicki L. Ruiz, Cannery Women, Cannery Lives: Mexican Women, Unionization, and the California Food Processing Industry, 1930-1950

Leila Rupp and Verta Taylor, Survival in the Doldrums: The

American Woman's Rights Movement, 1945 to the 1960s
John Rury, Education and Women's Work: Female Schooling and
    the Division of Labor in Urban America, 1870-1930
Jennifer Scanlon, Inarticulate Longings: The Ladies' Home Journal
    Gender, and the Promises of Consumer Culture
Lois Scharf, To Work and To Wed: Female Employment, Feminism
    and the Great Depression
Lois Scharf and Joan Jensen, eds. Decades of Discontent: The
    Women's Movement, 1920-1940
Virginia Scharff, Taking the Wheel: Women and the Coming of
    the Motor Age
Stephanie J. Shaw, What a Woman Ought to Be and to Do: Black
    Professional Women Workers during the Jim Crow Era
Judith Smith, Family Connections: Italian and Jewish Lives in
    Providence, Rhode Island, 1900-1940
Susan L. Smith, Sick and Tired of Being Sick and Tired: Black
    Women's Health Activism, 1890-1950
Rickie Solinger, Wake Up Little Susie: Single Pregnancy and Race
    before Roe v. Wade
_____, The Abortionist: A Woman Against the Law
Sharon Hartman Strom, Beyond the Typewriter: Gender, Class and
    the Origins of Modern American Office Work, 1900-1930
Amy Swerdlow, Women Strike for Peace: Traditional Motherhood
    and Radical Politics in the 1960s
Leslie Woodcock Tentler, Wage-Earning Women: Industrial Work
    and Family Life in the United States, 1900-1930
Cynthia Grant Tucker, Prophetic Sisterhood: Liberal Women
    Ministers of the Frontier, 1880-1930
David Tyack and Elisabeth Hansot, Learning Together: A History of
    Coeducation in American Public Schools
Susan Van Horn, Women, Work, and Fertility, 1900-1986
Winifred D. Wandersee, On the Move: American Women in the
    1970s
Susan Ware, Partner and I: Molly Dewson
_____, Beyond Suffrage: Women in the New Deal
Lynn Y. Weiner, From Working Girl to Working Mother: The
    Female Labor Force in the United States, 1820-1980
Barbara Meyer Wertheimer, ed., Labor Education for Women
    Workers
Marjorie Spruill Wheeler, New Women of the New South: The Leaders
    of the Woman Suffrage Movement in the Southern States
Susan M. Yohn, A Contest of Faiths: Missionary Women and
    Pluralism in the American Southwest
Patricia Zavella, Women's Work and Chicano Families: Cannery
    Workers of the Santa Clara Valley

AHR=American Historical Review   JSH=Journal of Social History
FS= Feminist Studies   JWH=Journal of Women's History
JAH=Journal of American History   WMQ=William & Mary Quarterly
G&H=Gender & History

VI. SOME NOTABLE FILMS

A. Feature Films

Heartland (based on the letters of Elinore Pruitt Stewart, a
    homesteader in early 20th-century Montana)
Daughters of the Dust (African American women in Gullah-speaking
    regions of the Carolinas in the early 20th century)
Hester Street (a Russian Jewish woman's experience in early 20th-
    century New York)
Come See the Paradise (a real mess of a movie, but contains good
    segments on the internment of a Japanese American woman
    during World War II)
Thousand Pieces of Gold (based on the life story of a Chinese-
    American woman in the 19th-century American West)
The Long Walk Home (an African American domestic worker and her
    white employer during the Montgomery Bus Boycott)
Salt of the Earth (controversial 1950s film on women's roles in
    a zinc miners' strike in New Mexico)
A League of Their Own (the story of the All American Girls'
    Professional Baseball League, inspired by the documentary
    film of the same name)
The Ballad of Little Jo (an interesting spin on standard male-
    oriented histories of the American frontier; deals with a
    woman who dresses as a man in order to survive)
If These Walls Could Talk (covers the stories of three women in
    three different eras -- 1952, 1974 & 1996 -- who considered
    abortions)

B. Documentary Films

Hearts and Hands: Quiltmaking in Women's Lives (covers women's
    history, 1820-1900)
The Life and Times of Rosie the Riveter (women and World War II)
Women of Summer: The Bryn Mawr Summer School for Women Workers
    in Industry, 1921-1939
A Passion for Justice: The Life of Ida B. Wells
Sentimental Women Need Not Apply: A History of American Nursing
All My Babies (a classic study of African American midwives in
    1950s Georgia)
Union Maids (women as union activists)
With Babies and Banners: The Story of the Women's Emergency
    Brigade (1930s auto workers)
Madame C. J. Walker: Two Dollars and a Dream (biography of the
    first African American woman millionaire)
Silver Wings and Santiago Blue (the Women's Air Service Pilots
    in World War II)
International Sweethearts of Rhythm and Tiny and Ruby: Hell
    Divin' Women (two films about an interracial women's jazz
    band from the 1940s and its trumpeter, Tiny Davis)
Fundi: The Story of Ella Baker (profile of a notable civil rights
    worker)
Freedom Bags (on African American women domestics and the Great

35

Migration)

Watsonville on Strike (Mexican American women cannery workers)

Radium City (white women workers in a radium dial plant in
Ottawa, Ill. during the 1920s, whose work was toxic to their
health)

The Willmar Eight (bank tellers in a small Minnesota town who
fought employer efforts to "downsize" them)

Slaying the Dragon (media portrayals of Asian-American women and
the stereotypes they reflect)

The Emerging Woman (good short, though somwhat dated, history of
the women's rights movement)

Indians, Outlaws, and Angie Debo (a pioneering historian of
the West and her role in documenting land fraud)

A League of Their Own (women's baseball league 1943-54; the
feature film with the same title was inspired by this one)

Beyond Imagining: Margaret Anderson and "The Little Review" (a
short biography of the literary editor and lesbian feminist)

Back-Alley Detroit (abortion in the era when it was illegal)

Last Call at Maud's (California lesbian life in the 1950s and
1960s, seen through reminiscences of a bar and its patrons)

Guerillas in Our Midst (chronicles the activities of the Guerilla
Girls, a group of activist women artists)

Heaven Will Protect the Working Girl (focuses on immigrant
garment workers in early 20th-century New York City)

One Woman, One Vote (a two-hour documentary on the fight for
women's suffrage)

When Abortion was Illegal (a 30-minute film featuring interviews
with women who had abortions in the 1950s and 1960s)

Leona's Sister Gerri (Gerri died as the result of an illegal
abortion; this film tells her story, that of her family, and
of a graphic photograph used in the cause of abortion
rights; 60 minutes)

With Fingers of Love (tells the story of a group of Mississippi
quilters who turned their domestic skills into a money-
making cooperative; 30 minutes)

Nobody's Girls: Five Women of the American West (90 minutes)

Alice Paul: We Were Arrested, Of Course (a 28-minute film
documenting the early life and suffrage activism of Alice
Paul and other members of the National Woman's Party)

A Midwife's Tale (interweaves historical reenactments with
coverage of historian Laurel Thatcher Ulrich as she re-
constructs the life of Martha Ballard, an 18th-century
Maine midwife; 80 minutes)

WOMEN IN UNITED STATES HISTORY

Lori Ginzberg   History 117
410 Weaver   Fall 1997
863-8947   email: LDG1@psu.edu

Office Hours: Wednesday 9-11

This course surveys the history of women in the United States from
the colonial period to the twentieth century. It focuses on
ideologies about women as well as women's actual experiences as
members of a class, a race, and an ethnic community. The course uses
primary and secondary materials in order to understand how these
factors, as well as the shared social experiences of gender, shaped
women's lives.

The class meets twice a week for lectures, films, and discussion. You
are responsible for:

1) Attendance and participation in class (10%)
2) 3-5 page paper due on Sept. 19 (15%)
3) In-class midterm on Oct. 10 (20%)
4) Biographical project due on Dec. 5 (25%)
5) Final exam (30%)

LATE PAPERS WILL BE GRADED DOWN.

The following are required reading, available in the bookstore and on
reserve in the library. Readings which are not in these books
(marked with a *) are available in a photocopy packet, which is on
sale at the bookstore.

        Nancy Cott, et al., Root of Bitterness (2nd edition)
        Constance Curry, Silver Rights
        Harriet Jacobs, Incidents in the Life of a Slave Girl
        Susan Ware, Modern American Women: A Documentary
            History

ASSIGNMENTS AND TOPICS:

Aug. 28:   INTRODUCTION TO THE COURSE

Sep. 2:   WHY WOMEN'S HISTORY?

             *Gerda Lerner, "Placing Women in History," in The
                Majority Finds its Past (145-59) (1974)

Sep. 4:   WOMEN AND CULTURAL CONTACT

             Root of Bitterness, pp. 36-41
             *Bush, "The Eye of the Beholder: Contemporary European
             Images of Black Women," in Slave Women in
             Caribbean Society (11-22)

Sep. 9:   GENDER AND COMMUNITY IN THE NORTHERN COLONIES

             Root of Bitterness, pp. 17-29; 42-46
             *Laurel Ulrich, "The Ways of her Household," chap. 1
             of Good Wives (NY: 1980) (13-34)

Sep. 11:   WITCHES AND OTHER "DEVIANTS"

             Root of Bitterness, pp. 3-16; 32-35
             *Carol Karlsen, "The Devil in the Shape of a Woman,"
             in Kerber & DeHart, Women's America (4th ed.)
             (57-72)

Sep. 16:   GENDER AND RACE IN THE SOUTHERN COLONIES

             Root of Bitterness, pp. 29-31

Sep. 18-23: TRANSITIONS TO A NEW REPUBLIC

             Root of Bitterness, pp. 49-70; 83-109
             *Cornelia Hughes Dayton, "Taking the Trade: Abortion
             and Gender Relations in an 18th-Century New
             England Village," Women's America (68-84)

Sep. 25:   WOMEN AND THE REVOLUTIONARY ERA

PAPER DUE!
             Root of Bitterness, pp. 71-82

Sep. 30:   WOMAN'S SPHERE AND WOMEN'S EMPLOYMENTS

             Root of Bitterness, pp. 113-173
             *Nancy Cott, "Passionlessness," A Heritage of Her Own
             (162-81)

Oct. 2:   ROSH HASHONAH: NO CLASS

Oct. 7:   THE DIFFERING BONDS OF WOMANHOOD

              Root of Bitterness, pp. 198-212
              *Smith-Rosenberg, "Female World of Love and Ritual,"
                 in Disorderly Conduct (53-76)
              *Stansell, "Women, Children, and the Uses of the
                 Street," in Women's America 4th ed (129-42)

Oct. 9-14:   SLAVERY AND SEX

              Root of Bitterness, pp. 239-73
              Jacobs, Incidents in the Life of a Slave Girl

Oct. 16:   IN-CLASS MIDTERM

Oct. 21:   WOMEN AND THE NATIONAL MISSION: IMMIGRANTS & PIONEERS

              Root of Bitterness, pp. 177-197; 213-235

Oct. 23:   HEALTH, MEDICINE AND SEXUALITY

              Root of Bitterness, pp. 293-340

Oct. 28:   WOMEN'S WORK IN AN INDUSTRIAL AGE

              Root of Bitterness, 347-395
              Modern American Women, 54-86

Oct. 30:   ORGANIZING WOMEN

              *Alice Kessler-Harris, "Where are the Organized Women
                 Workers?" in A Heritage of Her Own (343-66)

Nov. 4:   THE 'THREADBARE LIE': RACE, SEXUALITY & VIOLENCE

              FILM: "IDA B. WELLS: A PASSION FOR JUSTICE"

              Root of Bitterness, pp. 274-90
              *Excerpts from Selected Works of Ida B. Wells-Barnett,
                 compiled by Trudier Harris (Oxford, 1991), pp.
                 16-45; 216-39

Nov. 6-11:   THE NEW WOMAN: FEMINISTS AND RADICALS

               Root of Bitterness, pp. 399-440
               Modern American Women, pp. 3-53, 87-111, 112-136

Nov. 13:   THE DEPRESSION

               FILM: UNION MAIDS

Nov. 18:   THE DEPRESSION

               Modern American Women, 172-204

Nov. 20:   WORLD WAR TWO

               FILM: "ROSIE THE RIVETER"

               Modern American Women, 213-240

Nov. 25:   THE FIFTIES

               Modern American Women, 241-262
               Begin reading Constance Curry, Silver Rights

Nov. 27:   THANKSGIVING: NO CLASSES

Dec. 2:   BLACK WOMEN, WHITE WOMEN, AND CIVIL RIGHTS

               Curry, Silver Rights
               Modern American Women, 263-273

Dec. 4:   THE SECOND WAVE OF FEMINISM

               Modern American Women, 279-369

Dec. 9:   THE 1980S: BACKLASH

BIOGRAPHICAL PROJECTS DUE!

Modern American Women, 373-412

Dec. 11:   DISCUSSION OF BIOGRAPHICAL PROJECTS & REVIEW FOR FINAL

History 320:
United States Women's History Survey

Renée M. Sentilles
MW 11-12:20
office hours: Tues 1-4 pm, or by appointment
Phone: X3963; home: 391-5868
R_Sentilles@acad.fandm.edu

American Women's History is the study of American culture focusing attention on the experiences of women. Exploring women's history means attempting to make sense of American women's pasts: underlying patterns, overt themes, and events effecting women's legal, social, and/or political status. It is also important to us, as scholars looking to the past, to try and reconstruct the fabric of many women's everyday lives, and to remember that individuals make up our collective past. Because women and men live together, raise families together, use and are subject to the same legal and political system, and are held together as citizens under the same constitution--the history of women in the United States is American history with a gender-specific angle of inquiry.

The course will begin by coming to terms with the various meanings of "gender" and "sex." In the ensuing weeks, we will examine how those definitions change in American culture(s) and how they are shaped by class, race, and religion.

After the first week, the class will assume a "survey approach" to U. S. women's history. Readings will correspond with, but not replicate, the lectures. Students are invited to participate with questions and comments during the lectures, and are required to take part in class discussions.

Objectives:

By the end of this course students should exhibit an understanding of the overall chronology, key events, themes and underlying patterns characterizing American women's history. They should also be familiar with current debates in the study of gender, sexuality, women and the family. In both papers and discussions, students are expected to present clear, concise arguments supported with specific evidence. Students will read critically by interpreting and evaluating scholarly arguments. Finally, students should leave the course with a better understanding of gender, American women's history and our collective American past.

Attendance and Participation:

All class meetings are mandatory. Attendance and participation will make up 10% of your semester grade. For your own sake, let me know if you will be absent from class. Participation means both listening and joining in discussion. I will keep records on attendance and participation, and you should feel free to inquire about your record. This is *your* class and you are expected to be actively involved.

Assignments:
Journal writing: Students will keep journals *responding* to weekly class readings (that means analyzing, giving opinions, figuring things out --NOT SUMMARIZING). I may sometimes suggest a topic. Journals must be kept in either a spiral bound notebook (handwritten in pencil, blue or black ink) or a sturdy folder (typed). Names must be clearly written on the cover of the journal. Journals will be graded on content, not grammar. Students will be assigned to group A, B, or C, and turn in their journal on the date designated by the syllabus (approx. every 3 weeks). Journals are worth **30%** of the semester grade and will be graded with a check+ (=A to B+), check (=B to C), or check- (= C- to D). *Students will not need to write an entry for the week they work on the biography paper.*

Quizes: There will be two *short* quizes to make sure you are getting the basic information. Each quiz is worth **5%** of the semester grade.

Short Paper (4-5 pages + citations) **20%** of semester grade. See attached for details.

Final Paper (approx. 15 pages + citations): **30%** of semester grade. See attatched for details.

Writing: I expect to receive papers with clear, well supported theses. *Do not* turn in a paper with mispelled words or incorrect grammar. We will talk more about writing as we approach the paper assignments.
You are invited to come to me with drafts (the more polished, the more you will get out of our meeting) a week before the paper is due.

Grading: I use the scale designated in the F&M catalogue (A=4.0, A-=3.7, etc).
To get an 'A' in this course you must be excellent all-around (attend class, participate, turn in creative, well-written and inciteful papers, and engage material in your journal). You must do a good, solid job to earn a 'B' (turn in papers that satisfy the assignment, attend nearly every class, participate somewhat, and complete journal assignments). C students are slackers. D students are worse then slackers and will end up having several talks with me before the semester ends.

Required Texts:
Three Readers (Collections):
Mary Beth Norton, Major Problems in American Women's History **(MP)**
Nancy Cott, et al., Root of Bitterness: Documents of the Social History of Women (2nd edition, 1996) **[RB]**
Ellen Dubois, Vicki Ruiz, Unequal Sisters (2nd edition) **[UES]**

Four biographies:
Anzi Yezierska, Breadgivers
Nell and Robert Peters, Nell's Story
Ann Moody, Coming of Age in Mississippi
Florence King, Confessions of a Failed Southern Lady

Two short novels:
    Charlotte Perkins Gilman, The Yellow Wallpaper
    Kate Chopin, The Awakening

Optional (I will xerox chapters from the following, but it may be easier for you to buy the book): Susan Douglas, Where the Girls Are: Growing Up Female with the Mass Media.

Reserve Articles: Articles are placed on reserve at the library. I will also have a copy of the reserve readings in my office, another in the history department (just ask Mrs. Bender if you can see it), and I will "float" two copies among the students.

Notes on Reading:
    Reading in this class is moderate, but appears heavy because it tends to be scattered. With the exception of the biographies, most weekly readings will come in around 150 pages.
    Students are required to engage the material. For some of you this may mean reading every word, for others it may mean reading "objectively"--with a pencil and paper in hand, taking notes, but not reading everything in entirety. My requirements are that you 1) understand and critique the arguments made in secondary readings 2) can take a "historian's" approach to the primary documents--reading them to enhance your understanding and ability to critique lectures and secondary readings.

Extensions/Absences: Class time is sacred space. Do not schedule anything during class time unless you are willing to pay the penalty of absence. Extensions and excused absences will be given only if you are on your death bed or if you personally are coping with a family tragedy.

My contract with you: My job as a professor is to convey information, help you work on skills relevant to the historical discipline, and to encourage your intellectual growth. As your professor I will respect your right to make personal decisions, I will not hold classes over the designated time limit, nor add extra assignments or class meetings.   I am aware that you all live full and busy lives. Academic learning should be an integral and positive part of your life, not an activity that encourages you to disregard physical and/or emotional health.

January 22: Introduction to the Course
    READING: Introduction to RB; Lerner, MP; on reserve: Joan Wallach Scott, "Gender: A Useful Category of Analysis"

January 27: Gender and Conquest
    READING: Joan Jensen, "Native American Women and Agriculture: A Seneca Case Study," UES.

Women in Colonial and Revolutionary America, 1600-1820

January 29: Gender and Social Construction of Race
    READING: On Reserve: Evelyn Brooks Higginbotham, "African-American
Women's History and the Metalanguage of Race."

GROUP A Journals Due

February 3: Good Wives and Witches
    READING: Koehler, Norton, and Karlsen, MP; ; 3-10, 29-31,36-4, 59-60 RB.

February 5: Revolution
    READING: Wilson and Norton, MP; 77-82, 98-102, 113-137, RB; On Reserve:
Catherine M. Scholten, "On the Importance of the Obstetrick Art' Changing Customs of
Childbirth in America, 1760-1825."

GROUP B

Women and Domesticity in Industrializing America, 1820-1880

February 10: Domesticity and Wage Labor
    Quiz # 1: Through the Revolutionary Period.
    READING: Chapter 5, MP; 132-147, RB.

February 12: Class and Race in the South
    READING: 167-173, 239-242, RB; Deborah Gray White, "Female Slaves: Sex
Roles and Status in the Antebellum Plantation South" UES; Chapter 6, MP.

GROUP C

February 17: Women's Work
    READING: Bordon, MP; 208-217, RB. Jeanne Boydston, "To Earn her Daily
Bread," UES.

February 19: Abolition and Women's Rights
    READING: Truth, Grimke, DuBois, MP; 243-251, 263-267, RB.
GROUP A

February 24: Civil War and Its Aftermath
    Class Film Showing: *Women in American Life, Part I: 1861-1880: Civil
War, Recovery, and Westward Expansion* (fifteen minutes)
    READING: 268-290, RB.

February 26: Women and the West
    Quiz #2: New Nation to Reconstruction
    READING: 178-197, 218-235, RB; On Reserve: Sylvia Hoffert, "Childbearing
in the Trans-Mississippi West."

Group B

March 3: Female Health and Sexuality

Discussion: Yellow Wallpaper
Class Film Showing: *Women in American Life, Part II: 1880-1920: Immigration, New Work and New Roles* (16 minutes)
READING: Chapter 9, MP; Gilman, The Yellow Wallpaper; Part VI in RB.

Transformation of the Women's Sphere, 1880-1920

March 5: Discussion: Kate Chopin, The Awakening
READING: Kate Chopin's The Awakening

* * *   Spring Break!   * * *

March 17: Women and Work
Class Film Showing: *Women in American Life, Part 3: 1917-1942: Cultural Image and Economic Reality* (17 minutes)
READING: 353-395, 421-440 RB; Kathy Peiss, "Charity Girls and City Pleasure: Historical Notes on Working Class Sexuality, 1880-1920" in UES.

March 19: Race, Culture and Social Reform.
Class film showing: *Ida B. Wells: A Passion for Justice* (60 minutes)
READING: Linda Gordon, "Black and White Visions of Welfare," in UES; 400-422, RB.

GROUP C
RESEARCH TOPICS DUE

March 24: Discussion: Anzia Yezierska, Bread givers
READING: Bread givers

March 26: Suffrage
READING: Kraditor, MP; Paula Baker, "Domestication of Politics "; Joanne Meyerowitz, "Sexual Geography and Gender Economy" ; Kathy Peiss "Making Faces," in UES.

GROUP A

Women in Modern America, 1920-1990

March 31: After Suffrage
READING: On Reserve: Pamela Haag, "In Search of 'The Real Thing'" ; Vicki Ruiz, "'Star Struck"; Linda Gordon, "Family Violence, Feminism, and Social Control."

April 2: World War II
Class Film Showing: *Rosie the Riviter*
READING: Chapter 13, MP. Valerie Matsumoto, "Japanese American Women During World War II," in UES.

GROUP B

April 7: Crabgrass Frontier

Class Film Showing: *Women in American Life, Part 4: 1942-1955: War Work, Housework, and Growing Discontent* (15 minutes)
READING: Rickie Solinger, "Race and 'Value'" in UES; On Reserve: Joanne Meyerowitz, "Beyond the Feminine Mystique, 1946-1958"; Rickie Solinger, "Extreme Danger: Women Abortionists and Their Clients before Roe vs. Wade."

April 9: Discussion: Nell's Story
READING: Peters, Nell's Story. Reserve: Wini Breines, "The 'Other' Fifties."
GROUP C

April 14: Women and the Media
Class Film Showing:*Women in American Life, Part 5: 1955-1977: New Attitudes Force Dramatic Changes* (25 minutes)
READING: On Reserve (or available for purchase at Follet's) Susan Douglass, Where the Girls Are: Growing Up Female with The Mass Media, Chapters 1-3.

April 16: Discussion: Moody, Coming of Age in Mississippi
READING: Moody, Coming of Age

April 21: Women's Liberation: 1960s-70s
READING: Friedan, Brauer, NOW, and Evans, MP. On Reserve: Where the Girls Are, Chapters 9-10; Diana Pearce, "Welfare is Not for Women."

April 23: Discussion: King, Confessions of a Failed Southern Lady
READING: Donna Penn, "The Sexualized Woman"; King, Confessions.

April 28: 1980s-90s
READING: Paula Giddings, "The Last Taboo," in UES; On Reserve: Where the Girls Are,Chapters 11-Epilogue; Linda Gordon, "The New Feminist Scholarship on the Welfare State."
A, B, and C Journals Due for final grading

April 30: The Big Picture
Research Papers Due; Bring two copies to class.
READING: Tessie Liu, "Teaching the Differences Among Women," in UES. Reserve: Joan Wallach Scott, "Gender: A Useful Category of Historical Analysis" (reprisal)

Seniors' grades will be available May 12. Please include a self-addressed, stamped envelope if you want your paper returned to you!

Women in American Culture and Society: Short Paper Assignment

I will divide the class into four equal groups according to which biography you will read. Be prepared to rank the books on Monday, January 27, with number 1 as your first choice, and 4 as your last. After you are assigned a book, you may not switch. You will get a list of the other people writing on the same book, in case you would like to meet with them outside of class.

I am dividing the class this way for several reasons: 1)I will have more time to help you with drafts 2)everyone is required to read the book, but this means at least one-quarter of the class will have also analyzed the book.

Students turning in a paper should come to that class prepared to discuss how they approached the biography. These students should also have three compelling questions for the class. These students are also excused from writing a journal entry on the biography.

The paper should be 4-5 pages long, typed and double-spaced.

Students are invited to take any approach they believe will be most effective. I suggest looking at the biograpy within its contextual history, examining how it expresses issues for women (or a particular groups of women) at that time. But this is not the only possible approach. For example, you could explore how Nell's expression of sexuality is an extension of working-class discourse, as seen in several articles. You could analyze the purpose of humor in King's autobiography. Think about what you find most compelling about the book.

Biographies:

Anzi Yezierska, Bread givers. Jewish Russian immigrant Yezierska's compelling examination of ghetto culture in early twentieth-century New York. **Paper due March 24.**

Nell and Robert Peters, Nell's Story: A Woman from Eagle River. Nell Peters grew up on the wrong side of tracks in mid-twentieth-century Wisconsin. Peters's narrative shatters many of our preconceptions about white women of the 1950s. Very bawdy. **Paper due April 9.**

Anne Moody, Coming of Age in Mississippi. A young African-American woman's evocative account of growing up in the Civil Rights Movement. Long book, but worth every page. **Paper due April 16.**

Florence King, Confessions of a Failed Southern Lady. A comical autobiography of a working class white woman coming to terms with her southern heritage.   **Paper due April 23.**

*Sample footnotes:

Thomas Lacquer, Making Sex: Body and Gender from the Greeks to Freud (Cambridge, MA: Harvard University Press, 1990) 158-60.

Gerda Lerner, "Placing Women in History," in Major Problems in American Women's History, ed. Mary Beth Norton (Lexington: DC Heath & Co., 1989) 4.

Final Paper: Images of Women in American Pop Culture

Students will write a research paper focusing on images of women in popular culture. Students should design their own topic, but some possible topics include: "African-American Women in Five Box Office Hits of the 1940s," "The Role of Women During World War II According to *Ladies Home Journal*," "Images of Women in Franklin & Marshall's *College Reporter* during the move to coeducation," "Female Beauty in Advertising in the 1890s," or "Images of Women in the Music of Billy Holiday." In other words: skies the limit, just make sure your topic suits the length of the paper (approx. 15 pages, plus citations).

Topic is due March 19. Write down a brief paragraph outlining your proposed project to turn in during class.

Paper is due April 30, and you will be sharing it with two of your peers.

The paper should be typed and double-spaced. It should have a cover sheet with a title, your name, the course, and the date. Include a bibliography. Because this is a history research paper, you must use footnotes. *Not* parathetical citation. Refer to either Chicago Manual of Style.

Hints:

Be sure to spell-check your paper. Bad spelling in the age of computers just makes you look lazy.

Don't use passive voice. Don't write "The game was played until sunset by the children of the neighborhood." Write "The neighborhood children played the game until sunset." Don't write "She was known to all of Spain as a great ballroom dancer." Write "The Spanish hailed her as a great ballroom dancer."

Write strong sentences. Don't write, "I took a walk, by the way, to the Mr. Hooper's store, and back." Write, "By the way, I took a walk to and from Mr. Hooper's store."

Don't insert first person at the end of the paper. If you are going to bring yourself into the paper, do it from the beginning.

Take risks. The best skiiers fall on their bums a lot, but they also learn to fly; it's the careful ones who end up lost in snow drifts.

Challenge yourself to excel: be creative, take on difficult topics, press the boundaries, argue constructively.

If you want an A, then you have to rewrite. Good writing comes from rewriting. Read the paper outloud; revise it. Give it to a friend; revise it. Bring it to me; revise it. You should be your most critical reader.

2. Graduate and Undergraduate Survey Courses, Settlement to 1890

HISTORY 353:

WOMEN IN AMERICAN SOCIETY TO 1870

Professor: Teaching Assistant:

  Jeanne Boydston   Lisa Tetrault
  boydston@facstaff.wisc.edu   tetrault@students.wisc.edu
  263-0647   263-1939
  5120 Humanities Building   4272 Humanities
  Off. Hrs.: Wed. 11-1 (& by appt.)   Off. Hrs.: T 2:15-3:15/R 11-12

  Class email address: history-353@lists.students.wisc.edu

This course surveys the history of women in the United States from the colonial period to 1870. We will investigate how women understood their lives as individuals and as members of families and communities and how broad discourses of gender framed questions of colonization, nationalism, race, and class. This semester we will approach these issues through the theme of *"authority,"* examining the ways in which women attempted to construct a social authority for themselves (as females, as workers, as citizens, etc.) and the social discourses and institutions that supported and/or weakened those claims.

Books:
We have ordered the following books at **A Room of One's Own Bookstore**:

  Kathryn Sklar and Thomas Dublin, eds., Women and Power, Volume One
  Nancy Cott et al, Root of Bitterness
  Carol Karlsen, The Devil in the Shape of a Woman
  Christine Stansell, City of Women
  Mary Washington, Ed., The Narrative of Sojourner Truth

Also, we have ordered two packets at **Bob's Copy Shop, University Square Mall**:

  a Reading Packet
  a separate xerox packet containing the The Letters of Jerusha Swain.

We will use the Reading Packet throughout the course. Your second (5-page paper) will be on the Swain letters.

Grading:
We expect you to attend all classes and all discussion sections, to complete all assignments on time, and to participate in discussions. We will calculate your final grade as follows:

  Attendance/preparation/discussion \   averaged = 1/3 of final grade
  Reading Guides   /

  3-page paper and re-write   \   averaged = 1/3 of final grade
  5-page paper   /

  Final examination   \   averaged = 1/3 of final grade
  Mid-Term   /

Unexplained absences or late assignments will lower your grade.

January 21:   Introduction

COLONIAL ENCOUNTERS AND COMMUNITIES

January 23:   Pocahontas Revisited

  Root of Bitterness:
      "Carolina Women Observed," pp. 36-41.

January 28:   Race, Gender, and Labor in the Southern Colonies

  Women and Power:
      Lois Green Carr and Lorena Walsh, "The Planter's Wife"
  Root of Bitterness:
      "Ordinary Dealings at Colonial County Courts," Accomak-Northampton
      County, pp. 17-19.

January 30:   Settlement and Slavery

  Root of Bitterness:
      "Statutes on Slave Descent: Virgina and Maryland," 29-31
  Reading Packet:
      Julia Cherry Spruill, "Participation in Public Affairs" [Friedman and
      Shade, Our American Sisters (1973)]
February 4:   Reformation Spirituality

  Carol Karlsen, The Devil in the Shape of a Woman,
  Root of Bitterness:
      "The Examination of Anne Hutchinson," pp. 3-10

February 6:   Family Settlement in New England

  Carol Karlsen, The Devil in the Shape of a Woman
  Root of Bitterness,
      "Church Trial and Excommunication of Anne Hibbens," pp. 11-16
      "Ordinary Dealings at Colonial County Courts," Suffolk County, pp. 19-23

February 11:   Witches and Real Estate

  Carol Karlsen, The Devil in the Shape of a Woman

TRANSITIONS TO A NEW REPUBLIC

February 13:   Religion and Commerce in Eighteenth-Century America

  Women and Power
      Joan Jensen, "Butter Making and Economic Development"
  Root of Bitterness,
      "A Rape on the Body of Ann Eastworthy," pp. 42-43
      "A Law for Regulating Midwives," pp. 44-46
      "Sarah Osborne's Religious Conversion," pp. 49-53
      (Assignment continues next page)

"Query to the Philadelphia Baptist Association," pp. 54-55
"Diary of Mary Cooper," pp. 61-66

February 18: Prosecuting the War

> Root of Bitterness,
> "Abigail Adams' Letters from the Home Front, 1776, 1777," pp. 71-76
> "An Adolescent's Wartime Diary," pp. 77-82

February 20: Gender and the Promises of Liberty

> Women and Power
> Nancy Cott, "Divorce and the Changing Status of Women"
> Reading Packet
> Jean Soderlund, "Black Women in Colonial Pennsylvania," [**Shade and
>   Capozzoli, eds.** Our American Sisters, **4th ed.**, reprinted from
>   Pennsylvania Magazine of History and Biography, 107/1 (1983)]
> Root of Bitterness
> "A Father's Advice to His Daughter," pp. 91-97

*February 24: 3-page paper on Jensen, "Butter Making and Economic Development,"
     due.*

February 25: The Problems of Female Citizenship

> Reading Packet:
> Linda Kerber, "'I Have Don . . . much to Carrey on the Warr': Women and
>   the Shaping of Republican Ideology after the American Revolution"
>   [Applewhite and Levy, Democratic Politics in the Age of the
>   Democratic Revolution]
> Root of Bitterness
> "Moll Placket-Hole," pp. 67-70
> "Eliza Southgate Reflects Upon the Relation of the Sexes," pp. 98-102

WOMAN'S SPHERE AND WOMEN'S EMPLOYMENTS

February 27: Gender, Religion and Reform as a National Discourse

> Reading Packet:
> Lori Ginzberg, "The Business of Benevolence" [Women and the Work of
>   Benevolence]

March 4: Gender, Bodies, and Authority: The Power of Dis-embodiedness

> Reading Packet:
> Nancy F. Cott, "Passionlessness: An Interpretation of Victorian Sexual
>   Ideology," 1790-1850" [Cott and Pleck, A Heritage of Her Own, orig.
>   pub. Signs 4 (1978): 219-36.
> "Parallelism of the Sexes," Providence Ladies Museum (to be distributed)
> Root of Bitterness
> "The Peciliar Responsibilities of American Women," pp. 132-137

March 6:   Gender, Bodies and Power: Prices of Dis-embodiedness

    Reading Packet:
        "Essay on Criminal Abortion: Transactions--WI State Medical Society
           (1870)"
    Women and Power:
        James Mohr, "The Social Character of Abortion in America, 1840-1880"
    Root of Bitterness
        "The Murders of Marriage," pp. 303-308
        "Testimony as to the Insanity of Elizabeth Packard," pp. 309-314

March 11:   Womanhood and Labor

    Re-write of Jensen paper due.

    Christine Stansell, City of Women
    Women and Power:
        Carroll Smith-Rosenberg, "Beauty, the Beast, and the Militant Woman"

March 13:   Claiming Labor

    Christine Stansell, City of Women
    Women and Power
        Thomas Dublin, "Women, Work, and Protest" in Women and Power
    Root of Bitterness:
        "Women's Work in the Market Economy," 105-109
        "Striking Tailoresses Speak," 118-122

March 18:   Maternalism and Other Women's Bodies

    Christine Stansell, City of Women [finish reading]
    Women and Power:
        Lucie Chang, "Chinese Women in 19th-Century California"
    Root of Bitterness:
        "A Moral Reformer Makes Her Rounds," 198-203
        "An Afternoon Call," 204-207

March 20:   Mid-Term Examination

--------------------------------SPRING BREAK--------------------------------

WOMEN AND THE NATIONAL MISSION

April 1:   The Authority of the Land

    Root of Bitterness
        "Cherokee Women Address their Nation," 177-178
        Reading Packet: Lucy Eldersveld Murphy, "Autonomy and the Economic
           Roles of Indian Women of the Fox-Wisconsin River Region, 1763-1832"
           [Shoemaker, Negotiators of Change]

    Women and Power
        Joan Jensen, "Native American Women and Agriculture"

April 3: Gender and the Wars of Removal

    Root of Bitterness
        "Iron Teeth," 224-229
        SEPARATE XEROX PACKET: The Letters of Jerusha Swain (begin reading)

April 8: White Women's Frontiers

    SEPARATE XEROX PACKET: The Letters of Jerusha Swain (finish reading)
    Root of Bitterness:
        "Reaching Oregon," pp. 193-197
        "Since We Came to America," 218-223
    Reading Packet:
        Susan L. Johnson, "Sharing Bed and Board: Cohabitation and Cultural
            Difference in Central Arizona Mining Towns, 1863-1873" [Armitage
            and Jameson, The Women's West]

SLAVERY, WAR, AND EMANCIPATION

April 10: Gender and Slavery in Antebellum America

    Women and Power
        Deborah G. White "Female Slaves"
    Root of Bitterness:
        "James Curry's Mother," pp. 239-242
        "Narratives of Escaped Slaves," pp. 252-257
        "A Slave Writes to Her Former Mistress," pp. 260-261

April 14: 5-page paper on Jerusha Swain letters due.

April 15: Maria Stewart and the Authority of Black Women's Protest

    Root of Bitterness:
        "Maria Stewart Sees Chains on the Soul," pp. 113-117
        "Sarah Parker Remond on American Slavery"
    (Start reading Mary Washington, ed, The Narrative of Sojourner Truth)

April 17: Authoring the Self: Sojourner Truth

    Mary Washington, ed, The Narrative of Sojourner Truth (complete)

April 22: The Authority of White Women's Assault on Slavery

    Root of Bitternress:
        "An Appeal to the Women of the Nominally Free States," pp. 246-251
        "Virgina Ladies' Petition to Eliminate Slavery," pp. 243-245
    Women and Power
        Gerda Lerner, "The Political Activities of Antislavery Women"

April 24: From Reform Talk to Rights Talk

    Reading Packet:
        Lori Ginzberg, "Moral Suasion is Moral Balderdash" [Journal of American
           History]
        "Declaration of Sentiments"
    Root of Bitterness:
        "Sarah Grimke on the Condition of Women in the United States," 123-127
        "A Daughter of Temperance Exhorts Her Sex," pp. 208-212
        "Louisa McCord on Enfranchisement of Woman," pp. 262-267

April 29: War

    Root of Bitterness
        "Union Women in Wartime," pp. 268-273
        "Gertrude Clanton Thomas's Civil War Diary," pp. 274-280
    Reading Packet:
        Drew Gilpin Faust, "'Trying to Do a Man's Business': Slavery, Violence
           and Gender in the American Civil War" [Gender and History 4, No. 2
           (Summer 1992)]

May 1: Emancipation

    Root of Bitterness:
        "A Freedwoman before the Southern Claims Commission," pp. 281-285
        Letters of Sarah Chase and Lucy Chase (1866, 1868)

May 6: A Movement Asunder

    Reading Packet:
        (Woman suffrage documents to be distributed))
        Angela Davis, "Class and Race in the Early Women's Rights Campaign"
           [Women, Race and Class]

May 8: 1870 and After

HISTORY OF AMERICAN WOMEN, to 1890

This course examines the prevailing cultural constructions of
gender as related to major developments in the political economy:
European expansion and colonization; American independence and
the rise of industrial capitalism; U.S. continental and overseas
expansion. It emphasizes conceptual frameworks of the New
Scholarship in women's history, including interdisciplinary
methods and categories of analysis, such as race, class
ethnicity, and region. It includes a critical review of the
private/public, culture/politics dimensions of recent
interpretative schemas.

Student Requirements: attendance at lectures and participation in
weekly discussion sections. Three short papers (5-7 pp) due Feb.
9, Mar. 16, Apr. 20; and a final project during the Reading
Period due May 12.

BOOK LIST

Nancy F. Cott, *et. al.*, eds, Root of Bitterness: Documents of the
Social History of American Women, 2d ed., Northeastern University
Press 1996

Nancy F. Cott, The Bonds of Womanhood, 2d ed., Yale University
Press 1997

Sarah Elbert, ed., Louisa May Alcott: On Race, Sex, and Slavery,
Northeastern University Press 1997

Harriet Jacobs, Incidents in the Life of a Slave Girl, Harvard
University Press 1987

Susanna Rowson, Charlotte Temple, Oxford University Press 1987

Elizabeth Stuart Phelps, The Silent Partner, Feminist Press 1983

Maria Susanna Cummins, The Lamplighter, Rutgers University Press
1988

Kathryn Kish Sklar and Thomas Dublin, eds., Women and Power in
American History, Vol. I to 1880, Prentice Hall 1990

Lucy Larcom, New England Girlhood, Northeastern University Press
1985

SYLLABUS

I. INTRODUCTION

Jan. 21   Introductory Remarks
           Nancy Cott, *et. al.*, eds., <u>Root of Bitterness:</u>
           <u>Documents of the Social History of American Women</u>
           2d ed. (Boston: Northeastern University Press, 1996),
               Introduction, pp. xiii-xxi.
           Kathryn Kish Sklar and Thomas Dublin, eds., <u>Women and</u>
           <u>Power in American History</u>, Vol. I to 1880 (Englewood
           Cliffs: Prentice Hall, 1991), Introduction, pp. 1-7.

Jan. 23   Women's History: Old and New
           J. Kelly-Gadol, "The Social Relations of the Sexes:
           Methodological Implications of Women's History, <u>Signs</u>,
           1(Summer 1976), pp. 6-24.
           Evelyn Brooks Higginbotham, "African-American Women's
           History and the Metalanguage of Race," <u>Signs</u>, 17(Winter
           1992), pp. 251-74.

II. COLONIAL ENCOUNTERS

1/26   Farmers and Foragers
           Joan A. Jensen, "Native American Women and Agriculture:
           A Seneca Case Study," in Sklar and Dublin, eds., <u>Women</u>
           <u>and Power in American History</u>, pp. 8-23.

1/28   Mainspring of Empire: Slavery
           Allan Kulikoff, "The Beginnings of the Afro-American
           Family in Maryland," in Sklar and Dublin, eds., <u>Women</u>
           <u>and Power in American History</u>, pp. 72-89.

1/30   Social Relations & the Construction of Race & Gender
<SECTION   Joan Rezner Gundersen, "The Double Bonds of Race and
           Sex: Black and White Women in a Colonial Virginia
           Parish," <u>Journal of Southern History</u>, 52(August 1986),
           pp. 351-372.

Feb. 2   Help Meets, North and South
           Laurel Thatcher Ulrich, "'A Friendly Neighbor': Social
           Dimensions of Daily Work in Northern Colonial New
           England," in Sklar and Dublin, eds., <u>Women and Power in</u>
           <u>American History</u>, pp. 37-50.
           Lois Green Carr and Lorena S. Walsh, "The Planter's
           Wife: The Experience of White Women in Seventeenth-

Century Maryland," in Sklar and Dublin, eds., Women and
Power in American History, pp. 51-71

Feb. 6   A Midwife's Tale
            Video: A Midwife's Tale, produced by Laurie Kahn-
            Leavitt.

            Recommended: Laurel Thatcher Ulrich, A Midwife's Tale

Feb. 8   Goodwives, Shrews, and Witches
<SECTION   Cott, Root of Bitterness, Part I. Colonial Encounters
            and Community, pp. 3-46.
            Lyle Koehler, "The Weaker Sex as Religious Rebel," in
            Sklar and Dublin, eds., Women and Power in American
            History, pp. 24-36.

Feb. 9   Emerging Patterns of Gentility
            Nancy F. Cott, "Divorce and the Changing Status of
            Women in Eighteenth-Century Massachusetts," in Sklar
            and Dublin, eds., Women and Power in American History,
            pp. 90-105.

            Recommended: Nancy Cott, "Passionlessness: An
            Interpretation of Victorian Sexual Ideology, 1790-
            1850," Signs, 4(1978),219-236.

            First Essay Due

Feb. 11   The American Revolution --A Turning Point?
            Cott, Root of Bitterness, Part II. Transitions to a New
            Republic, pp. 49-111.

            Recommended: Debra L. Newman, "Black Women in the Era
            of the American Revolution in Pennsylvania," Journal of
            Negro History, 61(July 1976), 276-89.
            Linda J. Kerber, "'I have Don . . . much to Carrey on
            the Warr': Women and the Shaping of Republic Ideology
            after the American Revolution," Journal of Women's
            History, 1(Winter 1990), pp. 231-243.

Feb. 13   Discourses on Daughters
<SECTION   Susanna Rowson, Charlotte Temple

III. THE EXPANDING NATION

Feb. 16   Long Weekend -- No Class

Feb. 18   Race & Class Dimensions of the Cult of Domesticity

61

Nancy Cott, <u>Bonds of Womanhood</u>, Preface, Introduction,
and Chapters 1-4
James Oliver Horton, "Freedom's Yoke: Gender
Conventions among Antebellum Free Blacks," <u>Feminist
Studies</u>, 12(Spring 1986), 51-76.
Carol Lasser, "The Domestic Balance of Power: Relations
Between Mistress and Maid in Nineteenth-Century New
England, in Sklar and Dublin, eds., <u>Women and Power in
American History</u>, pp. 130-143

Feb. 20   Woman's Sphere: Friends & Lovers
<SECTION   Cott, <u>Bonds of Womanhood</u>, Chapters 5-6
            Carroll Smith Rosenberg, "The Female World of Love and
            Ritual: Relations between Women in Nineteenth-Century
            America," <u>Signs</u>, 1(August 1975), pp. 1-29
            Karen V. Hansen, "'No <u>Kisses</u> Is Like Youres': An Erotic
            Friendship between Two African-American Women during
            the Mid-Nineteenth Century," <u>Gender & History</u>, 7(August
            1995), pp. 153-182.

Feb. 23   "Marry, Stitch, Die, or Do Worse"
            Mary H. Blewett, "Work, Gender and the Artisan
            Tradition in New England Shoe-Making," in Sklar and
            Dublin, eds., <u>Women and Power in American History</u>, pp.
            119-129
            Cott, <u>Root of Bitterness</u>, III. Woman's Sphere and
            Women's Employments, pp. 113-175.

            Recommended: Gerda Lerner, "The Lady and the Mill Girl:
            Changes in the Status of Women in the Age of Jackson,
            1800-1840," in Lerner, <u>Majority Finds Its Past</u>, pp.
            15-30.

Feb. 25   A Community of Women: Lowell
            Thomas Dublin, "Women, Work, and Protest in the Early
            Lowell Mills: 'The Oppressing Hand of Avarice Would
            Enslave Us,'" in Sklar and Dublin, eds., <u>Women and
            Power in American History</u>, pp. 114-57.

Feb. 27   Reflections on Life at Lowell
<SECTION   Lucy Larcom, <u>New England Girlhood</u> (1889)

Mar. 2   The Plantation System
            Deborah G. White, "Female Slaves: Sex Roles and Status
            in the Antebellum Plantation South," in Sklar and
            Dublin, eds., <u>Women and Power in American History</u>, pp.
            158-171

            Recommended: Marli F. Weiner, <u>Mistresses and Slaves:
            Plantation Women in South Carolina, 1830-80</u> (Urbana:
            University of Illinois Press, 1997)

Mar. 4   The Slave Experience
           Thelma Jennings, "'Us Colored Women Had to Go Though a
           Plenty'" Sexual Exploitation of African-American Slave
           Women," Journal of Women's History, 1(Winter 1990), pp.
           45-73.

           Recommended: Jacqueline Jones, "'My Mother Was Much of
           a Woman': Black Women, Work, and Family under Slavery,"
           Feminist Studies, 8(Summer 1982), 235-69.

Mar. 6   Reflections of Life Under Slavery
<SECTION   Harriet A. Jacobs, Incidents in the Life of a Slave
           Girl, edited by L. Maria Child.

           Recommended: Deborah M. Garfield and Rafia Zafar,
           Harriet Jacobs and Incidents in the Life of a Slave
           Girl (Cambridge: Cambridge University Press, 1996)

Mar. 9   Internal Empire
           Glenda Riley, "Women and Indians on the Frontier," in
           Sklar and Dublin, eds., Women and Power in American
           History, pp. 216-228.
           Lucie Cheng, "Chinese Immigrant Women in Nineteenth-
           Century California," in Sklar and Dublin, eds., Women
           and Power in American History, pp. 244-258.

           Recommended: Elizabeth Jameson and Susan Armitage,
           eds., Writing the Range (Lincoln: University of
           Nebraska Press, 1997)

Mar. 11   Overseas Expansion
           Cott, Root of Bitterness, Part IV. Women and the
           National Mission, pp. 177-237.

Mar. 13   Categories of Analysis: Race, Class, Ethnicity, Region
<SECTION   Bonnie Thornton Dill, "Race, Class and Gender:
           Prospects for an All-Inclusive Sisterhood, Feminist
           Studies, 9(Spring 1983), pp. 131-150.
           Nancy Hewitt, "Beyond the Search for Sisterhood:
           American Women's History in the 1980s," Social History,
           10(October 1985)

IV. CULTURE AND POLITICS

Mar. 16   Her Sister's Keeper: Moral Reform and Benevolence
           Carroll Smith-Rosenberg, "Beauty, the Beast, and the
           Militant Women: A Case Study in Sex Roles and Social
           Stress in Jacksonian America," in Sklar and Dublin,
           eds., Women and Power in American History, pp. 185-98

           Second Essay Due

Mar. 18   The Politics of Sentimentality
           Nina Baym, ed., The Lamplighter, by Maria Susanna
           Cummins (New Brunswick, N.J.: Rutgers University Press,
           1988), Introduction, ix-xxi.

Mar. 20   "a production by a lady"
<SECTION   Maria Susanna Cummins, The Lamplighter (1854)

Spring Recess

Mar. 30   Anti-Slavery & Woman's Rights"
           Gerda Lerner, "The Political Activities of Antislavery
           Women," in Sklar and Dublin, eds., Women and Power in
           American History, pp. 172-184.
           Cott, Root of Bitterness, Part V. Slavery, War, and
           Emancipation, pp. 239-91.

Apr. 1   The Civil War & the Woman Movement
           Elisha Harris, "The United States Sanitary Commission,"
           in Sarah Elbert, ed., Louisa May Alcott: On Race, Sex,
           and Slavery (Boston: Northeastern University Press,
           1997), Appendix, pp. 87-101.
           Estelle Freedman, "Separatism as Strategy: Female
           Institution Building and American Feminism, 1870-1930,"
           Feminist Studies, 5(Fall 1979), pp. 512-29.

           Recommended: Drew Gilpin Faust, Mothers of Invention:
           Women of the Slaveholding South in the American Civil
           War (Chapel Hill: University of North Carolina Press,
           1996).

Apr. 3   The Author of Little Women
<SECTION   Sarah Elbert, ed., Louisa May Alcott: On Race, Sex, and
           Slavery (Boston: Northeastern University Press, 1997).

           Recommended: Elizabeth D. Leonard, Yankee Women: Gender
           Battles in the Civil War (New York: Norton, 1994).

Apr. 6   The Woman Question & The Labor Question
           Cott, Root of Bitterness, Part VII. Women's Work in an
           Industrial Age, pp. 347-97.

           Recommended: Wendy Gambler, The Female Economy: The
           Millinery and Dressmaking Trades, 1860-1930 (Urbana:
           University of Illinois Press, 1997).

Apr. 8   An American Radical
           Video: America's Victoria: The Victoria Woodhull Story
           (1995), by Victoria Weston

Apr. 10   Sisterhood Across the Classes
<SECTION   Elizabeth Stuart Phelps, The Silent Partner (1871)

Apr. 13   Body Politics
            Cott, Root of Bitterness, Part VI. Health, Medicine,
            and Sexuality, pp. 293-345.
            Kathryn Kish Sklar, "Victorian Women and Domestic Life:
            Mary Todd Lincoln, Elizabeth Cady Stanton, and Harriet
            Beecher Stowe," in Sklar and Dublin, eds., Women and
            Power in American History, pp. 229-243.
            James C. Mohr, "The Social Character of Abortion in
            America, 1840-1880," In Sklar and Dublin, eds., Women
            and Power in American History, pp. 259-271

            Recommended: Nancy M. Theriot, "Women's Voices in
            Nineteenth-Century Medical Discourse: A Step toward
            Deconstructing Science," Signs, 19(Autumn 1993), pp. 1-
            31.

Apr. 15   The Woman's Crusade
            Cott, Root of Bitterness, Part VIII. New Women, New
            Worlds, pp. 399-440.

            Recommended: Ruth Bordin, "'A Baptism of Power and
            Liberty': The Women's Crusade of 1873-1874," Ohio
            History, 87(Autumn 1978), 383-404.

Apr. 17   Culture & Politics Reconsidered
<SECTION   Ellen DuBois, et. al, "Politics and Culture in Women's
            History: A Symposium, Feminist Studies, 6(Spring 1980),
            pp. 26-64.
            Nell Irvin Painter, "Sojourner Truth in Life and
            Memory: Writing the Biography of an American Exotic,"
            Gender & History, 2(Spring 1990), 3-16.

V. REFLECTIONS

Apr. 20   Social Constructions/Cultural Constructions
            Linda J. Kerber, "Separate Spheres, Female Worlds,
            Woman's Place: The Rhetoric of Women's History,"
            Journal of American History, 75(June 1988), pp. 9-39.

            Third Essay Due

Apr. 22   Discussion of Final Project
            Due May 12

Apr. 24   No Class - Reading Period Begins

American Women I

HST 169   Fall 1997
Carr 135   TR 3:50-5:05

Dr. Nancy Hewitt   TA: Gwenn Miller
Office: 338 Carr   Office: 330 Carr
Off Hrs: Tues 2-3:30   Off Hrs: Thur 2-3:30
Phone: 684-2505   Phone: 684-2506
Email: newitt@acpub   Email: gam4@acpub

The purpose of this course is three-fold: (1) to introduce you to women's role in American History from c. 1600 through the Civil War; (2) to explore differences in women's experiences rooted in race, region, ethnicity and class; and (3) to analyze past events in order to better understand the development over time of gender roles, the sexual division of labor, sexual stereotypes, and women's attempts to shape themselves, their communities, and the larger society.

Written assignments for this course include an in-class midterm, a weekly journal, and a take-home final. For the midterm, you will be required to write a three-generation history of women living between 1600 and the American Revolution, based on course readings and discussions. You may prepare a one-page outline ahead of time, but the history itself will be written during the exam hour on Thursday, Oct. 9. You will also be asked to keep a journal during the semester, responding to the readings and class discussions each week. A description of the journal assignment appears at the end of this syllabus. Journals will be collected periodically throughout the semester. Your final written assignment will be a take-home final, handed out on the last day of class and due during exam week.

In addition to the written assignments, students will participate in several in-class projects, some relying on the assigned readings for the week and others requiring a small amount of library research. Performance on these group projects will be counted along with participation in class discussion toward your final grade. CLASS PARTICIPATION is the key to this course, and reading assignments must therefore be completed on time. The required books, listed below, are supplemented by articles on reserve. The reserve reading is also REQUIRED. Reserve readings may be obtained in hard copy at the Reserve Reading Desk in Perkins Library on West Campus, or they can be printed out via the web at http://devil.lib.duke.edu/

Each of the four major requirements for this course--midterm, journal, class participation, and final--will count 25% toward your final grade. If you have questions during the semester regarding your performance in any area of the course, please see Nancy Hewitt or Gwenn Miller to discuss your concerns. If you cannot see us during our regular office hours, please call or email us to arrange another appointment time.

The following books are required reading for this course and can be purchased at the Regulator Bookshop on 9th Street (which runs parallel to and one block over from the west border of East Campus):

Nancy Woloch, Women and the American Experience, vol. 1, 2nd edition (WAE)
Nancy Hewitt, ed., Women, Families and Communities: Readings in American History, vol. 1 (WFC)
Kathleen Brown, Good Wives, Nasty Wenches, and Anxious Patriarchs
Laurel Thatcher Ulrich, A Midwife's Tale: The Life of Martha Ballard based on Her Diary
Christine Stansell, City of Women: Sex and Class in New York, 1789-1860
Melton McLaurin, Celia, A Slave
Lillian Schlissel, ed. Women's Diaries of the Westward Journey

Topics and Assignments:

Tues Sep 2   Introduction: American History/Women's History
              Hand-out: Library assignment--Where Are the Women?

Thur Sep 4   On the Eve of Empire
              Read: Brown, Good Wenches, chpt 1
              Reserve: Jennifer Morgan, "Some Could Suckle Over Their Shoulder" (WMQ, January 1997)
              Judith Brown, "Economic Organization and the Position of Indian Women" (Ethnohistory 17, 1970)

Tues Sep 9   Women and Conquest I
              Read: Brown, Good Wenches, chpt. 2
              Lebsock, "No Obey," in WFC
              Library assignment due.

Thur Sep 11   Women and Conquest II
              Read: Woloch, WAE, chpt. 1, and chpt 2, pp. 33-37 only
              Reserve: Antonia Castaneda, "Sexual Violence in the Politics and Policies of Conquest"
              Sylvia Van Kirk, "The Role of Native Women in Fur Trade Societies"
              Handout: Mary Rowlandson's account of her captivity.
              Group Project: Contact, Conquest, and Conflict

Tues Sep 16   Race Matters
              Read: Brown, Good Wenches, chpts. 4-6

Thur Sep 18   Building Colonies: The South
              Read: Brown, Good Wenches, chpts 3 and 7
              Reserve: Lois Carr and Lorena Walsh, "The Planter's Wife"
              HAND IN JOURNALS

Tues Sep 23   Building Colonies: The North
              Read: Woloch, WAE, chpt. 2
              Reserve: Ulrich, "The Ways of the Household"
              Group Project: The Trial of Mistress Anne Hibbens

Thur Sep 25   Gender Conflicts: Witchcraft
              Read: Woloch, WAE, pp. 42-46 only
              Koehler, "Salem Village Cataclysm" in WFC
              Reserve: Carol Karlsen, "The Devil in the Shape of a Woman"
              Elaine Breslaw, "Tituba: The Reluctant Witch"

Tues Sep 30   Gender Conflicts: Plantation Labor
              Read: Woloch, WAE, chpt. 3
              Reserve: Barbara Stevenson, "Slavery," from Black Women in America: An
              Encyclopedia
              Handout: Eliza Lucas Pinckney and the Cultivation of Indigo
              Group Project: Rewriting History

Thur Oct 2   On the Eve of Revolution
              Read: Woloch, WAE, chpt. 4 to p. 80
              Brown, Good Wenches, chpt. 9
              Reserve: Allan Kulikoff, "The Beginnings of the Afro-American Family"
              HAND IN JOURNALS

Tues Oct 7   Women and Revolution
              Read: Woloch, WAE, pp. 80-94 only
              Kerber, "Politicizing the Household" and Scott, "Sisters, Wives and Mothers" in
              WFC
              Reserve: Jacqueline Jones, "Race, Sex and Self-Evident Truths"
              Lucy Eldersveld Murphy, "Autonomy and the Economic Roles of Indian
              Women"
              Group Project: Did Women Have a Revolution?

Thur Oct 9   MIDTERM

Tues Oct 14   FALL BREAK

Thur Oct 16   Birth of a Nation
              Read: Ulrich, Midwife's Tale, Intro to p. 234
              Scholten, "On the Importance of the Obstetrik Art" in WFC
              Helen Tanner, "Coocoochee: Mohawk Medicine Woman"
              Film: Selections from A Midwife's Tale

Tues Oct 21   Sex and Society
               Read: Ulrich, Midwife's Tale, p. 235 to end
               Reserve: Cornelia Huges Dayton, "Taking the Trade: Abortion and Gender
               Relations"
               Evelyn Blackwood, "Sexuality and Gender in certain Naitve American Tribes"
               Group Project: Family Values--the Old-Fashioned Way?

Thur Oct 23   Gender, Race and Class in the New Nation
               Read: Stansell, City of Women, Part I
               Johnson, "The Modernization of Greenleaf and Abigail Patch" in WFC
               Handout: Petitions of Jemima Hunt and Judith Hope

Tues Oct. 28   Working-Class Lives
               Read: Stansell, City of Women, Part III
               Dublin, "Building a Community of Labor," AND White, "Female Slaves" in
               WFC
               Reserve: Whittington Johnson, "Free African American Women in Savannah"
               Group Project: Making Choices, Making Do

Thur Oct 30   Piecing Together the Past
               Film: Hearts and Hands: A History of American Women through Quilting
               HAND IN JOURNALS

Tues Nov 4   Middle-Class Ideals
               Read: Woloch, WAE, chpt. 5 and chpt. 6 to p. 135
               Perdue, "Domesticating the Natives" in WFC
               Reserve: Carroll Smith-Rosenberg, "Female World of Love and Ritual"
               Karen Hansen, "No Kisses Is Like Youres"

Thur Nov 6   Ideals into Action
               Read: Woloch, WAE, chpt. 8 to p. 195; Stansell, City of Women, Part IV
               Smith-Rosenberg, "Beauty, the Beast, and the Militant Woman" in WFC
               Library Assignment: Godey's Ladies Book

Tues Nov 11   Woman's Rights
               Read: Woloch, WAE, pp. 195-200 only; Stansell, City of Women, Part II
               Hewitt, "Women's Anti-Slavery Activism" in WFC
               Reserve: Judith Wellman, "The Seneca Falls Woman's Rights Convention"
               Group Project: The Origins of Women's Rights

Thur Nov 13   Woman's Wrongs
               Read: McLaurin, Celia, A Slave
               Reserve: Brenda Stevenson, "Distress and Discord in Virginia Slave Families"

Tues Nov 18 In Their Own Voice
Read: Woloch, WAE, pp. 146-49 AND EITHER a Slave Narrative OR a
Plantaion Mistress's Diary
Group Project: Telling Stories of the Old South
HAND IN JOURNALS

Thur Nov 20 New Frontiers?
Read: Schlissel, Women's Diaries, Parts I and II, with diary excerpts
Woloch, WAE, pp. 142-46
Reserve: Sarah Winemucca Hopkins, Life Among the Pauites, selected pages

Tues Nov 25 Settlement and Upheaval
Read: Faragher, "Midwestern Farm Families" in WFC
Reserve: Jane Dysart, "New Mexican Women in San Antonio"
Albert Hurtado, "Between Two Grizzlies' Paws: Indian Women in the 1850s"
Group Project: Whose West?

Thur Nov 27 THANKSGIVING

Tues Dec 2 Civil War: White Women on the Homefront
Read: Woloch, WAE, pp. 222-225
Intro to Part V and Ginzburg, "A Passion for Efficiency" in WFC
Reserve: George Rable, "The Coming of Lucifer's Legions"

Thur Dec 4 Accommodation and Resistance
Group Project: A Women's War

Tues Dec 9 Freed Women?
Read: Woloch, WAE, pp. 226-30
Jones, "Freed Women?" in WFC
Reserve: Elsa Barkley Brown, "Negotiating and Transcending the Public
Sphere"
FINAL JOURNALS DUE

Thur Dec 11 Reviewing and Reconstructing Women's Place
Read: Woloch, WAE, pp. 231-48, 271-92, 326-38
Group Project: Women at the Nation's Centennial, 1876
Hand out Take Home Final

Dec 15-20 Final Exams: Take Home Due on Date for In-class Exam

Keeping a Journal for American Women I, Fall 1997

Each student will keep a journal in a notebook used exclusively for this assignment. The journal is intended to help you synthesize the materials from class discussions and readings over the course of the semester. It is also intended to help us (your teachers) understand your thinking on an on-going basis. The journals, for instance, allow us to see how you make sense of the course materials, even at those times when you do not speak up in class. In addition, writing out your ideas in a journal may help you develop thoughts so that you feel more comfortable joining in class discussions.

The word "synthesis" best describes what we are looking for in your journal. You may respond to individual reading assignments, but the more important function of this assignment is to help you expand upon persistent themes over the course of the semester. With this in mind, you will want to constantly review earlier entries, build connections among topics, problems, and themes that recur from week to week, and perhaps even draw links to materials from other courses. Above all, think critically about what you read and hear. What are an author's strengths and/or weaknesses? How did issues raised in class challenge or confirm your own interpretation of an article or document? How did class projects shape your thinking about an issue? How do class discussions relate to issues of importance today?

By the end of the semester, you should have compiled a journal of some 50-60 pages of legible writing (though there are no set minimum or maximum lengths). You will hand in your first set of entries on Sept. 18 and periodically thereafter as noted on the syllabus. You will receive comments on your journal over the course of the semester, a tentative grade after October 30, and a final grade at the end of the semester. On the days that journals are to be handed in, we may begin class discussions by asking a student or two to read from their entries.

There is ample opportunity for creativity and improvement in this assignment so try to enjoy your journal as well as learn from it.

HIS 352 American Women, 1600-1850

Spring 1996   Dr Nancy Hewitt
W 10:30-1:00   Hrs: W 2:30-4:00
Carr 229   Carr 232/x2505

This course is designed to introduce you to the history and
historiography of American women in the colonial and conquest
periods. Between 1600 and 1850, the lives of women in North
America, Latin America, and the Caribbean were transformed by the
coming together of Western Europeans, Native Americans and Africans
in the western hemisphere. Differing by race, region, religion,
class, sexualities, and nationalities, the experiences of these
women are nonetheless studied together here as a counterpoint to
the master narrative of the Americas. The assigned readings will be
employed to explore the histories and the historians of American
women.
        The primary assignment for this course is to analyze the
readings on a weekly basis. As part of this analysis, you will be
required to prepare discussion questions every other week and
participate in discussion every week. The writing assignments for
the course will include a 3 pp. response to Natalie Zemon Davis's
preface to Women on the Margins (due Jan. 24), a 5-pp. comparison
of two dissertations on women in colonial societies (due MONDAY,
March 18); and a 10 pp. critique of a major work on women and
gender in the Americas or an annotated syllabus for an
undergraduate course on American Women, 1600-1850 (due April 24).

The following books are required for the course and can be
purchased at the Regulator Bookshop on 9th Street:
        Merry Weisner-Hanks, Women and Gender in Early Modern Europe
        Claire Robertson and Martin Klein, eds., Women and Slavery in
        Africa
        Asuncion Lavrin, ed., Sexuality and Marriage in Colonial Latin
        America
        Carol Devens, Countering Colonization: Native American Women
        and Great Lakes Missions, 1630-1900
        Sylvia Van Kirk, Many Tender Ties: Women in Fur Trade
        Societies, 1670-1870
        Carol Karlsen, The Devil in the Shape of a Woman
        Hilary Beckles, Natural Rebels: A Social History of Enslaved
        Black Women in Barbados
        Susan Juster, Disorderly Women: Sexual Politics and
        Evangelicalism in Revolutionary New England
        Patricia Morton, ed., Discovering the Women in Slavery

In addition, students will be asked to read a dissertation by
Kathleen Brown, GENDER AND THE GENESIS OF A RACE AND CLASS SYSTEM
IN VIRGINIA, 1630-1750. A copy of this dissertation will be on
reserve at Duke and UNC. Other reserve readings can be found in
Lilly Library(*: listed under Jane Mangan; # under Nancy Hewitt) or
the Duke Graduate Student Lounge.

Jan. 17   Introduction

Jan. 24   The Eve of Conquest
           Read: Weisner-Hanks, Women in Early Mod. Eur.
           Reserve: Duke students read ONE article in Gender &
           History issue on Early Mod Eng and UNC students read ONE
           chpt. from Mary Elizabeth Perry, Gender and Disorder in
           Early Modern Seville
           Hand out: N. Z. Davis, "Preface" to Women on the Margins
           DUE: 3 pp. response to NZD's preface

Jan. 31   Gender, Race and Slavery
(DQ:A)   Read: R&K, Women and Slavery in Africa, Introduction and
           Part I
           Reserve: Tessie Liu, "Teaching the Difference Among
           Women" [DuBois and Ruiz, Unequal Sisters (2nd ed)];
           #Jerrold Casway, "Irish Women Overseas, 1500-1800" and
           #Ciaran Brady, "Political Women and Reform in Tudor Eng."

Feb. 7   The Americas: First Encounters
(DQ:B)   Read: Lavrin, S&M: Intro. and article by Gruzinski;
           VanKirk, Tender Ties, Intro. and ch. 1;
           Beckles, Natural Rebels, Intro. and chs. 1-3
           Reserve: *Antonia Castaneda, "Sexual Violence in the
           Politics and Policies of Conquest, Amerindian Women and
           the Spanish Conquest of Alta California"; Mary Louise
           Pratt, "Arts of the Contact Zone"; and *Steve Stern,
           "Paradigms of Conquest" (Journal of Lat Am Studies, 1992)

Feb. 14   Conquering Souls
(DQ:A)   Read: Lavrin, S&M: articles by Lavrin, Twinsam, and
           Waldron
           Deven, CC, Intro. and chs. 1 & 2
           Reserve: Natalie Zemon Davis, "Marie De L'Incarnation:
           New Worlds"; *Frank Salomon, "Indian Women in Early
           Modern Quito as seen through their Testaments" (Americas,
           January 1988)

Feb. 21   Women Possessed/Possessing Women
(DQ:B)   Read: Karlsen, The Devil in the Shape of A Woman
           Lavrin, S&M: article by Behar
           Reserve: Ruth Perry, "Colonizing the Breast"; and Lyndal
           Roper, "Witchcraft and Fantasy in Early Mod. Germany"

Feb. 28   SCaRs of Colonization and Control
           Read: Kathleen Brown, "Gender and the Genesis of a Race
           and Class System in Virginia, 1630-1750" (Dissertation)
           Reserve: Gary Nash, "The Hidden History of Mestizo
           America," (Journal of Am Hst, December 1995)

Mar. 6 & 13: Read a dissertation on gender, race and/or class in the Americas during the colonial period and write a 5 pp. comparison of this dissertation with that of Kathleen Brown on Virginia. Choose dissertations from list provided. CRITIQUE DUE MONDAY, MARCH 18 at 5 PM

Mar. 20   Ties That Bind
(DQ:A)   Read: VanKirk, Tender Ties, chs. 2-8;
           Lavrin, S&M: articles by Socolow, Boyer, Calvo, and Nizza de Silva;
           Morton, Discovering: article by Powell
           Reserve: Steve Stern, ch. 4, "Woman, Man and Authority" from The Secret History of Gender

Mar. 27   Enslavement and Resistance
(DQ:B)   Read: Beckles, Natural Rebels, chs. 4-9;
           R&K, Women and Slavery: article by Broadhead;
           Morton, Discovering: articles by Hangar, Gould, Hunt, and Schwartz
           Reserve: *Dignia Castaneda, "The Female Slave in Cuba during the First Half of the Nineteenth Century"

Apr. 3   Religion and Rebellion
(DQ:A)   Read: Devens, CC, chs. 3-5;
           Juster, Disorderly Women, Intro and chs. 1-5;
           Morton, Discovering: article by Lyerly
           Reserve: Cornelia Hughes Dayton, "Taking the Trade: Abortion in 18th c. New England" (WMQ, Jan. 1991)

Apr. 10   Antebellum Dilemmas
(DQ:B)   Read: Juster, Disorderly Women, ch. 6;
           Morton, Discovering: articles by Bynum, Kellow, Weiner, and Kattner
           Reserve: *Antonia Castaneda, "The Political Economy of Nineteenth Century Stereotypes of Californias"
           In addition, each student will read (or reread) a book on antebellum women from the attached list.

Apr. 17   1848: The Culmination of Early American Women's History??
           Collaborative reading/presentation on Anglo-American, Mexican and Mexican-American, Native American, OR Irish American women in the 1840s.

Apr. 24   NO CLASS: FINAL PAPERS DUE

74

3. Graduate and Undergraduate Survey Courses, 1850 to 1990

Hist/Amst/GSC 470
Fall, 1996

Professor Gail Bederman
255 Decio
Office Hours:
Thurs., 10:30-12:30
and by appointment
Office Phone 631-7789
Gail.Bederman.1@nd.edu

HISTORY OF AMERICAN WOMEN II, 1890-PRESENT

REQUIRED BOOKS:

Kerber and De Hart, eds.   Women's America: Refocusing the Past (4th ed.)

Susan Ware, ed.   Modern American Women: A Documentary History

Horowitz and Peiss, eds.   Love Across the Color Line : The Letters of Alice Hanley to
Channing Lewis

Anne Moody   Coming of Age in Mississippi

Susan Douglas   Where the Girls Are: Growing Up Female with the Mass Media

Students are also required to read a packet of xeroxed articles, which will be available for purchase at the
Copy Center in LaFortune Student Center. Articles marked * on the syllabus are included in this set.

All assigned books and articles are on reserve in the Hesburgh Library, as well.

Two valuable women's history textbooks are also on reserve : Rosalind Rosenberg's Divided Lives:
American Women in the Twentieth Century (1992) and Sara M. Evans's Born For Liberty (1989). These
books serve well as supplementary texts, especially for students with little background in American
history.

N.B. This syllabus is an outline, not a contract. As needed, readings or topics may be added, substituted,
or shifted to different days.

COURSE OBJECTIVES:

By the end of the course, students should be able to:
--understand the methodologies and vocabulary of American women's history.
--write a critical, analytical essay utilizing those methodologies and vocabulary.
--analyze primary source documents pertaining to women and gender in light of the frameworks women's
    historians have developed.
--understand how historians analyze gender as a cultural system which positions men and women
    differently, in relation to social power.
--appreciate some of the ways gender has changed between 1890 and 1996, in response to economic,
    social, political, and cultural forces
--appreciate the active part women and men of various classes, races, and regions have played in bringing
    about those historical changes.
--use historical analysis to discover useful perspectives on today's problems and issues, drawing on and
    speaking to their own political beliefs.

SYLLABUS

Week 1: Introduction and Methodology

Tues. August 27 Introductions

Thurs. August 29 What is the subject of women's history?

Fri. August 30 Section
> Linda Kerber & Jane S. De Hart, "Introduction" in *Women's America*, 3-25
> * Rosalind Rosenberg, "Chapter 1: The Family Claim", in *Divided Lives* (1992), 3-34
> Sarah Deutsch "Hispanic Village Women on the Southwest Frontier," in *Women's America*, 276-84
> "Documents: Struggling for Educational Opportunities," Zitkala-"Sa, Mary Anton, and M. Carey Thomas, *Women's America*, 265-76.

Week 2: Women in the Growing Cities: Immigration and Work

Tues. Sept. 3 Women's Work in the Cities

Thurs. Sept 5 New Women Immigrants : Italian and Jewish

Fri. Sept. 6 Section.
> Kerber & De Hart, "Industrializing America 1880-1920" in *Women's America*, 227-30.
> David M. Katzman, "Seven Days a Week: Domestic Work *Women's America*, 240-1
> Pauline Newman, "We Fought and we bled and we died..." 242-44
> Alice Kessler Harris, "Where are the Organized Women Workers?" *Women's America*, 244-57.
> Kathy Peiss, "Putting on Style: Working Women & Leisure in Turn-of-the-Century-New York," *Women's America*, 257-64
> Ware, *Modern American Women*, 19-27, 65-91, photos 95-8, 100-108.
> (Also see Kerber and DeHart's commentary on *Muller* vs. *Oregon* in *Women's America*, 576-7.)
> Look at graph: "Percentage of Men and Women in the Labor Force, 1890-2000" in *Women's America*, 562.
> *Charts on women's work at front of reader

Week 3: Middle Class Women Challenge the Victorian Gender Ideology

Tues. Sept 10: Middle-class "New Women" and the Transformation of American Culture

Thurs. Sept. 12: The Woman's Movement

78

Fri. Sept. 13: Section
Elsa Barkeley Brown, "Maggie Lena Walker and the Independent Order of Saint Luke: *Women's America*, 231-39.
Peggy Pascoe, "Home Mission Women, Race, and Culture: The Case of Native 'Helpers'" *Women's America*, 285-94
"Documents: Working for Economic and Racial Justice" by Florence Kelley and Ida B. Wells, *Women's America*, 295-303
*Gail Bederman, "Civilization, The Decline of Middle-Class Manliness, and Ida B. Wells's Anti-Lynching Campaign (1892-1894)" *Radical History Review* 52, Winter, 1992, 4-30.
Susan Ware, *Modern American Women*, 1-18; 28-65; photos on 92-4, 108-113.
Blanche Weisen Cook, "Female Support Networks & Political Activism: Lillian Wald, Crystal Eastman, Emma Goldman" in *Women's America*, 303-319

Week 4: Continuing Challenges to Victorian World Views

Tues. Sept 17 Women and Consumer Culture

Thurs. Sept 19 "Feminism," Modern Love, and the New Morality

Fri. Sept 20 Section.
Margaret Sanger, "I resolved that women should have knowledge of contraception..." *Women's America*, 335-42
Comstock Law, 1873, *Women's America*, 574-5
Birth rates chart, in *Women's America*, 563.
Susan Ware. *Modern American Women*, 120-130
Horowitz and Peiss, eds., Love Across the Color Line : The Letters of Alice Hanley to Channing Lewis especially 1-40; 55-107

Week 5: Suffrage and After Women and Politics in the 1910s and 1920s

Tues. Sept. 24 Domesticating the State.

Thurs. Sept 26 What Happened When Women got the Vote?

Fri. Sept. 27 Section:
MacKenzie v. *Hare* (1915), "Equal Suffrage (Nineteenth) Amendment," *Adkins* v. *Children's Hospital* (1923) in *Women's America*, 578-83
Suzanne Lebsock, "Woman Suffrage and White Supremacy: A Virginia Case Study" *Women's America*, 320-334
*Rosalyn Terborg-Penn, "Discontented Black Feminists: Prelude and Postscript to the Passage of the Nineteenth Amendment," in *Decades of Discontent: The Women's Movement, 1920-1940* (1983) 261-78
Nancy F. Cott, "Equal Rights and Economic Roles: The Conflict Over the Equal Rights Amendment in the 1920s *Women's America*, 355-65
Blanche Weisen Cook, "Eleanor Roosevelt as Reformer, Feminist, and Political Boss" *Women's America*, 365-74
Ware, *Modern American Women,* photo on 99, 131-156; 164-66;180-5.

Week 6: The "Modern Woman" of the 1920s.--Heterosociality and Consumer Culture

Tues. Oct. 1 The Cultural Work of the Flapper

First Paper Due Oct. 1

Wednesday, Oct. 2:   Evening Film Showing: It. 7:00 pm, 119 DeBart. Required!

Thurs. Oct. 3 Women, Work, and Consumerism in the 1920s-

Fri. Oct. 4 Section.

> Joan Jacobs Brumberg, "Fasting Girls: The Emerging Ideal of Slenderness in American
> Culture" *Women's America*, 374-82
> *Vicki L. Ruiz, "'Star Struck:' Acculturation, Adolescence, and Mexican-American
> Women, 1920-1950" in *Small Worlds*, Elliott West and Paula Petrik, eds.
> (University Press of Kansas, 1992), 61-80..
> * Two "flapper" cartoons by John Held and Art Young
> *Elizabeth Clark-Lewis, "This Work Had a End: African-American Domestic Workers
> in Washington, DC, 1910-1940," in To Toil The Livelong Day, Carol Groneman
> and Mary Beth Norton, eds. 196-212.
> Ruth Schwartz Cowan, "The 'Industrial Revolution' in the Home: Household
> Technology and Social Change in the Twentieth Century." in Women's America,
> 372-85.
> Ware, *Modern American Women*, 159-163; 172-80; 186-92; picture 230-31.
> *Dorothy Dunbar Bromley, "Feminist--New Style" *Harper's Monthly Magazine* 155,
> October 1927, 552-560
>
> *Optional but Highly Recommended:*
> Jacquelyn Dowd Hall, "Disorderly Women: Gender & Labor Militancy in the
> Appalachian South," *Women's America*. 394-406

Week 7: The 1930s

Tues. Oct. 8 Women, Work and Family in the Great Depression.

Thurs. Oct. 10 Women and the Welfare State.

Fri. Oct. 11 Section.

> Jacquelyn Jones, "Harder Times: The Great Depression, " *Women's America*, 407-11
> Linda Gordon, "'The Powers of the Weak:' Wife Beating and Battered Women's
> Resistance" *Women's America* 411-25
> Margaret Jarman Hagood, "Of the Tenant Child as Mother to the Woman," *Women's
> America*, 425-31
> Ware, *Modern American Women*, 193-210; 218-29; pictures 232-33.
> *Charts on women's work at front of reader

Week 8: World War II.

Tues. Oct. 15 Rosie the Riveter. Film. Meet in O'Shag 242.

Thurs. Oct. 17 Women in W.W.II

Fri. Oct. 18 Section:
    Kerber and De Hart, "Modern America 1920-1990" *Women's America,* 351-54.
    Beth Bailey and David Farber, "Prostitutes on Strike: The Women of Hotel Street During
        World War II" *Women's America* 431-440
    Valerie Matsumoto, "Japanese American Women During World War II," *Women's*
        America 440-446
    Ruth Milkman, "Gender at Work: The Sexual Division of Labor During World War II,"
        Women's America, 446-457.
    Statistics on work, chart in *Women's America,* 523.
    Ware, *Modern American Women,* 238-82, photos 234-35.
    *Charts on women's work at front of reader

October 19-27: Fall Break. Have a great vacation!

Week 9: The Feminine Mystique? 1945-1963.

Tues., Oct. 29 Homeward Bound: Cold War, Warm Hearths

Wednesday, Oct. 30:   **Evening Film Showing: The Thrill of It All! 7:00 pm, 242 O'Shag.**
    Required!

Thurs. Oct. 31 In-Class Discussion
    Ware, Modern American Women, 283-311; advertisement, 236.
    *Mirra Komarovsky, "Cultural Contradictions and Sex Roles" American Journal of
        Sociology 54, November 1946) 184-89.*
    Betty Friedan, The Feminine Mystique (1963) *Women's America,* 512-16 (beginning of
        Friedan's chapter 1)
    *Betty Friedan, "Chapter 1: The Problem that Has No Name" The Feminine Mystique
        (1963) pages 19-32 in reader. (End of Friedan's first chapter, not excerpted in
        textbook.)
    Regina G. Kunzel, "Unwed Mothers, Social Workers, and the Postwar Family: White
        Neurosis, Black Pathology" *Women's America* 457-467
    Susan K. Cahn, "'Mannishness,' Lesbianism, and Homophobia in U.S. American Sport"
        Women's America 468-77
    Amy Swerdlow, "Ladies Day at the Capitol: Women Strike for Peace versus HUAC,"
        Women's America, 493-506
    *Charts on women's work at front of reader

Fri. Nov. 1 No Class

Week 10 Women and the Civil Rights Movement

Tues. Nov. 5: Women in the Civil Rights Movement

Thurs., Nov. 7 Bridge to Feminism?

Fri. Nov. 8: Section.
    Pauli Murray and Jessie Lopez de la Cruz "Documents: Making the Personal Political:
        Becoming Feminist," *Women's America* 478-92
    Ware, Modern American Women, 312-19, photo 237.
    Anne Moody, *Coming of Age in Mississippi* (1968)

Week 11 Feminism

Tuesday, Nov. 12 The Rebirth of Liberal Feminism

Second Paper Due November 12!

Thurs. Nov. 14 The Founding of a Movement

Fri. Nov. 15 Section
> *Hoyt* v. *Florida* (1961) and *Taylor* v. *Louisiana* (1975); Civil Rights Act, Title VII (1964), Equal Rights Amendment (1972) *Frontiero* v. *Richardson* (1973) Women's America, 583-92
> Ware, *Modern American Women,* 329-40 . photos 402-03
> Susan J. Douglas, *Where the Girls Are: Growing Up Female with the Mass Media* 3-139.
> *Charts on women's work at front of reader

Week 12: Feminism, continued:

Tues. Nov. 19 Liberal vs. Radical Feminism

Thurs. Nov. 21 Women's Liberation

Fri. Nov. 22 Section
> * Robin Morgan, "Introduction" *Sisterhood is Powerful: An Anthology of Writings from the Women's Liberation Movement* (1970)
> Ware, *Modern American Women,* 341-74; 395-400
> Maxine Hong Kingston, "She said I would grow up a wife and a slave, but she taught me the song of a warrior woman." *Women's America,* 507-512
> Ellen Willis, "I see men who consider themselves dedicated revolutionaries, yet exploit their wives and girl friends shamefully without ever noticing a contradiction" *Women's America,* 516-18
> Susan J. Douglas, *Where the Girls Are: Growing Up Female with the Mass Media* 139-245.

Week 13:

Tues. Nov. 26: To Be Announced.

Thanksgiving Vacation, Nov. 28-29

Week 14: Conflict over Gender in the 1970s and 1980s

Tues. Dec. 3 Rightward Turn

Thurs. Dec. 5 Gender Conflict

Fri. Dec. 6 Section

"Document: Remembering Vietnam," *Women's America*, 519-22
Kristin Luker, "Abortion, Motherhood, and Morality," *Women's America*, 523-33
Roe V. Wade (1973); *Planned Parenthood* v. *Casey* (1992) *Rostker v. Goldberg* (1981),
Meritor Savings Bank v. Mechelle Vinson et. al. (1986) in *Women's America*,
592-604
Ware, *Modern American Women*, 375-89, 410-65, photos 404-09.
(Note that Ware and Kerber/DeHart excerpt different sections of the *Roe* decision; read
both.)
Phyllis Schlafly, "The thoughts of one who loves life as a woman," *Women's America*,
533-37
Susan J. Douglas, *Where the Girls Are: Growing Up Female with the Mass Media* 245-
307
*Charts on women's work at front of reader

Week 15: Conclusion

Tues. Dec. 10 *Last Class Day* Discussion and Assessment: Where do we stand, now?

Jane Sherron De Hart, "The New Feminism and the Dynamics of Social Change"
Women's America, 493-521

The take-home exam will be due at the time and location which the University schedules for the exam.

MECHANICS AND REQUIREMENTS

WRITTEN ASSIGNMENTS

Each student will write two short polished essays, (7-9 pages) which will be designed to investigate a conceptual theme developed within one unit of the course. They will be due

Tuesday, October 1
Tuesday, November 12

Topics will be assigned approximately ten days in advance.

Papers are due in class at 9:30 a.m.. After that moment, unless accompanied by a verified excuse from the Office of Residence Life, they will be downgraded a fraction of a grade for each day (24 hours or fraction thereof) they are late., until I receive them Late papers should be placed in my mailbox in 219 O'Shaughnessy, with a note indicating the date and time the paper was placed in the mailbox. This inflexible policy is designed to insure fairness.

FINAL EXAM

During examination week, students will be required to submit a final take-home paper/exam, which will cover themes developed during the entire course. The exam will be due in the room and at the time the university schedules for the final exam, which will probably be Wednesday, December 18, 10:30-12:30. (Check again in December for final confirmation re: this schedule.) No late final exams will be accepted.

MANDATORY ATTENDANCE POLICY AND PENALTIES

Attendance at all scheduled classes is **mandatory**. Attendance will be taken regularly. Students with more than three unexcused absences will be penalized a fraction of their final grade (i.e. their grade will drop from a B to a B-). Students with more than six unexcused absences will be penalized a full grade. Additional unexcused absences will be penalized proportionately.

DISCUSSION SECTIONS

Friday's classes have been designated as discussion sections. Students must complete the day's assigned reading, and be prepared to discuss all that week's previously-assigned reading.

Bring the assigned readings with you to discussions.

Attendance and **active participation** at all discussions is mandatory and will be graded. Section participation for each day will be graded as follows:

Student is absent: F
Student shows up but doesn't speak: C
Student has read and thought about the assigned reading,, and speaks two or three times per
    class: B
Student has read and thought about the assigned reading,, participates actively in discussion,
    listens carefully to other students, and responds to their comments: A

If you are shy or have a hard time getting to say what you want in section, please discuss this with me! Section discussions only work well when **everybody** participates, Students have repeatedly commented that hearing their peers discuss the readings really clarifies things for them. They really need you to express your ideas and ask your questions! **There is no such thing as a stupid question or bad comment on the course material.**

SECTION LEADERS

Each student must sign up to lead two discussion sections. Section leaders are encouraged to discuss their plans with me in advance, at my office hours, or by appointment.

JOURNAL ASSIGNMENTS

At the beginning of discussion sections, each student should turn in a brief journal entry, which should demonstrate that s/he has read and thought seriously about week's readings. These can be short--i.e. a half page, typed; or the equivalent amount of (legible) handwriting. Longer is OK, but not necessary. They don't need to be polished: first drafts are fine. However they do need to demonstrate that you have read and thought about the week's readings.

The content of your journal entry can vary, depending on your own needs and study methods. It might consist of one sentence summaries of the week's articles, or a series of questions you have about the readings, or your thoughts on some historical topic broached by some of the articles. **The more analytical, personal, and creative, the better!**

There are only two constraints on your creativity: First, since this is a history course, your focus should be mostly on the past. And second, your thoughts, questions, observations, etc. should grow out of your attempts to synthesize the readings for the week.

Journals will be graded pass/fail, and be part of your section grade.

Students are encouraged to turn in journal entries every week; but I must receive at least **ten** pass-quality journal entries from each student (There are 13 discussion meetings.)

EVENING VIEWING OF FEATURE FILMS

Two Hollywood feature films will be shown at 7:00 p.m. on <u>Wednesday, October 2</u> in 119 DeBartolo and on <u>Wednesday, October 30</u>, in 242 O'Shag. These films are an important and integral part of the course, and are **required**.

Those unable to attend the scheduled evening showings must make arrangements to view the films in the audio-visual room at the Hesburgh Library <u>before Friday's class in which they will be discussed</u>. Those unable to attend the scheduled evening showings will be required to turn in brief journal entries on the movies, in addition to their other journal entries.

GRADING

Section discussion and journal assignments will count for 15% of your grade. The final exam will count for 30% of the grade. The papers will each count for 27.5% of your grade. Intangibles, like improvement, will be taken into account.

INFORMAL CONFERENCES

All students are required to come to my office (255 Decio) at least once during the semester (preferably before mid-term) to discuss any questions (specific or amorphous) that have been raised by the course, to let me know how things are going, or just to check in and introduce themselves on a one-to-one basis If you have a class or other conflict during my office hours, contact me to make an appointment. I really enjoy getting to know my students, so please--come see me !

Hist 570
Fall, 1996
Tues 11:30-1:00

Professor Gail Bederman
255 Decio
Office Hours:
Thurs 10:30-1230 (255 Decio)
and by appointment
Office Phone 631-7789

HISTORY OF AMERICAN WOMEN II, 1890-PRESENT:
REVISED SUPPLEMENT FOR GRAD STUDENTS

Course Description:

This is a reading course intended to serve as an introduction to one of the most active, rapidly developing fields in U.S. history. It does not aspire to comprehensive coverage. Rather, it aims to give graduate students who are considering taking a field in American Women's women's history a basic background in some of the major methodological, historiographical, and topical issues current in twentieth-century women's history scholarship today.

As it happens, far more has been written on women's history prior to 1945 than on the later period. In order to keep our readings synchronized with the lectures as much as possible, most of our discussion meetings will take place during the first half of the semester. This will give you more time at the end of the semester to prepare the final review essay.

Requirements:

Students will be expected to attend each class (lectures, seminars, and the two required evening film viewings) unless prior arrangements have been made otherwise. Students are further expected to arrive thoroughly prepared to take an active (i.e. an informed, lively, critical, irreverent) part in each discussion. Seminar participation should demonstrate knowledge and understanding of all the assigned readings and lectures. (35% of the grade).

Each student will be responsible for two class sessions, in which s/he will open the discussion of the assigned readings for that week. This student will give a short (5-7 minutes) presentation outlining the major theoretical issues raised by the readings, and raising a set of questions for the class's discussion. As part of this assignment, students will prepare a 6-8 page critical essay analyzing the theoretical and historical themes and problems raised in the reading. The focus should be on analysis and critical thinking. These short papers, however, don't need to be polished--concentrate on raising ideas and issues to discuss. (Each paper--15% of the final grade) Last year, it worked well to distribute the essays to the rest of the group before class, and we may want to continue that practice this year.

Finally, each student will be required to write a polished, critical, analytical, 10-12 page review essay on a topic of her/his choice, which will be due on or before **12 noon, Monday, December 16**. (Roughly 5-6 books and/or the equivalent amount of articles should be covered.) (35% of the grade.) This topic should both appeal to your own interests *and* be one on which there has been significant recent scholarship. Please clear your subject and the books/articles you plan to discuss with me on or before **Tuesday, November 5.**

Books and Purchases

All assigned readings will be available in the reserve book room at the Hesburgh Library.

In addition, all the assigned books are for sale at the bookstore.

You are not required to read the undergraduates' assigned reading. Those with extra time or energy will get a broader picture of the historical narrative of women's history by doing as much as possible of that reading, particularly the secondary sources. Kerber and DeHart's textbook is on reserve at the Hesburgh Library.

Syllabus:

Tues. Sept 3:
>Sara M. Evans, *Born for Liberty* 1-143
>Linda Kerber & Jane S. De Hart, "Introduction" in *Women's America*, 3-25
>Gerda Lerner, "Placing Women in History: Definitions and Challenges," (1975) in *The Majority Finds Its Past*, 145-159.
>Baker, Paula, "The Domestication of Politics: Women and American Political Society, 1780-1920," *American Historical Review*, 89 (1984)

Tues. Sept 10:
>Kathy Peiss, *Cheap Amusements: Working Women and Leisure in Turn-of-the-Century New York* (Temple U. Press, 1986)
>Carroll Smith-Rosenberg, "The Female World of Love and Ritual" (1975) in Smith-Rosenberg, *Disorderly Conduct: Visions of Gender in Victorian America* (Note: this is the most reprinted and one of the most influential articles in women's history. It's about a different class and a different time period ; but see if you can see how Peiss's book was written in the context of a nineteenth century widely seen by historians as a "homosocial world")
>Hazel Carby, "Policing the Black Woman's Body in an Urban Context," *Critical Inquiry* 18 (Summer, 1992) 738-55.
>Joanne Meyerowitz, "Sexual Geography and Gender Economy," *Gender and History* 2:3, (Autumn 1990) 274-296

Tues. Sept 17:
>Peggy Pascoe, *Relations of Rescue: The Search for Female Moral Authority in the American West,* 1874-1939 (Oxford U. Press, 1990)
>Nancy A. Hewitt, "Beyond the Search for Sisterhood" American Women's History in the 1980s" *Social History* 10:3 (October 1985) 299-321
>Joan W. Scott, "Gender: A Useful Category of Historical Analysis " *American Historical Review*, 91 (1986): reprinted in Scott, *Gender and the Politics of History;*
>Gail Bederman, "Civilization, The Decline of Middle-Class Manliness, and Ida B. Wells's Anti-Lynching Campaign (1892-1894)" *Radical History Review* 52, Winter, 1992, 4-30.
>Sara M. Evans, *Born for Liberty* 145-173

Tues. Sept 24 -- *no class*

Tues., Oct 1:
Nancy F. Cott, *The Grounding of Modern Feminism* (Yale U. Press, 1987)
Estelle Freedman, "Separatism as Strategy: Female Institution Building and American Feminism" *Feminist Studies* 5 (Fall 1979) 512-29
Rosalyn Terborg Penn, "Discontented Black Feminists: Prelude and Postscript to the Passage of the Nineteenth Amendment," in *Decades of Discontent: The Women's Movement 1920-1940* eds. Lois Scharf and Joan Jensen, (1983) 261-68.
Christina Simmons, "Companionate Marriage and the Lesbian Threat" *Frontier* 4:3 (1979) 54-59.
Sara M. Evans, *Born for Liberty* 175-196

Tues., Oct. 8:
George Chauncey, *Gay New York: Gender, Urban Culture, and the Making of the Gay Male World, 1890-1940* (Basic: 1994)
Joan W. Scott, Experience'" in *Feminists Theorize the Political* Judith Butler and Joan Scott, eds. (1992) 22-40.
Christina Simmons, "Modern Sexuality and the Myth of Victorian Repression" in *Passion and Power*, Kathy Peiss and Christina Simmons, eds. (1989) 157-177.

Tues., Oct. 15:
Gordon, Linda, *Pitied But Not Entitled: Single Mothers and the History of Welfare* (Free Press, 1994)
Nancy Fraser and Linda Gordon. "A Genealogy of Dependency: Tracing a Keyword of the U.S. Welfare State." *Signs* 19, no. 2 (December 1994): 309-336.
Sonya Michel and Robyn Rosen. "The Paradox of Maternalism: Elizabeth Lowell Putnam and the American Welfare State." *Gender & History* 4, no. 3 (1992): 364-386.
Sara M. Evans, *Born for Liberty* 197-218

Tues, Oct. 22: *Fall Break*

Tues., Oct. 29:
Judy Yung, *Unbound Feet: A Social History of Chinese Women in San Francisco* (U. of California, 1995)
Tessie Liu, "Teaching the Differences Among Women from a Historical Perspective: Rethinking Race and Gender as Social Categories,"(1991) reprinted in *Unequal Sisters*, 2nd edition.
Iris Berger, Elsa Barkely Brown, and Nancy A. Hewitt, "Symposium--Intersections and Collision Courses : Women, Blacks, and Workers Confront Gender, Race, and Class," *Feminist Studies* 18:2, (Summer 1992) 283-326.
Sara M. Evans, *Born for Liberty* 219-241

Tues Nov. 5,
>Rickie Solinger, *Wake Up Little Susie: Single Pregnancy and Race Before Roe v. Wade*
>>(Routledge, 1992)
>Ruth Feldstein, "'I Wanted The Whole World To See': Race, Gender, & Constructions of
>>Motherhood in the Death of Emmett Till" in Joanne Meyerowitz, ed. *Not June
>>Cleaver: Women and Gender in Postwar U.S., 1945-1960*, (1994, Temple
>>University Press.)
>Fleming, Cynthia Griggs. "Black Women Activists and the Student Nonviolent
>>Coordinating Committee: The Case of Ruby Doris Smith Robinson." *Journal of
>>Women's History.* 1993 Dec; 4(3): 64-82.
>Sara M. Evans, *Born for Liberty* 243-62

Make sure you have cleared the subject of your review article with me by this date!

Tuesday, Nov. 12: *No Class*

Tues. Nov. 17 Susan Douglas
>* Douglas, Susan J. Where the Girls Are: Growing Up Female with the Mass Media
>>(Times Books, 1994)
>Lynn Spigel, "Television in the Family Circle" in Logics of Television, ed. P. Mellencamp.
>Sara M. Evans, *Born for Liberty* 263-314

Tues, Nov. 26: *No Class*

Tues, December 3: *No Class*

Final Paper will be due Monday, December 16, by 12 noon.

Readings in Modern American Women's History & Politics
History 201: AM

Jane S. De Hart   Fall, 1997
HSSB 4252   HSSB 3202
Office Hours: Wed. 5-6   Tu. 2-5 p.m.
  & by appointment
e mail: dehart@humanitas.ucsb.edu

Course Overview:

This course focuses on the political experiences of American women in the twentieth century, drawing on a multidisciplinary literature[1] that demonstrates why gender,[2] no less than class and race, has become an indispensible category of analysis for students of politics, policy, and the state.

We will begin with introductory readings on the politics of scholarship, social construction and the "new" history, and feminist political theorists' critique of liberal theory. Exploring next the political meanings of gendered citizenship, we will examine the gendered political cultures of the early twentieth century and the role of politically active women in the creation of the welfare state. The main body of the course will focus on gender (and often race) in relation to: interest group politics and political parties (suffragists before and after suffrage); the state and the reproduction of difference (wage inequity and workplace stratification prior to and during World War II); the state, sexuality, and reproduction (homosexuality and prostitution in the early years of the Cold War and fetal rights in the later Cold War years); mobilization politics, cultural politics, and the amendment process (the feminist movement, antifeminists, and the Equal Rights Amendment); equality and rights theory (law and the difference dilemma); and state institutions and policy (the military).

While there will be attention to chronology, the course aspires neither to comprehensive coverage of women's political experience in the twentieth century nor to exhaustive treatment of issues relating to gender and politics. There will be, for example, little attention to women candidates or to gender consciousness and politics since the 1970s—both important topics. Rather the course will provide brief exposure to critical issues, a rich body of literature, and some newer

---

[1] Of the core books listed, four are authored by political scientists, three are the work of historians, and two are written by sociologists.

[2] Gender, much misused as a synonym for sex, is the social organization of sexual difference—the knowledge that establishes meanings for bodily differences between men and women.

theoretical perspectives, inviting much more extensive scrutiny. Suggested readings provide only a small sample of the extensive material available.

Class Format and Discussion Preparation:

Emphasis will be placed on close, careful reading of the texts. To stimulate and focus discussion, questions on the required reading will be e-mailed to the entire class prior to meeting. The purpose of these questions will be to generate analysis of the author's thesis, arguments, and insights, and to lay out substantive, methodological, and theoretical issues for discussion. In order to increase exposure to key material, each member of the class will report on a book or articles most relevant to your own work in the suggested reading list at least once during the quarter.

Please complete all required reading prior to the seminar meeting for which it is due. Attendance is essential and any unavoidable absences should be cleared with me in advance.

Note that **there is reading assigned for the first class meeting** at which we will not only take care of organizational business, but engage in substantive discussion. This acceleration is necessary because there is **no class meeting the week of Oct.** 21 when I have to be out-of-town for professional purposes.

Essay Assignments:

There will be one short paper (8 pp.), due October 28, and one longer (15 pp.) paper, due during exam week, if possible; if not, then on the first day of classes in 1998. For the first paper, you may choose option A, B or C. Neither essay requires formal footnoting of common reading--provision of author and date of publication is adequate. A full first citation should be provided for all other reading. I also expect strong organization, carefully constructed paragraphs, and clear, concise prose. Your grades on both essays will reflect the quality of your organization and writing as well as the content. For effective writing, use a guide such as William Shrunk, Jr. and E. B. White, The Elements of Style or The Chicago Manual of Style.

Essay #1:

Option A: Political Biography. After reading relevant portions of Sara Alpern's The Challenge of Feminist Biography: Writing the Lives of Modern American Women (1992), choose **one** of the following biographies, all of which are on Reserve in the Library: Elizabeth Israels Perry, Belle Moskowitz: Feminine Politics & the Exercise of Power in the Age of Alfred E. Smith (1987), Jacquelyn Dowd Hall, Revolt Against Chivalry: Jessie Daniels Ames and the Women's Campaign Against Lynching, rev. ed. (199); Blanche Cook, Eleanor Roosevelt Vol. I, 1884-1933 (1994);

Susan Ware, Partner and I: Molly Dewson, Feminism and New Deal Politics (1987); Ingrid Winther Scobie, Center Stage: Helen Gahagan Douglas, A Life (1992).

Your essay should contain some discussion of the relative merits of the biography (what is it that makes it an example of good scholarship, if indeed it is). Primarily, however, the focus should be on whether and how the writing of the biography has been affected by gender analysis (and familiarity with field of women's history insofar as you have been exposed to it). Are there methodological and/or interpretive differences? Are different questions posed in relation to the data? To put the problem differently, irrespective of whether the subjects are female or male, feminist or nonfeminist, what would prompt a reviewer in the New York Times, for example, to term some-- possibly all--of these biographies "feminist"? Needless to say, the answer will require you to draw on matters discussed during the first weeks of the course as well as the criteria for sound scholarship you have developed through other coursework not focusing on gender.

Option B: New Scholarship on Woman Suffrage.
Within the past two years, historians and political scientists have published five new studies on the suffrage struggle and its immediate aftermath. They are: Sarah Hunter Graham, whose Woman Suffrage and the New Democracy (1996) focuses on the National American Suffrage Association and interest groups politics; Elna Green, whose Southern Strategies: Southern Women and the Woman Suffrage Question (1997) is the first to examine the socio-economic base and ideology of grass-roots suffragists and antisuffragists in the South; Susan Marshall, whose Splintered Sisterhood: Gender and Class in the Campaign Against Woman Suffrage (1997) also focuses on antisuffragists. Others are: Suzanne Marilly, whose Suffrage and the Origins of Liberal Feminism,1820-1920 (1996) identifies three dissenting ideologies of equal rights; and Kristi Anderson, whose After Suffrage (1996) examines the efforts of newly enfranchised women to participate in male-dominated political parties and the polity.

Supplementing Hunter and Anderson (which are assigned) with Green and/or Marshall prepare a review essay that assesses this new scholarship. Be sure to note points of agreement and disagreement in the treatment of the various issues surrounding the suffrage movement and its tactics, ideology, leadership, constituency, and opposition. To the extent possible, indicate whether differences in these works with respect to questions, methodology, or interpretation reflect disciplinary differences or are the result of other factors. By way of conclusion, think about what you might have said about new directions in woman suffrage scholarship had you been among the historians and political scientists addressing this question at the 1995 APSA panel on woman suffrage and had you been given page proofs of these books.

Option C: New Scholarship on Gender and the State
Of the topics covered thus far, many remain relatively
unexplored for reasons of time. For example, the Kerber chapter
on the obligation to pay taxes introduces the role of gender in
nineteenth century tax policy, but there is no subsequent
assigned reading on gender and tax policy in the second half of
the twentieth century. Another topic introduced is gender and
the welfare state. The focus, however, is on the early 20th
century U.S., omitting any comparative focus on early welfare
state history or gender and welfare regimes.
Making your essay a review essay, pursue an aspect of a
topic of your choice further. If, for example, your interest is
20th century tax policy, begin with Edward J. Mc Caffery's
impressive study, Taxing Women (1997). Or if your interest is in
gender and the welfare state, take a look at the comparative
literature, beginning with Seth Koven and Sonya Mitchels, eds.
Mothers of a New World (1993) and Diane Sainsbury, ed., Gendering
Welfare States (1993). Those interested in the concept of regime
types might go in that direction. Focusing on Jane Lewis whose
1992 article on gender and regime types in The Journal of
European Social Policy helped to put gender on the analytic
agenda, explore the debate her work has inspired as reflected in
the 1977 (summer) issue of Social Politics. Look also at
subsequent work attempting to develop analytic frameworks that
capture the effects of state social provisions on gender
relations. (For a review of literature on gender and the welfare
state, see Ann Shola Orloff, "Gender and the Welfare State,"
Annual Review of Sociology 22 (1996):51-78.)

Essay # 2, is based on discussion and reading throughout the
course and is not a research paper. Rather it provides an
opportunity to focus on a topic of your design that utilizes,
criticizes, or in some way responds to the readings from the
course. Some possibilities are: an essay on a particular topic
or topics that illustrate how gender--as a mechanism of social
differentiation, order, and control--adapts, reconfigures, or
declines in a particular chronological period; an essay that
experiments with some of the readings as a conceptual model for
your own work; or a historiographical essay that develops further
your understanding of a particular topic or theme.

Required Reading:

Books listed below are available at Student Stores in
paperback editions whenever possible. They are also available at
the reserve desk in the Library. In addition, a list of articles
and other assigned readings will be available as a coursepack at
the Alternative in Goleta. **With respect to those books starred
(Green, Marshall, and Marilley), you need purchase one of the
three only if you doing Option B for Essay #1.**
If you do not have a working knowledge of the basic
contours of women's history, you may wish to consult an overview

of the period such as William H. Chafe, The Paradox of Change:
American Women in the 20th Century (1991). For reference works
and further reading, see the appended list of "Selected Sources
for the Study of American Women's History." A highly selective
list of recent historical publications on women and politics is
available for the period 1880-1990 in Kerber and De Hart, eds.
Women's America (4th ed., 1995) and in the suggested readings
listed in the final version of the syllabus. For a counterpart
in political science, see Lois Lovelace Duke, Women in Politics
(2nd ed., 1996).

Core Reading:

Anderson, Kristi, After Suffrage (1996)
Daniels, Cynthia R., At Women's Expense: State Power and the
     Politics of Fetal Rights (1993)
Echols, Alice, Daring to Be Bad: Radical Feminism in America,
     1967-75 (1989)
*Green, Elna, Southern Strategies and the Woman Suffrage
     Question (1996)
Kessler-Harris, Alice, A Woman's Wage: Historical Meanings and
     Social Consequences (1990)
Graham, Sara Hunter, Woman Suffrage and the New Democracy (1996)
*Marshall, Susan E., Splintered Sisterhood: Gender and the
     Campaign Against Woman Suffrage (1997)
Mathews, Donald G. and Jane Sherron De Hart, Sex, Gender, and the
     Politics of ERA: A State and the Nation, (1990)
*Marilly, Suzanne, Suffrage and the Origins of Liberal Feminism,
     1820-1920 (1996)
Milkman, Ruth, Gender at Work: The Dynamics of Job Segregation by
     Sex during World War II (1987)
Mink, Gwendolyn, The Wages of Motherhood: Inequality in the
     Welfare State, 1917-1942 (1995)
Pateman, Carol, The Sexual Contract (1988)
Stiehm, Judith Hicks, Arms and the Enlisted Woman (1993)

Class Schedule:

**Sept.30   Women, the Academy and the Impact of the Feminist
Movement: The Politics of Scholarship and the Uses of Social
Construction**

Echols, Alice, Daring to Be Bad: Radical Feminism in America,
     1967-1975, chaps. 1-4.
Scott, Joan W., "American Women Historians,1884-1984" in Scott,
     Gender and the Politics of History (1988) 178-98.
Scott, Joan W., "Women's History" in New Perspectives on
     Historical Writing, ed. Peter Burke (1991), 42-66 (review).
De Hart, Jane Sherron, "Women's History and Political History:
     Bridging Old Divides" in American Political History: Essays
     on the State of the Discipline, eds. John Marszalek and
     Wilson D. Miscamble (1996):25-53.

Jones, Kathleen B., "Towards the Revision of Politics," in The
Political Interests of Gender, eds. Kathleen B. Jones and
Anna G. Jonasdottir (1985), pp. 11-32.
Lopez, Ian F. Haney, "The Social Construction of Race" and "White
by Law" in Critical Race Theory, ed. Richard Delgado (1995):
191-203, 542-48.5.

**Oct. 7 Critiquing Political Theory/ Exploring the Gendered and
Racialized Meaning of the Rights and Obligations of Citizenship**

Pateman, Carol, The Sexual Contract (1988).
Kerber, Linda, The Right to be Ladies: American Women and the
Obligations of Citizenship (forthcoming 1998), chap. 3.

Suggested Reading:

For further critiques of Western political theory:
Elshtain, Jean Bethke, Public Man, Private Woman: Women in Social
and Political Thought (1981).
Okin, Susan Moller, Women in Western Political Thought (1979)
Pateman, Carol and Marl L. Shanley, eds. Feminist Critiques of
Political Theory (199).

For a critique of justice theory:
Okin, Susan Moller "Are Our Theories of Justice Gender-Neutral?"
in The Moral Foundation of Civil Rights eds. Robert
Fullinwider and Claudia Mills (1986)
Okin, Susan Moller, Justice, Gender, and the Family (1989)
Young, Iris Marion, Justice and the Politics of Difference (1990)

**Oct. 14 Gendered and Racialized Meanings of Citizenship--II:
Gendered Political Cultures and Women's Role in the Creation of
the Welfare State and Early Social Policies**

Skocpol, Theda and Gretchen Ritter, "Gender and the Origins of
Modern Social Policies in Britain and the United States,"
Studies in American Political Development 5 (1991):36-93.
Sklar, Kathryn Kish, "The Historical Foundations of Women's Power
in the Creation of the American Welfare State, 1830-1930" in
Mothers of a New World: Maternalist Politics and the Origins
of the Welfare State, eds. Seth Koven and Sonya Michel
(1993), pp. 43-93.
Mink, Gwendolyn, The Wages of Motherhood: Inequality, Inequality
in the Welfare State, 1917-1942 (1995)
Gordon, Linda, "Black and White Visions of Welfare: Women's
Welfare Activism, 1890-1945," Journal of American History
(1991): 559-590.
Orloff, "Gender in Early U.S. Social Policy, Journal of Policy
History 3 (1991):249-81
Polsky, Andrew J. "Welfare State History: The Limits of the New,"

Jill Quadagno, "A Reply to Andrew Polsky" and Linda Gordon, "A Reply to Andrew Polsky" and Andrew J. Polsky, "A Reply to the Authors," all in Journal of Policy History 7 (1995) 441-66.

Suggested Reading:
A classic on gendered political cultures of the 19th century:
Baker, Paula, "The Domestication of Politics: Women and American Political Society, 1780-1920," American Historical Review 89 (1984): 620-47.
On gender, race, class and the formation of the welfare state:
Gordon, Linda, "The New Feminist Scholarship on the Welfare State" and
Mink, Gwendolyn "The Lady and the Tramp: Gender, Race and the Origins of the American Welfare System," both in Women, the State, and Welfare, ed. Linda Gordon (1990), 9-35, 92-122.
Nelson, Barbara J., "The Gender, Race, and Class Origins of Early Welfare Policy and the Welfare State: A Comparison of Workmen's Compensation and Mothers' Aid," in Women Politics and Change, eds. Louise A. Tilly and Pat Gurin (1990), 413-456.
Gordon, Linda, "Social Insurance and Public Assistance: The Influence of Gender in Welfare Thought in the United States, 1890-1935," American Historical Review 97 (1992): 19-54.
Sapiro, Virginia, "The Gender Basis of American Social Policy," Political Science Quarterly 101 (1986):221-38
Skocpol, Theda, Protecting Soldiers and Mothers (1994)
Muncy, Robin, Creating a Female Dominion in American Reform, 1890-1935 (1991).
Fraser, Nancy and Linda Gordon, " A Genealogy of Dependency: Tracing a Keyword of the U.S. Welfare State," in Signs (1994):309-36; Yvonne Zyland "Comment on Fraser and Gordon" and Nancy Fraser, "Reply to Zylan" in Signs (1996) 21: 515-536.

Oct. 21/28 Gendered and Racialized Meanings of Citizenship-III: Suffrage, Interest Group Politics, and Women's Political Participation After Suffrage

Graham, Sara, Woman Suffrage and the New Democracy (1996).
Anderson, Kristi, After Suffrage (1996).

Essay # 1 Due

Suggested Reading:

On African-American women and the vote:
Lebsock, Suzanne, "Woman's Suffrage and White Supremacy: A Virginia Case Study," in Visible Women: New Essay in American Women's Activism, eds. Nancy Hewitt and Suzanne Lebsock (1993), 62-100.

Gordon, Ann, ed. African-American Women and the Vote (1997)

On the political integration of women into electoral politics,
the gender gap, and gender and governance:
Shapiro, Virginia, The Political Integration of Women: Roles,
    Socialization and Politics (1983)
McGlen, Nancy E. and Karen O'Connor, Women, Politics, and
    American Society (1995)
Baxter, Sandra and Marjorie Lansing, Women and Politics: The
    Visible Majority (1983)
Witt, Linda, Karen M. Paget and Glenna Mathews, Running as a
    Woman: Gender and Power in American Politics (1994)
Carroll, Susan J.,Women as Candidates in American Politics (1985)
Burrell, Barbara C., A Woman's Place is in the House: Campaigning
    for Congress in the Feminist Era (1996)
Mueller, Carol M., ed., The Politics of the Gender Gap: The
    Social Construction of Political Influence (1988)
Rinehart, Sue Tolleson, Gender Consciousness and Politics (1992)
Thomas, Sue, How Women Legislate (1994)
Duerst-Lahti and Rita Mae Kelley, eds., Gender Power, Leadership,
    and Governance (1995).

**Nov. 4   The State and the Reproduction of Difference: The
Political Economy of Gender and Racial Stratification in the
Workplace During World II**

Kessler-Harris, Alice, A Woman's Wage: Historical Meanings and
    Social Consequences (1990), chaps. 1,3,4, especially.
Milkman, Ruth, Gender at Work: the Dynamics of Job Segregation by
    Sex during World War II (1987).
Janiewski, Dolores, "Southern Honor, Southern Dishonor:
    Managerial Ideology and the Construction of Gender, Race,
    and Class Relations in Southern Industry" in Work
    Engendered: Toward a New History of American Labor, ed. Ava
    Baron (1991), pp. 70-91.
Baron, Ava, "On Looking at Men: Masculinity and the Making of a
    Gendered Working-Class History, in Feminists Revision
    History, ed. Ann-Louise Shapiro (1994), pp. 146-71.

Suggested Reading:

On gendering of work and gender analysis in labor history:
Baron, Ava, Work Engendered: Toward a New History of American
    Labor (1991), esp. pp. 1-46

On labor market segmentation:
Gordon, David M., Richard Edwards, and Michael Reich, Segmented
    Work, Divided Workers: The Historical Transformation of
    Labor in the U.S. (1982).

On the state's role in the reproducing of social relations and

difference, there is an early (1970s & early 80s) literature
on the state and gender oppression signaled by the term "state
patriarchy" exemplifed by:
McIntosh, Mary, "The State and the Oppression of Women" in
Feminism and Materialism, eds. Annette Kuhn and AnnMarie
Volpe (1978), pp. 254-89.
Boris, Eileen and Peter Bardaglio, "The Transformation of
Patriarchy: The Historic Role of the State," in Families,
Politics, and Public Policy, ed. Irene Diamond (1983)
Abramovitz, Mimi, Regulating the Lives of Women: Social Welfare
Policy from Colonial Times to the Present (1988)

There is also a growing literature on state feminism that should
also be taken into account including:
Hernes, Helega Maria, Welfare State and Women Power: Essays in
State Feminism (1987)

**Nov. 11 The State, the Reproduction of Difference, and the
Regulation of Sexuality: Gender and Sexuality in Cold War America**

Smith-Rosenberg, "The Body Politic," Coming to Terms: Feminism,
Theory & Politics, ed. Elizabeth Weed (1989), 101-121.
Solinger, Rickie, "Extreme Danger: Women Abortionists and Their
Clients before Roe v. Wade" and
Penn, Donna, "The Sexualized Woman: The Lesian, the Prostitute,
and the Containment of Female Sexuality in Postwar America"
both in Not June Cleaver: Women and Gender in Postwar
America, 1945-1960, ed. Joanna Meyerowitz (1994), chs.14-15.
De Hart, Jane Sherron, "Containment at Home: Gender, Sexuality,
and National Identity in Cold War America" in The Cold War
and American Culture, eds. James B. Gilbert and Peter J.
Kusnick (forthcoming 1998).
Ericcson, Lars O. "Charges Against Prostitution: An Attempt at a
Philosophical Assessment," and
Pateman, Carole, "Defending Prostitution: Charges Against
Ericcson" both in Applications of Feminist Legal Theory to
Women's Lives: Sex, Violence, Work, and Reproduction, ed. D.
Kelly Weisberg (1996), pp. 208-221.
Zatz, Noah D., "Law, Labor, and Desire in Constructions of
Prostitution," Signs (1997) 22:277-308.
Daniels, Cynthia R. At Women's Expense: State Power and the
Politics of Fetal Rights (1993).

Suggested Reading:

On gender, sexuality and the state in the early Cold War years,
use the footnotes in the De Hart essay; the place to begin,
although the role of the state is not much emphasized, is:

May, Elaine Tyler, Homeward Bound: American Families in the Cold
War Era (1988).
Decker, John F., Prostitution: Regulation and Control (1979)

Corber, Robert J., Homosexuality in Cold War America: Resistance and the Crisis of Masculinity (1997)
Mc Cann, Carole R., Birth Control Politics in the United States, 1916-1945 (1994)

On more recent decades:

Jaffe, Frederick, Barbara Lindheim and Philip Lee, Abortion Politics: Private Morality and Public Policy (1981)
Petchevsky, Rosalind, Abortion and Woman's Choice: The State, Sexuality, Reproductive Freedom (rev. ed., 1990)
Lawson, Annette and Deborah L. Rhode, The Politics of Pregnancy: Adolescent Sexuality and Public Policy (1993)
Luker, Kristin, Dubious Conceptions: The Politics of Teenage Pregnancy (1996)
Estrich, Susan, Real Rape (1987)
Shapiro, Thomas, Population Control Politics: Women, Sterilization, and Reproductive Choice (1985)
Glendon, Mary Ann, Abortion and Divorce in Western Law (1987)
Eisenstein, Zillah R.,The Female Body and the Law (1988)

Nov. 18 Gender, Equality, and Law: Feminist Mobilization, the American Political System, and the Critique of Rights Theory and Practice in the Law

Echols, , Alice, Daring to Be Bad: Radical Feminism in America, 1967-1975 (1989), review chaps. 1-4 & read remaining chaps.
Mathews Donald G. and Jane Sherron De Hart, Sex Gender and the Politics of ERA: A State and the Nation (1990), chs. 3-8.
De Hart, Jane Sherron, "Equality Challenged: Equal Rights and Sexual Difference," Journal of Policy History 6 (1994): 40-72.
-----, "Rights and Representation: Women, Politics and Power" in U.S. History as Women's History Linda K. Kerber, Alice Kessler-Harris, and Kathryn Kish Sklar, eds., (Chapel Hill: University of North Carolina Press, 1995), 224-42, 403-14.
Rhode, Deborah L. "The Politics of Paradigms: Gender Difference and Gender Disadvantage," in Beyond Equality and Difference Gisela Bock and Susan James, eds. (1992)

Suggested Reading:

On the feminism and women's issues between the first and second feminist movements:
Rupp, Leila J. and Verta Taylor, Survival in the Doldrums: The American Women's Rights Movement, 1945 to the 1960s (1987).
Harrison, Cynthia, On Account of Sex: The Politics of Women's Issues, 1945-1968 (1988).
Gabin, Nancy, Feminism in the Labor Movement: Women and the United Auto Workers, 1935-1975 (1990).
Evans, Sara, Personal Politics: The Roots of Women's Liberation

in the Civil Rights Movement and the New Left (1979).
Klein, Ethel, Gender Politics: From Consciousness to Mass
    Politics (1984).
Castro, Ginette, American Feminism: A Contemporary History (1990)

On feminism and women of color:
Mirande, Alfredo and Evangelina Enriquez, "Chicana Feminism" in
    La Chicana: The Mexican-American Woman (1979), 233-43.
Garcia, Alma, "The Development of Chicana Feminist Discourse,
    1970-1980" Gender and Society 3 (1989):
The Cambahee River Collective, "A Black Feminist Statement," in
    All the Women are White, All the Black are Men, But Some of
    Us are Brave Gloria Hall, Patricia Bell Scott, and Barbara
    Smith, eds.,(1982), 13-22.
Collins, Patricia Hill, Black Feminist Thought: Knowledge,
    Consciousness, and the Politics of Empowerment (1990)

On the ERA struggle and the Mobilization of Gender Consciousnes:
Mansbridge, Jane J. Why We Lost the ERA (1986)
Boles, Janet, The Politics of the Equal Rights Amendment:
    Conflict and the Decision PRocess (1979)
Berry, Mary Frances, Why ERA Failed (1986)
Jones, Kathleen B. and Ann Jonasdottir, The Political Interests
    of Gender (1985), chap. 6
Rhinehart, Sue Tolleson, Gender Consciousness and Politics (1992)
On the critique of rights theory & practice with respect to •
gender, see notes for sec. 3 of De Hart, "Equality Challenged" &:
Minow, Martha, Making all the Difference: Inclusion, Exclusion,
    and American Law (1990)
Bock, Gisela and Susan James, Beyond Equality and Difference:
    Citizenship, Feminist Politics and Female Subjectivity
    (1992)

On sex discrimination, the difference debate and the Courts, some
of the most important scholarship is encompassed in:
Rhode, Deborah L., Justice and Gender: Sex Discrimintion and the
    Law (1989)
Goldstein, Leslie Friedman, Feminist Jurisprudence: The
    Difference Debate (199)
Koppleman, Andrew, Antidiscrimination Law and Social Equality
    (1996)

**Nov. 25 State Institutions and Equality Policy: Gender,
Sexuality and the Military**

Stiehm, Judith Hicks, Arms and the Enlisted Woman (1989), pp. 11-
    27, 47-107, 181-241.
Franke, Linda Bird, Ground Zero: The Gender Wars in the Military,
    chaps. 3,6, and 9.

Suggested Reading: accounts by nonscholars are starred (*)

On women in the military:
Becraft, Carolyn, <u>Women in the U.S. Armed Services: The War in the Persian Gulf</u> (1991)
Holm, Jeanne, <u>Women in the Military: An Unfinished Revolution</u> (1992)
*Franke, Linda Bird, <u>Ground Zero: The Gender Wars in the Military</u> (1997)
Stiehm, Judith, <u>Bring Men and Women: Mandated Change at the U.S. Air Force Academy</u> (1981)

On sexuality, sexual orientation and the military:
Herek, Gregory M., Jared B. Jobe, and Ralph M. Carney, eds. <u>Out in Force: Sexual Orientation and the Military</u> (1996)
*Shilts, Randy, <u>Conduct Unbecoming: Gays and Lesbians in the U.S. Military</u> (1993)
Zimmerman, Jeane, <u>Tailspin: Women at War in the Wake of Tailhook</u> (1995)

On women, militarism, and war:
Elshtain, Jean Bethke, <u>Women and War</u> (1987)
Elshtain, Jean Bethke and Sheila Tobias, eds. <u>Women, Militarism and War: Essays in History, Politics, & Social Theory</u> (1990)
Weinstein, Laurie and Christie C. White, eds. <u>Wives and Warriors: Women and the Military in the United States & Canada</u> (1997)

On militarized masculinity:
Enloe, Cynthia, <u>Does Khaki Become You: The Militarization of Women's Lives</u> (1988)
_____, <u>Bananas, Beaches & Bases: Making Femionist Sense of International Politics</u> (1990)
_____, <u>The Morning After: Sexual Politics at the End of the Cold War</u> (1993).
Jeffords, Susan, <u>The Remasculinization of America: Gender in the Vietnam War</u> (1989).

Dec. 2 Revisiting Old Problems and Assumptions, Reexamining Gender, and Theorizing the Political

Option I: Revisiting Problems:
Mouffe, Chantal, "Feminism, Citizenship, and Radical Democratic Politics"
Schultz, Vicki, "Women 'Before' the Law: Judicial Stories about Women, Work, and Sex Segregation on Job,"
Cornell, Drucilla L. "Gender, Sex, and Equivalent Rights," all in <u>Feminist Theorize the Political</u>, eds. Judith Butler and Joan W. Scott (1992), pp. 280-338, 369-84.

Option II: Reexaming Gender and Theorizing the Political:
Nicholson, Linda, "Interpreting Gender," <u>Signs</u> 20 (1994):79-10
Hawkesworth, Mary, "Confounding Gender" and "Comments by Wendy McKenna and Suzanne Kessler, Joan Wallach Scott, et al on

Hawesworth and Hawesworth's Reply" all in <u>Signs</u> 22 (1997): 686-713

Penn, Donna, "Queer: Theorizing Politics and History" in <u>Radical History Review</u> 24-42

Walters, Suzanna Danuta, "From Here to Queer: Radical Feminism, Postmodernism, and the Lesbian Menace (Or, Why Can't a Woman Be More Like a Fag?), <u>Signs</u> 21 (1996): 830-869.

Option III: Reexamining Disciplinary Assumptions and Borders:

De Hart, Jane, "Oral History and Contemporary History: Dispelling Old Assumptions" in <u>Journal of American History</u> 80 (1993):582-95

Petchesky, Rosalind Pollack, "Fetal Images: The Power of Visual Culture in the Politics of Reproduction," in <u>Theorizing Feminism: Parallel Trends in the Humanities and Social Sciences</u>, eds. Anne C. Herrmann and Abigail J. Stewart (1990),pp. 401-423.

Cooke, Miriam, <u>Women and the War Story</u>, 1-43, 291-300.

HIS 351.40 American Women's History, 1850-1990
Wed. 7-9:30 PM in Carr 132

Dr. Nancy Hewitt   Office: Carr 232
                          Hrs: W 4:00-6:00
Phone: 684-2505

During the fall 1994 semester, we will explore a series of topics
in American women's history covering the period from the mid-19th
through the late 20th century. The overall purpose of the course is
to introduce students to the history and historiography of American
women and to key theoretical and conceptual essays relevant to that
history. This year our readings will focus primarily on the US; on
issues of gender, race/ethnicity, class, and sexuality; and on
women's personal and political activism. We will examine these
issues in national contexts for the mid-19th and mid to late-20th
centuries and in a global context at the turn of the twentieth
century. Issues of diversity, power, and struggle (between women
and men and among women) will be emphasized throughout the course.
In addition, we will evaluate the different questions, sources,
methodologies, and frameworks employed by the scholars whose works
we study.

ASSIGNMENTS: You must complete the reading for each week; class
participation will account for 1/3 of your final grade in the
course. Students will be divided into two groups, As and Bs, and on
alternate weeks (by 5:15 PM Tuesday) the As and Bs will hand in
discussion questions drawn from the assigned readings. These
questions will be evaluated as part of your class participation
grade. Each student will also prepare an annotated bibliography of
selected readings (c.15-20) related to one week's assignment. You
should provide each member of the class with a copy of this
bibliography at the appropriate seminar meeting. On October 5, each
student will prepare a 7-10 pp. essay, based on the documents
published in Free at Last, analyzing the significance of gender for
the study of slavery and freedom. (The bibliography and essay will
account for 1/3 of your grade.) The final written assignment for
the course will be negotiated with me individually. It can be a
research paper, annotated bibliography, historiographical essay, or
equivalent. Papers of about 20-25 pages are anticipated. (This will
account for the final 1/3 of your grade.) Bibliographies and the
final written assignment can focus on US women's history
exclusively or on American women's history more broadly conceived.

READINGS: The following books (listed in the order in which they
will be used) can be purchased at the Regulator Bookshop on Ninth
Street:

        Ellen DuBois and Vicki Ruiz, eds., Unequal Sisters, SECOND
        EDITION (DR)
        Lori Ginzberg, Women and the Work of Benevolence: Morality,
        Politics and Class in the 19th C. United States
        Linda Gordon, Woman's Body, Woman's Right: A Social History
        of Birth Control in America

Jean F. Yellin and John VanHorne, eds., The Abolitionist
Sisterhood: Women's Political Culture in Antebellum America
Ira Berlin, et al, eds., Free At Last: A Documentary History
of Slavery, Freedom, and the Civil War
Evelyn Brooks Higginbotham, Righteous Discontent: The Women's
Movement in the Black Baptist Church
William Chafe, Paradox of Change: American Women in the
20th Century
Elizabeth Lasch-Quinn, Black Neighbors: Race and the Limits
of Reform in the Settlement House Movement
Julia Blackwelder, Women of the Depression: Caste and Culture
in San Antonio
Joanne Meyerowitz, ed., Not June Cleaver: Women and Gender in
Postwar America
Elizabeth Kennedy and Madeline Davis, Boots of Leather,
Slippers of Gold: The History of a Lesbian Community
Kim Chernin, In My Mother's House: A Daughter's Story

Students will also be assigned Tera Hunter's dissertation,
"Household Workers in the Making: Afro-American Women in Atlanta
and the New South" (Ph.D. Diss, Yale University, 1990), which can
be ordered from University Microfilms.

In addition there will be articles on reserve in the Graduate
Student Lounge at Duke, and one copy will be made available as well
to be placed in a convenient location at UNC.

WEEKLY ASSIGNMENTS

Aug. 31   Introduction

Sep. 7   Gender, Class and Culture in Antebellum America
           Read: Ginzberg, Women and the Work of Benevolence,
           intro and chs. 1-4; Gordon, Woman's Body, ch. 5
           In DR, Intro.,(4) Boydston, (8) Stansell, (9) VanKirk
           Reserve: Louis B. Gimelli, "'Borne Upon the Wings of
           Faith': The Chinese Odyssey of Henrietta Hall Shuck"

Sep. 14   Racial Bonds and Gender Frontiers
           Read: Yellin and Van Horne, Abolitionist Sisterhood
           In DR, (1) Hewitt, (3) Perdue, (5)Gonzalez
           Reserve: Joanne Meyerowitz, "American Women's History:
           The Fall of Women's Culture"
           Library Project: Mapping the Dissertation Landscape

Sep. 21   Breaking the Bonds
           Read: Berlin et al, Free At Last (selections);
           Ginzberg, chs. 5 & 6
           In DR, (2) White and (36) Liu
           Reserve: Hewitt, "Feminist Friends"; DuBois, "Taking
           the Law into Our Hands"; Edwards, "Sexual Violence,
           Gender, Reconstruction, and the Extension of the
           Patriarchy"; and Schultz, "Race, Gender and Bureaucracy

Sep. 28   Crossroads of Race and Gender
Read: Brooks Higginbotham, <u>Righteous Discontent</u>
In DR, (22) Hine and (17) Barkley Brown
Reserve: Elsa Barkley Brown, "What Is Happening Here?";
Deborah G. White, "The Cost of Club Work, the Price of
Black Feminism" OR "The Slippery Slope of Class in
Black America"

Oct. 5   Speak Softly and Carry a Big Stick? Bible? Notebook?
Read: Gordon, <u>Woman's Body</u>, chs. 6-8
In DR, (6)Jensen & (10)Pascoe OR (18)Sanchez & (19)Ruiz
On reserve, Joan Jacobs Brumberg, "The Ethnological
Mirror"; Thomas Dyer, "Race Suicide"; Donna Haraway,
"The Teddy Bear Patriarchy"; Louise Newman, "Coming of
Age, But Not in Samoa,"; AND Kim Emery, "Steers, Queers
and Manifest Destiny"

Oct. 12   In Pursuit of Power
Read: Chafe, <u>Paradox</u>, Part One
In DR, (7) Baker, (14) DuBois, and (16) Azize
Reserve: Hewitt, "In Pursuit of Power: The Political
Economy of Women's Activism in 20th C. Tampa"

Oct. 19   Community and Control
Read: Lasch-Quinn, <u>Black Neighbors</u>
In DR, (11) Gordon
Reserve: Kathryn Kish Sklar, "Hull House in the 1890s";
Nancy MacLean, "'Cleaning Up' Morality" and
"Paramilitary Paternalism"; Jessie Rodrique, "The Black
Community and the Birth Control Movement"

Oct. 26   Working It Out
Read: Hunter, "Household Workers in the Making"; Chafe,
<u>Paradox</u>, Part Two
In DR, (13)Tax, (23)Hall, (25)Weber, & (26)Nakano Glenn
Reserve: Sarah Deutsch, "Gender, Labor History, and
Chicano/a Ethnic Identity" and Robin Kelley, "'We
Are   Not What We Seem': Rethinking Black Working-Class
Opposition"

Nov. 2   Sex and Society
Read: Gordon, <u>Woman's Body</u>, chs. 9-12
In DR, (12) Meyerowitz, (20) Posadas, (21) Carby, (24)
Peiss, and (35) Giddings
Reserve: Esther Newton, "The Mythic Mannish Lesbian,"
Nancy MacLean, "The Leo Frank Case Reconsidered," AND
Joan Jacobs Brumberg, "Coming of Age in the 1920s"

Nov. 9   Depression
Read: Blackwelder, <u>Women of the Depression</u>
Reserve: Ruth Milkman, "Women's Work and the Economic
Crisis" and Lois Helmbold, "Beyond the Family Economy:
Black and White Working-Class Women in the GD"

Nov. 16   World War, Cold War, and Postwar
          Read: Chafe, _Paradox_, Part Three and ch. 10;
          Meyerowitz, _Not June Cleaver_ (selections)
          In DR, Swerdlow and Solinger
          Reserve: Leila Rupp & Verta Taylor, "The 'Isolationism'
          of the Women's Right Movement" and Kathy Nasstrom,
          "Down to Now: The Gendered Memory of Leadership in the
          Civil Rights Movement"

Nov. 23   The 'L' Word
          Read: Davis and Kennedy, _Boots of Leather_
          Reserve: Judith Bennett, "The 'L' Word in Women's
          History"

Nov. 30   What's Left?
          Read: Chernin, _In My Mother's House_; Chafe, _Paradox_,
          chs. 11 & 12
          In DR, (31) Kelly, (32) Tsosie, (33) Garcia, and (34)
          Kessler-Harris
          Reserve: Selections from Toni Morrison, ed., _Race-ing
          Justice, En-gendering Power: Essays on Anita Hill,
          Clarence Thomas, and the Construction of Social Reality_

Dec. 12   PAPERS DUE

History 72B

Gender, Society and Culture in Twentieth Century America

Spring Quarter, 1997
University of California, Davis
Office Hours: Tuesday 1:00-2:30
Thursday 4:30-6:00
And by appointment
Email: rerosen@ucdavis.edu

Professor Ruth Rosen
3234 Social Science/Hum
Office Phone: 752-6380
Messages: 752-0776

History 72B will deal thematically and chronologically with topics in the social, economic and cultural history of women, gender, sexuality, and the family during the twentieth century in the United States. The course will emphasize how ideas and experience of family life, gender roles and sexuality changed as American society became increasingly industrialized and urbanized and its culture dominated by mass culture, consumer values, rapid technological change and the transformation to a post-industrial, post-modern global economy.

The major goals of this course are to improve students' critical reading and writing skills, and to how to analyze why change occurs. To achieve these goals, I have assigned quite a variety of different writing assignments and readings that will encourage students to think about modern history from different perspectives, using different sources.

Course Requirements:
Please note that students must complete all requirements in order to pass the course.

1) Lectures will raise important issues and perspectives and provide background and analysis. Sections offer a forum for debate, discussion and collective problem solving. **Sections are mandatory and all students must enroll in and attend the same section throughout the quarter.**

2) A midterm in class, on May 1st

3) A seven page paper based on an oral interview with an individual who is at least twenty years older than yourself. The purpose of this assignment is to understand and analyze the impact of historical change on a particular person. Some examples might include interviewing a woman who worked during World

War II, a man who avoided the Vietnam draft, a man who fought in the Vietnam War, a woman who felt pressured by the Feminine Mystique during the 1950's, a woman who was affected (or not) by the contemporary women's movement during the 60 or 70's, a person who fought in the civil rights movement, a woman who entered the labor force as the "first woman" in her field, or a man who is a combat veteran of a war. Guidelines for the interview will be handed out and the paper will be due **June 5 in lecture. No exceptions unless my permission is granted or you have a doctor's note.**

5) A one page critique of any film shown in class. During the quarter I will be showing you a number of documentaries that illustrate important aspects of 20th century history. Students should choose one film and write a one-page critique of that documentary. The critique should include a statement of the film maker's thesis or argument, the evidence used to buttress that thesis, and the student's assessment of the film maker's bias and conclusion(s). The purpose of this assignment is to teach students to watch films critically, to recognize bias and cinematic argumentation. **The film critique will be due on May 29th.** You may hand it in earlier to your T.A. **Also, please note that both the midterm and final exams will likely have questions that draw upon the information and perspective of documentaries shown in class.**

5) A Final exam that covers the material of the course. Study questions will be given out by the last day of class and review sessions will be organized for students to study together. The final exam will include identifications, short essays and one long essay. All questions that will be on the final exam appear on the study questions.

Grading:
Midterm: 20%
Oral History Interview Paper: 30%
Film Critique: 10%
Attendance and Participation in Section: 10%
Final Exam: 30%

Required Reading:
Nancy Woloch, *Women and American Experience* -Text
Susan Ware, *Modern American Women*--Documents
Anzia Yezierska, *The Bread Givers*
Charlotte Perkins Gilman, *The Yellow Wallpaper*
Barbara Ehrenreich, *Hearts of Men*
Margaret Atwood, *The Handmaid's Tale*
Ann Moody, *Coming of Age in Mississippi*

And please, --read a daily newspaper with national and international news.

Schedule of Lectures and Readings:
Please Note: Readings should be completed before the lecture.

April 1   Introduction

April 3   **The Legacy of the Nineteenth Century**
Reading: Charlotte Perkins Gilman, *The Yellow Wallpaper.*

April 8   **The New Woman, Women Reformers and Progressivism**
Reading: Ware, In Part One, "Visions of the New Woman" and
Part Two"Expanding Horizons for Education Women; " read only
"Dance Hall Madness;" "The New Restlessness;" M.Carey
Thomas at Cornell; Alice Hamilton;   Mary Beard, "Women and
Progressive Politics"
Woloch: Ch11, "The Founding of Hull House" and Ch 12, "The
Rise of New Woman"

April 10   **African American Women, Race Relations and The Anti-
Lynching Movement**
Reading: Ware, Part One, "Black Women Enter the Teaching
Profession"
Part Two,"Black Women Plan to Lead the Race."   Woloch p.
226-231.
Film: "Ida B. Wells"

April 15   **Suffrage, Feminism and Social Feminism**
Reading: Ware, Part Four , " Feminsts, Anarchists and other
Rebel Girls (Optional: Ware: Part Five) Woloch Ch. 13 The Crisis
of the NWSA and Ch 14, Feminism and Suffrage, I860-1920.

April 17   **The Gendered Immigrant Experience:, Working-Class Culture,
Tradition and the Promised Land**
Reading: Yezierska, *The Bread Givers*
Woloch, p. 231-235

April 22   **The Politics of Prostitution: Reformers, Prostitutes, and
Cultural Symbol**
Reading: Ware, Part Three, "Women at Work."

April 24   **The Politics of Sex: Margaret Sanger, Birth Control, The Rise**

of Companionate Marriage and the Celebration of
Heterosexuality
Reading: Woloch: Ch15, Margaret Sanger's Crusade; Ch16,
Cross Currents in the I920's.

April 29   Working class women, Class Conflict and Class Alliance
Ware, Part Three: "Women at Work:
Woloch, Ch.9, The Shirtwaist Strike of I909, p.235-248;
Film: Women of Summer"

May 1   MIDTERM IN CLASS

May 6   The Gendered Depression: Women Reformers, The New Deal
and the Rise of the Welfare State
Reading: Ware, Part Seven, , "Women Face the Depression"
Woloch, Ch.17, "Humanizing the New Deal" and Ch.18
Emergencies: p.439-456.

May 8   World WAR II: The Gendered War and the Home Front:
Reading: Ware, Part Eight
Woloch, p. 459-473;
Film: "The Life and Times of Rosie the Riveter"

May 13   The Feminine Mystique and the Cold War:
Reading: Ware, Part Nine (Except excerpts by Anne Moody and
Rosa Parks); Ehrenreich, Hearts of Men, ch.1-6

May 15   The Civil Rights Movement
Reading: Ware, Part Nine "Civil Rights Activists"
Moody, Coming of Age in Mississippi
Woloch p. 509-523

May 20   The Origins of Contemporary Feminism and American
Political Culture
Finish Ehrenreich, Hearts of Men:
Woloch, Ch19 Turning Points The Early 60's, and Ch 20 High
Expectations I950-I975;
Ware: Part10. "The Revival of Feminism"
And Part 11" Women Organizing For Social Change."

May 22   The Hidden Injuries of Sex: The Uneasy Alliance Between
the Sexual Revolution and Feminism.

Reading: Ware, Part Twelve: "New Issues of Sex and Sexuality."
Woloch, Ch.21 The Thomas Hearings and Ch 22 "In Search of Equality"

May 27   **The Politics of Beauty and Appearance**
          Film: "Still Killing us Softly"

May 29   **From Sisterhood to Superwoman**
          One page Film Critique Due

June 3   **Feminism Redefined; Backlash and Global Explosion**
          Ware, Part Thirteen, "Conflicting Visions"
          Film: Vienna Tribunal

June 5   **Last Lecture: Gender, Feminism, and the Cultural Wars.**

          Oral History Paper DUE

**FINAL EXAM STUDY QUESTIONS HANDED OUT: All students must
   bring empty blue books to final exam.**

Professor Vicki L. Ruiz
Office: Women's Studies Program
Office Hours: M/T 1-3
or by appointment
965-3656
vruiz@asuvm.inre.asu.edu

HISTORY 598

"AND MILES TO GO":
WOMEN AND MODERN AMERICA, 1920-1990

This course will highlight some of the most exciting feminist approaches in twentieth century U.S. women's history. Focusing on theory, methodology, and resources, it will examine the ways in which scholars have embodied issues of race, class, culture, region, and sexuality in formulating new interpretations of women's experiences. I have also selected monographs which I hope engage students to the extent that they feel they are "curling up with a good book" rather than drudging through the required readings. The dynamics of oral history, fiction, and autobiographical narrative will also be explored.

REQUIRED READINGS

Sara Evans, Born For Liberty

Susan Ware, Still Missing: Amelia Earhart and the Search for Modern Feminism

Valerie Matsumoto, Farming the Home Place

Elaine Tyler May, Homeward Bound

Jo Ann Robinson, The Montgomery Bus Boycott and The Women Who Made It

Liz Kennedy, Boots of Leather, Slippers of Gold: The History of a Lesbian Community

Rickie Solinger, Wake Up Little Susie: Single Pregnancy and Race Before Roe v. Wade

Susan Douglas, Where The Girls Are: Growing Up Female with the Mass Media

Mary Crow Dog, Lakota Woman

Janice Radway, Reading the Romance

Pierette Hondagneu-Sotelo, Gendered Transitions: Mexican Experiences of Immigration

Stephanie Coontz, The Way We Never Were: American Families and the Nostalgia Trap

Ellen DuBois and Vicki L. Ruiz, Unequal Sisters: A Multicultural Reader in U.S. Women's History 2nd edition.

COURSE OUTLINE

Week 1
1/22   Introduction
            Film: A Century of Women, Part One: Work and Family

Week 2
1/29   Synthesis and Women's History
            Reading assignment: Born for Liberty

Week 3
2/4   Field Trip: Heard Museum 1 p.m.
2/5   Gender, Biography, and Iconography
            Reading assignment: Still Missing

Week 4
2/12   Oral History and Community Studies
            Reading assignment: Farming The Home Place

Week 5
2/19   The "State of Domesticity"
            Reading assignment: Homeward Bound

Week 6
2/26   Civil Rights and Gender
            Reading assignment: The Montgomery Bus Boycott

Week 7
3/4   Creating Community, Creating Family
            Reading assignment: Boots of Leather

Week 8
3/18   Race, Sexuality, and the State
            Reading assignment: Wake Up Little Susie

Week 9
3/25   Gender and Popular Culture
            Reading assignment: Where The Girls Are
            Film and Food: Mystic Pizza

Week 10
4/1   Representation and Autobiography
            Reading assignment: Lakota Woman

Week 11

113

4/8   Literature and Ethnography
            Reading assignment: Reading the Romance
            Film: The Desert Is No Lady

Week 12
4/15   The Politics of Work and Family
            Reading assignment: Gendered Transitions

Week 13
4/22   Contextualizing The Present
            Reading assignment: The Way We Never Were

Week 14
4/29   Voice, Power, and Gender
            Reading assignment: Unequal Sisters, 2nd edition

COURSE EXPECTATIONS

The Readings

Each student will be expected to give an in-class presentation of
one monograph in which she or he discusses the author's thesis,
narrative line, evidence, and interpretation. The presentation
should not be a rehash of the book, but a thoughtful review of its
contributions to our understanding of women's experiences. For
every monograph, students will prepare a one page synopsis or
precís summarizing the author's major points. Also, bring to class
one scholarly review of the monograph under discussion.

Historiographical Essay

The major portion of the student's grade will be based on a 20-25
page historiographical essay which draws upon the books selected
for this course. In addition to discussing the comparative merits
and limitations of particular approaches, students will be expected
to address specific themes and paradigms emerging out of feminist
discourse.   How can we grapple with women's consciousness and
agency? Whose voices count and who decides? How do we get at
issues of power?   Should a balance exist between structure and
agency? representation and lived experience?
Paper is due by Tuesday, May 7th at 4 p.m.

Attendance
Given the time constraints of this course, attendance at every
class is mandatory.

Grading

30% Monograph Presentation
20% Class Participation
50% Historiographical Essay

History 368
History of American Women in the 20th Century

Fall 1997; Lecture Hall 10   Professor K. K. Sklar
Lectures Mon & Wed 12-1   Library Tower 607
Teaching Assistant: Office Hrs. Wed. 1-3
    Jan Doolittle   and by appointment
    Office hrs: Phone: 777-6202
        M 1-3; F 11-12

COURSE DESCRIPTION

    The second of a two-semester sequence, this course focuses on themes
related to power in the lives of United States women during the past
hundred years, and the ability of women to control their life
circumstances. The course will compare different groups of women, such
as African-American and white women, in various social movements and in
relationship to various public policies. Particular emphasis will be
given to women and public life. Chronologically, the course will focus
on two periods, 1900-1930 and 1960-1990.

COURSE GOALS -- to help students understand continuity and change in:

-- women's ability to control the circumstances of their lives;
-- sexuality and reproductive rights;
-- family life;
-- the relations between women and men;
-- women's paid work;
-- women's legal status;
-- women's political activism;
-- women as active agents of social change;
-- how differences among women are structured and contested;
-- women's ability to control the distribution of social resources.

REQUIRED READING:

    Sklar and Dublin, eds., Women and Power in American History, Vol. II
    Susan Ware, Modern American Women: A Documentary History
    Andrea Tone, ed., Controlling Reproduction
    Rose Cohen, Out of the Shadow
    Anne Moody, Coming of Age in Mississippi

RECOMMENDED READING: Nancy Woloch, Women and the American Experience
(This textbook will provide an overview.)

Books are available for purchase at Bookbridge, Vestal Plaza, where a
discount is offered. Take Blue Bus #5. Bookbridge will deliver books
to any handicapped student; receipts are valid for reimbursements by
financial aid agencies. Books are also on reserve.

COURSE REQUIREMENTS:
    Attendance at lectures and discussion sections is required.
Students should arrive at discussion section prepared to discuss the
week's reading. Midterm and final examinations will stress essay
questions, but will also include brief identifications. A term paper of
10-15 pages is due in discussion section no later than Friday, Dec. 5.
Progress reports on term papers are due on Friday Nov. 7 and Friday Nov.
21. A report on two films in the course film series is due in
discussion section no later than Dec. 12. Because it is unfair to
students who complete their work on time, no extensions will be granted
on written work.

Course grades will be determined as follows:

-- participation in discussion section -- 20%
-- report on 2 films in film series -- 10%
-- midterm examination -- 20%
-- term paper -- 25%
-- final examination -- 25%

TERM PAPER: A term paper of 10-15 pages is due no later than discussion
section, Friday, Dec. 5. Each student is asked to write a paper based
on oral interviews with at least two generations of women in her/his
family born before 1960 or if family members are not available, with
other older women. Students should try to complete their interviews by
midpoint in the course, Monday, October 20 (week 8). Progress reports
on term papers are due in discussion section on Nov. 7 (week 10) and
Nov. 21 (week 12). The first progress report should identify who you
have interviewed and what themes have emerged in your interview. The
second report should present a rough draft of your term paper. These
will be graded pass/fail and will become part of term paper grades. For
further information, see GUIDE TO WRITING ASSIGNMENTS IN HISTORY 368.

WRITING CREDIT: The required work for the course meets the requirements
for the university's Intensive Writing Credit. However, if you wish
writing credit to be entered on your transcript, you must enroll in the
course for writing credit.

FILMS: A film series is offered in connection with the course on
Tuesdays, 7pm in Lecture Hall 10. Attendance at all films is
encouraged, but attendance at one film is required--"Tues. Oct. 14,
Women of Summer: The Bryn Mawr Summer School for Women Workers." Also
required is a brief (3-5 page) report about any two other films,
discussing the relationship of two films to themes raised in the course.
Film reports are due in discussion section no later than Friday, Dec.
12.

DEBATE: Students who volunteer to participate in the recreation of the
1920-1926 debate over the ERA on Monday, October 14, will receive extra
course credit in the form of an improved grade on the midterm
examination (to the next grade higher; for example from B to B+).

WORLD WIDE WEB: The course's homepage is under construction. Course
materials and links to related World Wide Web sites will soon be
available on the Web.

116

COURSE SCHEDULE

Throughout this syllabus an asterisk (*) indicates that the article is in Sklar & Dublin, Women and Power in American History, Vol. II.

Week 1: Sept. 3-5 -- Introduction

Wed. -- Introduction to Course;
Women and Economic Dependency, 1890-1990

Friday.--Discussion Section

Reading:

*Bianchi and Spain, "Women in the Labor Force, 1950-1980," Table 1 and Figure 1, 264 & 265

*Kathy Peiss, "'Charity Girls' and City Pleasures: Historical Notes on Working-Class Sexuality," pp. 88-100

Week 2: Sept 8-12--Fertility decline: 1830-1940

Mon. Women control their bodies, 1830-1880:
the Demographic Transition

Wed. The cultural consequences of fertility decline, 1880-1920

Friday: Discussion Section

Reading

Tone, Controlling Reproduction
I. Birth Control and Abortion in Early America, pp. 3-20
Documents, pp. 20-29
II. The Medicalization of Reproduction, pp. 33-58
Documents, pp. 58-74
III. Fertility Control in 19th-Century America, pp. 77-98
Documents, pp. 99-105

Modern American Women:
Anzia Yezierska, "An Immigrant Daughter," pp. 18-21
Belle Lindner Israels, "Dance Hall Madness," 21-24
Kate Simon, "Female Adolescence," pp. 166-171

Tues: FILM -- "Indians, Outlaws, and Angie Debo." Angie Debo's research on Oklahoma history brought her to a disturbing discovery about how Indians were swindled out of their land. Banned from publication until the 1950s, her work became the cornerstone of new scholarship on American Indians.

Week 3:   Sept. 15-19 -- Changes in Women's Economic Dependency, 1890-1920

Mon. -- Women's Economic Dependency
        and Women's Response to Economic Dependency

Wed. -- The Feminization of the Clerical Labor Force, 1880-1920

Friday--Discussion Section

Reading:
  *Carole Turbin, "And We Are Nothing But Women:
   Irish Working Women in Troy," pp. 25-40

  *Dana Frank, "Housewives, Socialists, & the Politics of Food:
   The 1917 New York Cost-of-Living Protests," pp. 101-114

Ware, Modern American Women:

   Nellie Bly, "Girl Reporter Derring Do" 5-8
   Edith Eudora Ammons "A Woman Homesteader" 25-29
   "Women at Work," pp. 54-56.
   "Buffalobird Woman's Story" 58-60
   "The Harsh Conditions of Domestic Service" pp. 60-64
   Agnes Nestor, "The Story of a Glove Maker," 67-70
   "Working Women Write the Jewish Daily Forward" 70-74
   pictures, 82-86
   Meredith Tax, "Housewives Protest High Food Prices," 89-93
   Josephine Conger-Kaneko, "Wages for Housework" 97-100

Tues: FILM "Fast Food Women" -- Penetrating documentary about women
in the low-wage work of fast-food restaurants in the 1980s, which in
some ways resemble women's low-wage work of the 1910's, except that the
1980s women are trying to support themselves and their children.

Week 4: Sept. 22-26 -- Migration and Immigration

   Mon. -- Rural-Urban Migration, American and Euro-American

   Wed. -- Japanese and Chinese Women Immigrants, 1850-1950

   Friday--Discussion section

   READING:

   Rose Cohen, Out of the Shadow
   *Mary J. Oates, "Organized Voluntarism: The Catholic
    Sisters in Massachusetts, 1870-1940"

   Ware, Modern American Women
   Monica Sone, "Japanese Relocation," 231-236

Tues: FILM -- "A Family Gathering" -- A young Japanese-American women
explores her family history through the lens of their detention in
concentration camps during World War II.

Week 5: Sept. 29 -- African-American women migrate north, 1880-1940

Mon. -- Migration North, Black Women's Associations, 1880-1940; Black and White Women Crusade against Lynching, 1890-1940

Wed. -- Rosh Hashanah -- no class

Friday: Rose Hashanah -- no discussion section

READING:
*Elizabeth Clark-Lewis, "This Work Had a End": African-American Domestic Workers"

*Julie Roy Jeffrey, "Women in the Southern Farmer's Alliance"

Ware, Modern American Women:
  Anna J. Cooper, "Black Women Plan to Lead," 12-15
  Mamie Garvin Fields, "Black Women Enter the
    Teaching Profession," 42-46
  "Female Perspectives on the Great Migration" 64-67

Read ahead in assignments for Week 7 and prepare for midterm exam

Tues: FILM -- "Ida B. Wells: A Passion for Justice"--
Documentary about Wells's crusade against lynching in the South and her organizing of Black club women in the North (60 mins).

Week 6: Oct. 6-8 -- The Woman Suffrage Movement, 1900-1920

Mon. -- White women and the Woman Suffrage Movement, 1900-1922

Wed. -- Black women and the Woman Suffrage Movement, 1900-1922

Friday: YOM KIPPUR -- NO DISCUSSION SECTION

READING:

*Rosalyn Terborg-Penn, "Discontented Black Feminists: Prelude and
    Postscript to the Passage of the Nineteenth Amendment"

Ware, Modern American Women:
  C.P. Gilman, "Feminist Challenge," 93-97
  "The Final Push for Suffrage," 112-114
  Abigail Scott Duniway, "A Western Suffragist Talks," 114-117
  Florence Luscomb, "Open-Air Meetings," 117-120
  Marie Jenny Howe, "An Anti Suffrage Monologue" 120-125
  Lenora O'Reilly, "A Labor Organizer Speaks," 125-128
  Maud Wood Park, "Front Door Lobbying," 128-131
  "Alice Paul goes to Jail," 131-136

Read ahead in assignments for Week 7 and prepare for midterm exam

Tues: FILM-- "One Woman, One Vote," documentary on suffrage movement.

Mon. -- I. Women's political culture during the Progressive Era, 1890-1920

Tues. - 7pm FILM IS REQUIRED VIEWING

Wed. -- II. Social Democratic harvest, 1900-1914

Friday--Discussion Section

READING:

*Ruth Bordin, "Women's Mighty Realm of Philanthropy"
*Estelle Freedman, "Separatism as Strategy"
*K. K. Sklar, "Hull House in the 1890s as a Community
  of Women Reformers"

Ware, Modern American Women:
   Bertha Palmer, "The Fair Women, Chicago, 1893," 8-12
   Frances Willard, "Learning to Ride a Bicycle," 15-18 & 79
   M. Carey Thomas at Cornell, 32-36
   Jane Addams, "After College, What?" 36-40
   Alice Hamilton, "Exploring The Dangerous Trades," 40-42
   Lucy S. Mitchell, "A Pioneering Dean of Women," 46-50
   Mary Beard, "Women and Progressive Politics," 50-53
   U.S. Supreme Court decision in "Muller v. Oregon," 74-78
   pictures, 79-81
    Carrie Chapman Catt, "New Voters," 143-145
   "Anxious Mothers write the Children's Bureau," 161-166

For more letters to the Children's Bureau, see (ON RESERVE) Molly
Ladd-Taylor, Raising a Baby the Government Way: Mother's Letters
to the Children's Bureau, 1915-1932 (Rutgers Press 1986)

PREPARE FOR ERA DEBATE

Tues: FILM: "Women of Summer: The Bryn Mawr Summer School for Women
Workers." Documentary about a reunion in the 1970s of working class
women and teachers who first met at the Bryn Mawr Summer School for
Women Workers in the 1920s. THIS FILM IS REQUIRED VIEWING.

Week 8: Oct. 20-24 --

Mon. -- The decline of women's political culture, 1920-1930

Wed. -- DEBATE over the Equal Rights Amendment:
          New Feminists vs. Old
          (Students who volunteer to participate in this recreation of the
          1920-1926 debate over the ERA will receive extra course credit.)

Friday--Discussion Section

READING

*K. K. Sklar, "Why Were Most Politically Active Women
     Opposed to the ERA in the 1920s?"

Review course readings and prepare for midterm exam

FILM -- Tues. Oct. 21: "Madame Secretary," Documentary on Frances
Perkins, Secretary of Labor under FDR and the first woman cabinet
member. (57 mins.)

Week 9: Oct. 27-31 --midterm exam

Mon. -- MIDTERM EXAM--

Wed. -- The new sexual order of the 20th century:
          (Jan Doolittle lecturing)

Friday: Discussion section

READING:

*Christine Simmons, "Companionate Marriage and the Lesbian Threat"

Modern American Women:
    Pictures, 86, 205-206
    "Individual Choice, Collective Progress," 139-143
    Dorothy Bromley, "Generational Conflicts," 145-149
    Crystal Eastman, "Creating a Feminist Lifestyle 149-155
    Eudora Ramsey Richardson "The New Woman in Fiction" 155-161

Tues: FILM -- "Diamonds" Frontline production, Public Broadcasting
System report about the false basis of the economic value of the
"forever" mineral (50 mins.)

121

Mon. -- The Criminalization of Abortion & Contraception, 1840-1940
       (Jan Doolittle lecturing)

Wed. -- Margaret Sanger and the Birth Control Movement, 1914-1936

Friday: Discussion section

          FIRST REPORT ON TERM PAPER DUE IN DISCUSSION SECTION

READING:

*James Mohr, "The Social Character of Abortion in
       America, 1840-1880" (in Sklar & Dublin, Vol. I, on reserve)
*Linda Gordon, "The Professionalization of the
       Birth Control Movement [in the 1920's]"
*Jessie M. Rodrique, "The Black Community and the Birth Control
       Movement," 160-74

Tone, Controlling Reproduction
 IV. Regulating Reproduction, pp. 109-138
       Documents, 138-144
  V. Birth Control Revolution: Reproductive Freedom or Social
       Control? pp. 147-154
       Documents, pp. 154-170

VII. The Political Economy of Birth Control, pp. 211-232

Modern American Women:
   "Margaret Sanger's Epiphany," 100-106
   Emma Goldman, "A Radical View," 106-111

Tues: FILMS "Margaret Sanger: A Public Nuisance," (25 mins.) and "When
Abortion was Illegal"(25 mins). Fairly uncritical documentary about
Sanger's early career before 1930; testimony about illegal abortions
before 1973.

Mon. -- Changes in Women's Labor Force Participation, and Union Organizing, 1950-1995: women's growing economic independence

Wed. -- "Women Strike for Peace" and the Cold War

Friday: Discussion section

Reading:

*Coyle, Hershatter and Honig, "Women at Farah: an Unfinished Story," 248-62

*S. Bianchi & D. Spain, "Labor Force Participation and Occupational Composition," 263-75

*Ruth Milkman, "Redefining 'Women's Work': The Sexual Division of Labor in the Auto Industry During World War II, 209-222

Modern American Women:
I.   THE CRISIS OF THE 1930S AND 40S
     "The Burdens of Rural Women's Lives," 56-58
     "Women Face the Depression," 172-174
     Meridel LeSueur, "The Despair of Unemployed Women," 174-180
     "American Women Ask Eleanor Roosevelt for Help," 180-186
     Ann Marie Low, "The Dust Bowl," 186-189
     Margaret Jarman Hagood, "White Southern Farm Women," 189-195
     Carlotta Silvas Martin "A Mexican-American Childhood During the Depression" 195-199
     Genora Johnson Dollinger, "Women and Labor Militancy," 199-204
     Pictures, 207-208
     "Rosie the Riveter and Other Wartime Women," 213-215
     Fanny Christina Hill, "Rosie the Riveter," 215-219
     Marion Stegeman, "Women in the Armed Forces," 219-225
     Harriette Arnow, "Wartime Migration," 225-231
II. WOMEN'S WORK IN POST-WAR AMERICA
     Helen Hovey "Female Entrepreneurship" 257-260
     "Women, Work, and Social Change," 313-315
     Cathy Tuley, "Clerical Workers Unite," 315-320
     Crystal Lee Sutton, "The Real 'Norma Rae'" 320-324
     Jessie Lopez De La Cruz, "Organizing Farm Workers," 330-334
     Jonnie Tillmon, "Women on Welfare," 334-338
     Pictures, 341-343
III. Ethel Barol Taylor, "Women Strike for Peace" 260-263

Tues: FILMS -- "The Memorial Day Massacre of 1937,"--Footage of the police shooting of steel industry unionists at a picnic. (16 mins.) "With Babies and Banners" -- Documentary with Genora Dollinger and other women of the Women's Emergency Brigade during the 1937 sit-down strike in Flint, Michigan, that established the United Automobile Workers. (55 mins.)

Week 12: Nov. 17-21--Women & the Civil Rights Movement of the 50s & 60s

Mon. -- Black Women in the Civil Rights Movement

Wed. -- White Women in the Civil Rights Movement

Friday: Discussion section

READING:

Anne Moody, *Coming of Age in Mississippi*

*Mary Aickin Rothschild, "White Women Volunteers in
    the Freedom Summers"

Modern American Women:
    Rosa Parks and Virginia Foster Durr, "Civil Rights Activists,"
      263-269
    Charlayne Hunter-Gault "Desegregating the University of Georgia,
      1961" 269-273

    SECOND REPORT ON TERM PAPER DUE IN DISCUSSION SECTION

Tues: FILM -- "Fundi" -- A study of the life of Ella Baker and her
contribution to the Civil Rights movement, through the NAACP, the SCLC,
and SNCC. (45 mins). "Eyes on the Prize" -- excerpts featuring women
from the multi-hour series. (50 min.)

Week 13: Nov. 24--The Reemergence of Feminism, 1963-1966

Mon. -- Founding of NOW:
            married women question the Feminine Mystique

Tues. FILM-- "Corita" -- Documentary about a nun influenced by the
Sister Formation movement following Vatican II.

        Wed. -- THANKSGIVING -- No Class and NO DISCUSSION SECTION
                        HAPPY HOLIDAY

READING:
Modern American Women:
    "The Fifties," 241-243
    Betty Friedan, "The Feminist Mystique," 243-252
    Betty Jeanne Boggs, "Balancing Work and Family in the 1950s,"
      252-257
    Pictures, 339-340, 343, 344

    PREPARE TERM PAPER

    PREPARE FILM REPORT

124

Mon. -- The Anti-War Movement among College Women
        and The Merging of Two Generations of Feminists

Wed. -- Reproductive Rights, 1965-1977

Friday: Discussion section

READING:

*Sarah Evans, "The Rebirth of the Women's Movement in the 1960s"

Ware, Modern American Women:
    "The Personal Becomes the Political," 277
    "The Revival of Feminism," 279-281
    "Founding the National Organization for Women, 1966," 281-286
    Robin Morgan, "Feminist Guerilla Theater, 1968," 286-289
    Pat Maninardi, "The Politics of Housework," 289-292
    Kate Shanley, "Thoughts on Indian Feminism," 292-296
    Combahee River Collective, "Black Feminism," 296-305
    Michele Wallace, "A More Personal View of Black Feminism,"
        305-312
    Susan Eisenberg "Hard Hatted Women" 324-330
    "New Issues of Sex and Sexuality," 347-349
    Helen Gurley Brown, "Sex and the Single Girl," 349-353
    Margaret Cruikshank, "Coming Out," 356-362
    Mariah Burton Nelson, "Sex and Sports" 362-369
    Lisa Tiger "Women and AIDS," 369-372

    Tone, Controlling Reproduction
    VI. Reproductive Rights, pp. 173-182
        Documents, pp. 182-208
    VII. Documents, pp. 233-240

Tues: FILM -- "JANE: An Abortion Service" -- From 1969 through 1973 a
group of ordinary women did an extraordinary thing. They formed JANE,
an underground Chicago-based women's health service that facilitated and
performed nearly 12,000 safe, illegal abortions. In this documentary
the women of JANE talk frankly about their actions then and the issue of
reproductive choice in the 1990s.

                TERM PAPERS DUE IN DISCUSSION SECTION

Mon. -- Gender war as a surrogate for class war:
     the ERA and reproductive rights

Wed. -- Can women be both equal to and different from men?
     The future of feminist legal theory

Friday: Discussion section

READING:

*Christine Littleton, "Equality and Feminist Theory"

Ware, Modern American Women
    "Abortion as a Legal and Feminist Issue," 353-358
    "Conflicting Visions from the 1970s and 80s," 373-375
    "Houston, 1977," 373-378
    Phyllis Schlafley, "The Positive Woman," 378-382
    Susan Faludi, "The Backlash Against Feminism" 383-389
    Anita Hill, "A Woman of Conscience" 389-394
    Abra Fortune Chernic, "The Voice of an Anorexic"   400-404
    Gloria Anzaldua, "The Borderlands" 404-412

Tues: FILM -- "Global Assembly Line" -- Documentary about the
working conditions for women in the global economy (60 mins.)

FILM REPORTS DUE IN DISCUSSION SECTION

FILM SERIES
organized by History 368, fall 1997
History of American Women in the 20th Century
FREE***FREE***FREE***FREE***FREE***FREE
ALL FILMS AT 7pm TUES, Lecture Hall 10

Tues. Sept. 9--"Indians, Outlaws, and Angie Debo." Angie Debo's research on
Oklahoma history brought her to a disturbing discovery about how Indians were
swindled out of their land. Banned from publication until the 1950s, her work
became the cornerstone of new scholarship on American Indians. (55 mins.)

Tues. Sept. 16--"Fast Food Women." Gripping documentary about women
in the low-wage work of fast-food restaurants in the 1980s, which in some ways
resembles women's low-wage work of the 1910's. (45 mins.)

Tues. Sept. 23--"A Family Gathering." A young Japanese-American women
explores her family history through the lens of their detention in concentration
camps during World War II. (55 mins.)

Tues. Sept. 30--"Ida B. Wells: A Passion for Justice." Wells's crusade against
lynching in the South and organizing of Black club women in the North. (60 mins.)

Tues. Oct. 7--"One Woman, One Vote." Documentary on suffrage movement. (90 mins.)

Tues. Oct. 14--THIS FILM IS REQUIRED VIEWING. "Women of Summer: The Bryn Mawr
Summer School for Women Workers." Documentary of a reunion in the 1970s of working
class women and teachers who first met at the Bryn Mawr Summer School for Women
Workers in the 1920s (60 mins).

Tues. Oct. 21-- "Madame Secretary." Documentary on Frances Perkins, Secretary of
Labor under FDR and the first woman cabinet member. (57 mins.)

Tues. Oct. 28--"Diamonds." Frontline production, Public Broadcasting System report
about the false basis of the economic value of the "forever" mineral (50 mins.)

Tues. Nov. 4--"Margaret Sanger: A Public Nuisance," Uncritical but informative
documentary about Sanger's early career before 1930 (25 mins.); and "When Abortion
was Illegal" gripping testimony about illegal abortions before 1973 (28 mins).

Tues. Nov. 11--"The Memorial Day Massacre of 1937,"--Real time footage of the police
shooting men at a union picnic. (16 mins.) "With Babies and Banners" --
Documentary with Genora Dollinger and other women of the Women's Emergency Brigade
during the 1937 sit-down strike in Flint, Michigan, that established the United
Automobile Workers. (55 mins.)

Tues. Nov. 18--"Fundi." A study of the life of Ella Baker and her contribution to
the Civil Rights movement, through the NAACP, the SCLC, and SNCC. (45 mins). "Eyes
on the Prize" -- excerpts featuring women. (60 min.)

Tues. Nov. 25--"Corita." Documentary about a nun influenced by the Sister
Formation movement following Vatican II.

Tues. Dec. 2--"JANE: An Abortion Service." From 1969 through 1973 a group of women
formed JANE, an underground Chicago-based women's health service that facilitated
and performed nearly 12,000 safe, illegal abortions. The women of JANE talk frankly
about their actions then and the issue of reproductive choice in the 1990s.

Tues. Dec. 9--"Global Assembly Line." Documentary about the working conditions for
women in the global economy (60 mins.)

127

4. Graduate and Undergraduate Topics Courses and Seminars

Ann Braude   Religion 360
                                              Spring, 1996

WOMEN IN AMERICAN RELIGIOUS HISTORY

Required Texts:

William Andrews, Sisters of the Spirit
Carol Karlsen, The Devil in the Shape of a Woman
Marabel Morgan, The Total Woman
Harriet Beecher Stowe, The Minister's Wooing
Susan Grossman and Rivka Haut, Daughters of the King
Ann Braude, Radical Spirits
Robert Orsi, The Madonna of 115th Street
Rosemary Curb and Nancy Manahan, Lesbian Nuns

METHODOLOGICAL INTRODUCTION: SISTERHOOD AND BEYOND

Feb 8 Introduction

Feb 15 Gerda Lerner, The Majority Finds Its Past, ch. 10-12.
       Gloria Hull and Barbara Smith, "The Politics of Black Women's Studies," in
           Hull, Scott and Smith, But Some of Us Are Brave.
       Paula Gunn Allen "Kochinnenako in Academe," in The Sacred Hoop
       Valerie Saiving, "Androcentrism in Religious Studies," Journal of Religion 56
           (1976): 177-197.
       **Bibliographic instruction with women's studies reference librarian Emily Bel-
           cher.

PIETY AND FEMININITY IN PROTESTANT CULTURE

Feb 22 Colonial gender norms and those who broke them
       Carol Karlsen, The Devil in the Shape of A Woman

Feb 29 Nineteenth-century domestic ideology
       Harriet Beecher Stowe, The Minister's Wooing

WOMEN IN RELIGIOUS LEADERSHIP

Mar 4 (Monday) **Paper topics and bibliography due.

Mar 7 African American evangelists
       William Andrews, Sisters of the Spirit
       Nell Irvin Painter, "Representing Truth: Sojourner Truth's Knowing and Bec-
           oming Known," JAH (Sept. '94)

Mar 14 Reform vs. Utopia
Mary Farrell Bednarowski, "Outside the Mainstream: Women's Religion and Women's Leadership in Nineteenth-Century America," JAAR, 48 (1980), 207-231.
Mary Ryan, "A Woman's Awakening," in Janet James, Women and Religion in America
**Primary Source Analysis due.

March 15 "Sojourner Truth, A Life, A Symbol," Center for the Study of American Religion Symposium on Nell Painter's forthcoming book. 10 a.m.-3 p.m.

Mar 21 No class--Spring Break

Mar 28 Spirit mediums and radical reformers
Ann Braude, Radical Spirits

WOMEN AND CULTURAL CONFLICT AND CONTINUITY

Apr 4 What does devotion to the Madonna mean in women's lives?: Italian Catholicism in East Harlem
Robert Orsi, The Madonna of 115th Street

Apr 11 Women in Jewish ritual
Grossman and Haut, Daughters of the King, pts. 2 and 3.

THE FEMINIST CRITIQUE OF THE CHURCHES AND THE RELIGIOUS CRITIQUE OF FEMINISM

Apr 18 Women on the religious right
Marabel Morgan, The Total Woman
Guest speaker: R. Marie Griffith

Apr 25 The rejection of patriarchal religion
Rosemary Curb and Nancy Manahan, Lesbian Nuns
Mary J. Oates, "Organizing for Service: Challenges to Community Life and Work Decisions in Catholic Sisterhoods, 1850-1940"

May 2 Conclusion

COURSE REQUIREMENTS

This class will be taught on a seminar format, so careful reading of all assignmnets and readiness to participate in a critical discussion of the texts are essential.

Each student will pursue a research topic throughout the term, and will report on the project at several stages.

Two page description of the topic with bibliography of primary and secondary sources, due on Monday March 4.

8-10 page analysis of a primary source, analyzing its content, placing it in historical context, and discussing its significance and usefullness to the research topic. Due on March 14.

Oral presentation of research topic and preliminary findings in class. Presentations will be scheduled at appropriate points in the term.

15-20 page paper due May 14.

The Welfare State in 20th Century America:
Social Policy and Social Differences
History 201 AM

Jane S. De Hart   Winter, 1995
Office Hours: Tu., Th. 1-2   Thurs. 2-5 p.m.
Ellison 5816   Phelps 3508

Course Overview:

Examining the development of the welfare state, welfare
politics, and the current reconfiguring of social policy
offers a superb opportunity to explore rich, new scholarship
on the interaction of gender, race, ethnicity and class. We
will pay particular attention to such questions as: 1) what
characteristics of nineteenth century politics and the
polity made possible female civic activism and how a
maternalist politics of reform figured in the creation of
the welfare state; 2) what ideas about social citizenship,
social differences, social control and social benefits were
incorporate into welfare policy and how those ideas were
shaped by gender, race, ethnicity and class; 3) how
policies have reflected and reinforced notions about
dependency, duty, entitlement and responsibility and why
current connotations of dependency have becomes so negative;
4) how the contemporary consensus on welfare developed, and
5) what strengths and limitations characterize the new
welfare scholarship.

Class Format and Discussion Preparation:

Emphasis will be placed on close, careful reading of
the texts, most of which are among the most recent works in
the field--an especially important factor in a field where
the pace of scholarly development is exceedingly rapid. Each
of you is expected to have completed all required reading
prior to the seminar meeting for which it is due. (Suggested
reading is optional.)

Class discussion will focus on the themes, issues, and
key questions raised in the reading. Quality of discussion
is critical and attendance is essential. Any unavoidable
absences should be cleared with me in advance.

To stimulate and focus discussion, each member of the
class will periodically choose a particular set of readings
on which she or he will provide synopses and questions that
will be made available to the class prior to each meeting.
The purpose of these 2-page statements is to generate
analysis of the author's thesis, arguments, and insights and
to lay out substantive, methodological, and theoretical
issues for discussion and also to facilitate review of the
readings at the end of the course.

Essay Assignment:

The paper required is a twenty-page (double-spaced) essay that could serve as a mini version of a book you are preparing to write entitled, "The Deserving and Undeserving Poor: From Mother's Pensions to the War on Welfare." Your purpose in this book (and essay) is to highlight social differences based on class, gender, race, and ethnicity as they have shaped policies and, as those policies have in turn, either lessened or reinforced differences. In this paper, be sure to explore in whatever order you choose: 1) continuities and changes in conceptions of who is deserving and undeserving, 2) how those conceptions have limited or constrained attempts to reform welfare policy, and especially 3) to what extent these conceptions and constraints have been shaped by gendered, ethnicized and racialized constructions of social citizenship.

In making your points, provide concrete examples drawn from the years: a) prior to World War I b) the New Deal, c) the Great Society and d) the 1980s and 1990s.

The assignment requires of you no additional reading, but rather sufficient mastery of the material to allow you to step back and look at it as a whole, rethinking and reorganizing it for purposes of this essay. **Do not wait until you have completed all the assigned reading to begin the organizing process. The challenge posed by this assignment lies not merely in demonstrating that you understand the material assigned, or that you are informed about the various topics you are asked to address. Rather it lies in the care and skill with which you select appropriate material, the effectiveness of your organization and the elegance of your presentation.**

The essay does not requires formal footnoting of common reading; however, **I do expect strong organization, carefully constructed paragraphs, and clear, concise prose.** Your grade will reflect the quality of your organization and writing as well as the content. For effective writing, use a guide such as William Shrunk, Jr. and E.B. White, The Elements of Style (1959) or The Chicago Manual of Style.

Required Reading:

Books listed below are available at Student Stores in paperback editions whenever possible. They are also available at the reserve desk in the Library for two-hour loan. In addition, a list of articles and other assigned readings will be available as a coursepack, which can be purchased at The Alternative in Isla Vista.

Gordon, Linda, Pitied But Not Entitled: Single Mothers and

the History of Welfare, 1890-1935, (1994) and Women,
the State, and Welfare (1990)
Handler, Joel F., and Yeheskel Hasenfeld, The Moral
Construction of Poverty: Welfare Reform in America,
(1991)
Mink, Gwendolyn, The Wages of Motherhood: Inequality in the
Welfare State, 1917-1942, (1995)
Muncy, Robyn, Creating a Female Dominion in American Reform,
(1991)
Murray, Charles, Losing Ground: American Social Policy,
1950-1980, (1984)
Olasky, Marvin, The Tragedy of American Compassion, (1992)
Quadagno, Jill, The Color of Welfare: How Racism Undermined
the War on Poverty, (1994)
Shklar, Judith N., American Citizenship: The Quest for
Inclusion, (1991)
Skocpol, Theda, Protecting Soldiers and Mothers: The
Political Origins of Social Policy in the United
States, (1992)
Wilson, William Julius, The Truly Disadvantaged: The Inner
City, the Underclass, and Public Policy, (1987)

Evaluation of Work:

At the end of the quarter, I will ask you to evaluate
you own and your compatriots' participation in the course.
The purpose of these evaluations will be to increase your
awareness of various contributions--your own and others--and
to correct any biases and misperceptions on my part.

Office Hours:

Please see me during my office hours if you have
problems with any of the reading or other assignments or if
you have suggestions as to how to make the course more
effective. If you need to get in touch with me at other
times, feel free to call me at home (568-0068).

Class Schedule:

Jan 4: Organizational Meeting

Handler, Joel F., and Yeheskel Hasenfeld, The Moral
Construction of Poverty: Welfare Reform in America,
(1991) ch. 1: What is Welfare Policy?.

Jan 11: Citizenship

Marshall, T.H., "Citizenship and Social Class and Other

Essays," (1950), Part 1.
Shklar, Judith N., American Citizenship: The Quest for
    Inclusion, (1991).
Boris, Eileen, "The Racialized Gendered State: Constructions
    of Citizenship in the United States," Social Politics,
    Summer 1995: 160-180.
Fraser, Nancy, and Linda Gordon, "Contract Versus Charity:
    Why Is There No Social Citizenship in the United
    States?," Socialist Review, 22:3 (July-Sept. 1992):
    45-67.
Pateman, Carole, The Disorder of Women: Democracy,
    Feminism, and Political Theory, (1989), Chapter 8.

Additional Reading:
Piven, Frances Fox, "Ideology and the State: Women, Power,
    and the Welfare State," in Women, the State, and
    Welfare, (1990), pp. 250-264.
Lister, Ruth, "Tracing the Contours of Women's Citizenship,"
    Policy and Politics, 21:1 (Jan. 1993): 3-16.
O'Conner, Julia S., "Gender, Class, and Citizenship in the
    Comparative Analysis of Welfare State Regimes:
    Theoretical and Methodological Issues," The British
    Journal of Sociology, 44:3 (Sept. 1993): 501-518.
Orloff, Ann Shola, "Gender and the Social Rights of
    Citizenship: The Comparative Analysis of Gender
    Relations and Welfare States," American Sociological
    Review, 58:3 (June 1993): 303-328.
Sarvasy, Wendy, "From Man and Philanthropic Service to
    Feminist Social Citizenship," Social Politics, Fall
    1994: 306-325.

Jan. 18: The Polity, Politics and Female Civic Activism

Skocpol, Theda, Protecting Soldiers and Mothers: The
    Political Origins of Social Policy in the United
    States, (1992), Introduction and Chs. 1 - 2.
Baker, Paula, "The Domestication of Politics: Women and
    American Political Society, 1780-1920," in Women, the
    State, and Welfare ed. by Linda Gordon (1990), pp. 55-
    91.
Sklar, Kathryn Kish, "The Historical Foundations of a
    Women's Power in the Creation of the American Welfare
    State, 1830-1930," in Seth Koven and Sonya Michel,
    eds., Mothers of a New World, pp. 43-93.
Muncy, Robyn, Creating a Female Dominion in American Reform,
    (1991), chs.xxx .
Gordon, Linda, "Black and White Visions of Welfare: Women's
    Welfare Activism, 1890-1945," Journal of American
    History, 78:2 (Sept. 1991): 559-590.
Handler, Joel F., and Yeheskel Hasenfeld, The Moral
    Construction of Poverty: Welfare Reform in America,
    (1991), Chapter 2.

Additional Reading:

Sklar, Kathryn Kish, Florence Kelley and the Nation's Work:
    The Rise of Women's Political Culture, 1830-1900,
    (1995)
Gordon, Linda. Pitied But Not Entitled: Single Mothers and
    the History of Welfare, 1890-1935, (1994), ch. 3.
Michel, Sonya, "The Limits of Maternalism: Policies toward
    American Wage-Earning Mothers in the Progressive Era,"
    in Seth Koven and Sonya Michel, eds., Mothers of a
    New World: Maternalist Politics and the Origins of
    Welfare States, (1993), pp. 277-320.
Mink, Gwendolyn, "The Lady and the Tramp: Gender, Race, and
    the Origins of the American Welfare State," in Women,
    the State, and Welfare ed. by Linda Gordon (1990), pp.
    92-122.

**Jan. 25: Maternalist Welfare Policies and the Origins of
the Two-Channel Welfare State**

Skocpol, Theda, Protecting Soldiers and Mothers: The
    Political Origins of Social Policy in the United
    States, (1992), chs. 6, 7, 8 and 9.
Mink, Gwendolyn, The Wages of Motherhood: Inequality in the
    Welfare State, 1917-1942, (1995), chs. 1-5.
Weiner, Lynn Y., Eileen Boris, and Molly Ladd-Taylor,
    "Maternalism as a Paradigm," Journal of Women's
    History, 5 (Fall 1993): 96-98, 104-113.
Gordon, Linda, "Putting Children First: Women, Maternalism
    and Welfare in the Early 20th Century," in U.S.
    History as Women's History, ed. by Linda K. Kerber,
    Alice Kessler-Harris, and Kathryn Kish Sklar (1995),
    pp. 63-86.
Nelson, Barbara J., "The Origins of the Two-Channel Welfare
    State: Workmen's Compensation and Mothers' Aid," in
    Women, the State, and Welfare ed. by Linda Gordon
    (1990), pp. 123-151.
Orloff, Ann Shola, "Gender in Early U.S. Social Policy,"
    Journal of Policy History, 3:3 (1991): 249-81.

Written assignment:
    You should volunteer in advance for **either** one of the
following topics: protective labor legislation, mother's
pensions, maternal and infant health care, child welfare,
and education **and** address the following questions: 1) what
was the perception of the problem, 2) what specific
programs/actions were undertaken and at whose initiative and
to what purpose, 3) who were the beneficiaries, 4) what were
the limitations and were those limitations the result of
factors that were: a) intellectual and/or ideological, b)
economic, c) political, and d) cultural? Finally what
insight does each provide about maternalism?
    Or for a short essay on one of the following in which

you indicate clearly what the issues are with respect to:
maternalism as a concept and the origins of the two-tier
welfare state.

Whatever your topic, convey clearly the different
emphases and interpretations in those instances where more
than one author covers your topic.

The paper should be 1-2 typed pages single-spaced.
**Be familiar with your topic so that you can speak definitely
about it in class.**

Additional Reading:
Kessler-Harris, Alice, "The Paradox of Motherhood: Night
    Work Restrictions" in Protecting Women: Labor
    Legislation in Europe, the United States and Australia,
    1880-1920, ed. by Ulla Wikander, Alice Kessler-Harris
    and Jane Lewis (1995), 337-58
Gordon, Linda, Pitied But Not Entitled: Single Mothers and
    the History of Welfare, 1890-1935, (1994), Ch. 4.
Goodwin, Joanne, "An American Experiment in Paid Motherhood:
    The Implementation of Mother's Pensions in Early
    Twentieth Century Chicago," Gender and History 4:3
    (Autumn 1992): 323-342.
Howard, Christopher, "Sowing the Seeds of 'Welfare': The
    Transformation of Mothers' Pensions, 1900-1914,"
    Journal of Policy History, Vol. 4, No. 2, (1992): 188-
    227.
Ladd-Taylor, Molly, Mother Work: Women, Child Welfare, and
    the State, (1994).
Sklar, Kathryn Kish, Florence Kelley and the Nation's Work:
    The Rise of Women's Political Culture, 1830-1900,
    (1995).
Skocpol, Theda, Protecting Soldiers and Mothers: The
    Political Origins of Social Policy in the United
    States, (1992), chs. 8 and 9.
Michel, Sonya, and Robyn Rosen, "The Paradox of Maternalism:
    Elizabeth Lowell Putnam and the American Welfare
    State," Gender and History, 4:3 (Autumn 1992): 364-386.

**Feb. 1: Gender, Race and Welfare in the New Deal and
World War II**

Gordon, Linda, Pitied But Not Entitled: Single Mothers and
    the History of Welfare, 1890-1935, (1994), Chs. 7-8.
Skocpol, Theda, "The Limits of the New Deal System and the
    Roots of Contemporary Welfare Dilemmas," in The
    Politics of Social Policy in the United States, ed.
    Margaret Weir, Ann Orloff, and Theda Skocpol (1988):
    293-311.
Mink, Gwendolyn, The Wages of Motherhood: Inequality in the
    Welfare State, 1917-1942, (1995), ch. 6-7.
Harris, Alice-Kessler, "Designing Women and Old Fools: The
    Construction of the Social Security Amendments of
    1939," in U.S. History as Women's History, ed. by Linda
    K. Kerber, Alice Kessler-Harris, and Kathryn Kish Sklar

(1995), pp. 87-106.
Handler, Joel F., and Yeheskel Hasenfeld, The Moral
    Construction of Poverty: Welfare Reform in America,
    (1991), pp. 82-106.

Additional Reading:
Cohen, Lizabeth, Making a New Deal: Industrial Workers in
    Chicago, 1919-1939, (1990).
Law, Sylvia, "Women, Work, Welfare, and the Preservation of
    Patriarchy," University of Pennsylvania Law Review,
    131, no. 6 (1983): 1249-1339.
Lopata, Helena Znaniecka, and Henry P. Brehm, Widows, and
    Dependent Wives: From Social Problem to Federal
    Program, (1986).
Quadagno, Jill, "Welfare Capitalism and the Social Security
    Act of 1935," American Sociological Review 49 (1984):
    632-647.
_____. The Transformation of Old Age Security, (1988).
Sapiro, Virginia, "The Gender Basis of American Social
    Policy," in Women, the State, and Welfare ed. by Linda
    Gordon (1990), pp. 36-54.
Wandersee, Winifred, "A New Deal for Women: Government
    Programs: 1933-1940," in Wilbur J. Cohen, ed., The
    Roosevelt New Deal: A Program Assessment Fifty Years
    After, (1986), pp. 185-197.

**Feb. 8: Illegitimacy, Motherhood, and Families in the
    "Long '50s"**

Glenn, Evelyn Nakano, "Social Construction of Mothering: A
    Thematic Overview," in Mothering: Ideology, Experience,
    and Agency, ed. by Evelyn Nakano Glenn, Grace Chang,
    and Linda Rennie Forcey, (1994), pp. 1-29.
Solinger, Rickie, "Race and 'Value': Black and White
    Illegitimate Babies, 1945-1965," in Mothering:
    Ideology, Experience, and Agency, ed. Evelyn
    Nakano Glenn, Grace Chang, and Linda Rennie Forcey,
    (1994), pp. 287-310.
Kunzel, Regina, Fallen Women, Problem Girls: Unmarried
    Mothers and the Professionalization of Social Work,
    1890-1945, ch. 6.
Roberts, Dorothy, "Racism and Patriarchy in the Meaning of
    Motherhood," Journal of Gender & the Law 1:1 (1993):
    1-38.
Moynihan, Daniel Patrick, The Negro Family: The Case for
    National Action, (1965).

Additional Reading:
Chodorow, Nancy The Reproduction of Mothering, (1976).
Collins, Patricia Hill, "Shifting the Center: Race, Class,
    and Feminist Theorizing About Motherhood," in
    Mothering: Ideology, Experience, and Agency, ed. by
    Evelyn Nakano Glenn, Grace Chang, and Linda Rennie

Forcey, (1994), pp. 45-66.
Rothman, Barbara Katz, <u>Recreating Motherhood</u>, (1989).
Stack, Carol B., and Linda M. Burton, "Kinscripts:
    Reflections on Family, Generation, and Culture," in
    <u>Mothering: Ideology, Experience, and Agency</u>, ed. by
    Evelyn Nakano Glenn, Grace Chang, and Linda Rennie
    Forcey, (1994), pp. 33-44.

**Feb. 15: The Discovery of Structural Poverty, the Culture
and Feminization of Poverty and the War on Poverty**

Patterson, James T., <u>America's Struggle Against Poverty,
    1900-1994</u>, (1994), chs. 6, 7 and 11.
Rowe, Audrey. "The Feminization of Poverty: An Issue for the
    90's." <u>Yale Journal of Law and Feminism</u> 4:73-79.
Bane, Mary Jo. "Politics and Policies of the Feminization of
    Poverty," in <u>The Politics of Social Policy in the
    United States</u>, ed. Margaret Weir, Ann Orloff, and Theda
    Skocpol (1988), pp. 381-396.
Joanne L. Goodwin, "'Employable Mothers' and 'Suitable
    work': A Reevaluation of Welfare and Wage-Earning for
    Women in the Twentieth-Century United States,"<u>Journal
    of Social History</u> 29:2 (Winter, 1995): 253-74.
Brauer, Carl M., "Kennedy, Johnson, and the War on Poverty"
    <u>Journal of American History</u> (June, 1982) 98-119.
Nicholas Lemann, "The Unfinished War" <u>Atlantic Monthly</u>
    (December, 1988), 37-56.
Matusow, <u>The Unraveling of America</u>, (1984), pp.   .
Quadagno, Jill, <u>The Color of Welfare: How Racism Undermined
    the War on Poverty</u>, (1994).

Written assignment:
For this assignment, each member of class should choose one
of the following policy areas: education, jobs, housing,
health care, community action, welfare and childcare. In a
2-page typed paper, please answer the following question
with respect to that area: 1) what was the perception of
the problem, 2) what specific programs/actions were
undertaken and what was the purpose of each, 3) how well did
they succeed and 4) were the problems which developed the
result of constraints that were: a) intellectual and/or
ideological, b) economic, c) political and d) cultural?

**Be sure to follow the above format precisely and come to
class thoroughly prepared to be THE authority on your topic.**

Additional Reading:
Burton, Linda M., and Robin L. Jarret, "Studying African-
    American Family Structure and Process in Underclass
    Neighborhoods: Conceptual Considerations," (Unpublished
    manuscript, Pennsylvania State University, 1991).
Neckerman, Kathryn M., Robert Aponte, and William Julius
    Williams. "Family Structure, Black Unemployment, and

American Social Policy," in <u>The Politics of Social Policy in the United States</u>, ed. Margaret Weir, Ann Orloff, and Theda Skocpol, (1988), pp. 397-419.

Pearce, Diane, "Welfare Is Not for Women: Why the War on Poverty Cannot Conquer the Feminization of Poverty," in <u>Women, the State, and Welfare</u> ed. by Linda Gordon (1990), pp. 265-279.

Feb. 22: Rising Welfare Role, the Racialization of Poverty and the Problem of Dependency

Amott, Teresa L., "Black Women and AFDC: Making Entitlement Out of Necessity," in <u>Women, the State, and Welfare</u> ed. by Linda Gordon (1990), pp. 281-298.

Simms, Margaret C. "Black Women Who Head Families: An Economic Struggle," in <u>Slipping Through the Cracks: The Status of Black Women</u>, eds. Margaret C. Simms and Julianne Malveaux (1986), pp. 139-151.

Darity, Jr., William A. and Samuel L. Myers, Jr. "Does Welfare Dependency Cause Female Headship? The Case of the Black Family," in *Journal of Marriage and the Family*, 46:4 (November 1984): 765-779.

Fraser, Nancy, and Linda Gordon, "A Genealogy of Dependency: Tracing a Keyword of the U.S. Welfare State" *Signs: Journal of Women in Culture and Society* 19 (1984): 309-36.

Additional Reading:

Aschenbrenner, Joyce, <u>Lifelines: Black Families in Chicago</u>, (1975).

Jones, Jacqueline, <u>Labor of Love, Labor of Sorrow: Black Women, Work, and the Family from Slavery to the Present</u>, (1985).

Roberts, Dorothy. "Race, Gender, and the Value of Mothers' Work," *Social Politics*, 2:2 (Summer 1995): 195-207.

Feb. 29: The Building Backlash: The Underclass and American Politics through the Reagan/Ford Era

Edsall, Thomas Byrne with Mary D. Edsall, "Race," *The Atlantic Monthly*, (May 1991): 53-86.

Murray, Charles, <u>Losing Ground: American Social Policy, 1950-1980</u>, (1984).

Takaki, Ronald, "A Dream Deferred: The Crisis of 'Losing Ground,'" in <u>From Different Shores: Perspectives on Race and Ethnicity</u> (1994), pp. 247-253.

Wilson, William Julius, <u>The Truly Disadvantaged: The Inner City, the Underclass, and Public Policy</u>, (1987).

Collins, Patricia Hill, "A Comparison of Two Works on Black Family Life," *Signs,* 14: 14 (Summer, 1989): 875-884.

Additional Reading:

Edsall, Thomas and Mary Edsall. Chain Reaction: The Impact of Race, Rights, and Taxes on American Politics, (1991).

Harpham, Edward J. "Fiscal Crisis and the Politics of Social Security Reform," in The Attack on the Welfare State, eds. Anthony Champagne and Edward J. Harpham, (1984), pp. 9-35.

Katz, Michael, The Undeserving Poor: From the War on Poverty to the War on Welfare, (1989).

Zinn, Maxine Baca. "Family, Race, and Poverty in the Eighties," Signs, 14 (Summer 1989):856-874.

March 7: The Attack on the Welfare State: the Politics of Social Policy in the 1980s and 1990s

Champagne, Anthony, and Edward J. Harpham. "The Attack on the Welfare State: An Introduction," in The Attack on the Welfare State, eds. Anthony Champagne and Edward J. Harpham (1984), pp. 1-7.

Dunn, Patricia. "The Reagan Solution for Aiding Families with Dependent Children: Reflections of an Earlier Era," in The Attack on the Welfare State, eds. Anthony Champagne and Edward J Harpham (1984), pp. 87-109.

Patterson, James T., America's Struggle Against Poverty, 1900-1994, (1994), ch. 14.

Olasky, Marvin, The Tragedy of American Compassion, (1992).

Fiscal Federalism and the Partnership Act of 1987

Handler, Joel F., and Yeheskel Hasenfeld, The Moral Construction of Poverty: Welfare Reform in America, (1991), ch. 5

Clinton's Work and Responsibility Act and Related Hearings

Republican's Personal Responsibility Act and Related Hearings.

"The Personal Responsibility Act: An Analysis" and "The Kassebaum Federalism Proposal: Is It a Good Idea?"

Fraser, Nancy, "After the Family Wage: Gender Equity and the Welfare State," Political Theory, 22:4 (November 1994): 591-618

Press Comentary:

Abramovitz, Mimi, and Frances Fox Piven, "Scapegoating Women on Welfare," The New York Times, September 2, 1995.

Bragg, Rick, "Child-Support Crackdown Shows Success and Limits," New York Times, April 14,1995.

Fund, John H., "Welfare: Putting People First," The Wall Street Journal, June 14, 1994.

Henneberger, Melinda, "State Aid Is Capped, but to What Effect?," New York Times.

Kaus, Mickey, "The Welfare Mess--How It Got That Way," The Wall Street Journal, September 12, 1994.

Pear, Robert, "GOP Governors Urge Big Changes For Welfare Bill," New York Times, April 13, 1995.

Skocpol, Theda, and William Julius Wilson, "Welfare As We Need It."

Additional Reading:
Handler, Joel F., and Yeheskel Hasenfeld, <u>The Moral
    Construction of Poverty: Welfare Reform in America</u>,
    (1991), ch. 4.
Slessarev, Helene. "Racial Tensions and Institutional
    Support: Social Programs during a Period of
    Retrenchment," in <u>The Politics of Social Policy in the
    United States</u>, ed. Margaret Weir, Ann Orloff, and Theda
    Skocpol (1988), pp. 357-379.
Minow, Martha. "The Welfare of Single Mothers and Their
    Children." *Connecticut Law Review,* 26: 817-42.
Roberts, Dorothy E. "Punishing Drug Addicts Who Have Babies:
    Women of Color, Equity, and the Right of Privacy."
    Harvard Law Review 104: 1419-50.
White, Lucie E., "On the 'Consensus' to End Welfare: Where
    Are the Women's Voices?," *Connecticut Law Review,* 26:3
    (Spring 1994): 843-56.
Williams, Lucy A., "The Ideology of Division: Behavior
    Modification Welfare Reform Proposals," *The Yale Law
    Journal,* 102:3 (December 1992): 719-46.

March 14: Discussion of Essays

WOMEN AND PUBLIC POLICY IN TWENTIETH-CENTURY AMERICA

History 163A   Jane De Hart
Spring, 1993   5816 Ellison
5820 Ellison   T/Th 11-12:00
T/Th 9:30-10:45

Course Description and Goals

History 163A & B focuses on gender issues and public policy.
Our primary emphasis is not on the technical aspects of the
policymaking process. Rather we will probe the implicit and often
explicit assumptions about gender incorporated into policy and
examine the context and and causes of policy shifts over time.
While the status of women has always been shaped by public
polices, it is in the decades since 1960 that women have been
particularly active as political claimants seeking to influence
policies that affect their lives. Taking into account that all
women do not experience the same policies in the same way, we
will examine such issues as reproductive technology and control,
sexual violence, workplace problems (discrimination, pay equity,
fetal protection, childcare), legal rights, welfare, and military
obligation. (Cnly a few of these topics can be covered in a
single quarter; therefore 163A & 163B will focus on different
ones.)

Our ultimate goal is to better understand: (1) the problems
and challenges involved in developing gender-just public polices
(assuming we can agree on what gender justice means) and (2) the
role of historians in that process. The course is also intended
as background for students who wish to use the proseminar
experience (History 163P) to explore a particular issue in a
research project that combines traditional historical sources
with oral interviews with key community and state leaders.

My hope is that you emerge from the course (and especially
the proseminar) with: (1) a new appreciation of the challenges
involved in creating social policies that genuinely meet the
needs of today's women and men and their families, and (2) a
better understanding of the workings of the political system and
the policy process. In sum: insights, information, and skills
that can be used to enhance our private and public lives.

Course Expectations

The course consists of lectures and discussions, some of
which are indicated on the syllabus as "Discussion". The
advantage of a small class, however, is the opportunity it allows
for some portion of almost every class session to be devoted to
discussion. For this format to work, the reading must be done on
time. By UCSB standards, the assignments are not light,
especially since the reading draws on a variety of disciplines
other than history. Unless you are prepared to take very
seriously the responsibility for prompt completion of the

assigned reading on schedule, this course is not for you. If you are prepared to make that commitment, previous students have found it well worth the effort.

All reading is contained in a course packet available at the Alternative Copy Shop in Goleta. No texts are assigned.

Grades

Grades will be based on 3 short (approximately 2-4 pp.) essays (45%), a final, for which you will have essay questions in advance (40%), and class participation (15%). We are all pressed for time and sometimes have difficulty meeting deadlines. Unless there is a genuine emergency, 4 points will be substracted for each day an assignment is overdue.

Office Hours

Do drop by or, better yet, make an appointment during the hours listed above so that you will not have to wait. My office phone is 893-2730. I am also available by appointment on days I am on campus. If you need to reach me when I am not on campus, call 568-0068 before 9 p.m.

Course Schedule and Assignments

Mar. 30 Organizational Meeting

I.   INTRODUCING KEY CONCEPTS: GENDER, HEGEMONY, AND THE
     DIFFERENCE DILEMMA

Before we can study policy and the policy process, we must understand the importance of culturally based assumptions about gender. The very way we structure our conceptions of femininity and masculinity, and the way these notions permeate both our conscious and unconscious thinking and behavior may have an emormous impact on a wide range of social areas, including policy. In this section, we will discuss gender socialization and asymmetry, how it develops within specific types of historical circumstances, how it is maintained over time. Some of the contemporary consequences of this historical interaction can be seen in a court case brought by EEOC against Sears, Roebuck & Co. in which the new scholarship in women's history figured prominently. Examining the testimony in the Sears case allows us to begin exploring the relationship of history to policy decisions raising, in the process, some critically important questions. It will also get us thinking about the usefulness of hegemony as a concept as well as introducing us to the "difference dilemma."

Apr. 1 Theories of Gender Formation, Difference and Asymmetry

Gender--what it is and what difference it has made historically--is the thrust of the first readings. How gender asymmetry is reproduced within the family is focus of Chodorow who is writing from a psychological perspective. Pay particular attention to Gottlieb's criticism of her theory. Sapiro, a political scientist, focuses on the difference gender has made in the political arena and why women have not historically played a role as policy makers.

Assignment
Jane De Hart and Linda Kerber, "Gender and Equality in the American Experience" in Luther Leudtke, ed., Making America
Nancy Chodorow, "Family Structure and Feminine Personality," in Rosaldo and Lamphere, eds., Women, Culture and Society, 43-46.
Roger S. Gottlieb, "Mothering and the Reproduction of Power," in Socialist Review. (1984), 93-119. (A critique of Chodorow)
Virginia Sapiro, "Political Marginality and Political Integration" in The Political Integration of Women: Roles, Socialization and Politics, 27-53.

Apr. 6 Reproducing Gender Asymmetry and Understanding Hegemony

Because sexual difference, like racial difference, has been the basis for different and unequal treatment historically, Chafe explores the two. In what ways has the past subordination of both women and blacks been similiar? different? How was control maintained? What role did women and blacks play in their own subordination? Williams enlarges our understanding of how relationships of subordination and domination are maintained and reproduce in this short, important, but difficult article on hegemeny. Read it carefully, using as a guide the questions in the coursepack to help you understand it. Gordon provides as example of hegemony in operation that helps us understand its workings.

Assignment
William H. Chafe, "Sex and Race: The Analogy of Social Control," in Women and Equality, 45-78.
Raymond Williams, "Hegemony," in Marxism and Literature, 108-114.
Robert W. Gordon, "New Developments in Legal Theory" in David Kairys, ed., The Politics of Law: A Progressive Critique, 287-92.

Apr. 8 The Sears Case: A First Look at the Relationship of History, Theory and Policy

Assignment
Jacquelyn Dowd Hall, "Women's History Goes To Trial: EEOC

v. Sears, Roebuck and Company" _Signs: Journal of Women in Culture and Society_ (1986) 751-779.

Paper: Taking the role of the judge in this case, prepare a 2-3 page **typed** paper in which you explain the decision you made in this case with reference to the historical testimony. For purposes of your paper consult **very carefully** the list of Discussion Questions on the Sears Case as well as background material in your course pak. Do **not** include any information not contained in the Sears case material. Be sure to explain which of the arguments of the other side you accept and which ones you reject and why you find for the plaintiff (or why you find for the defendant).

Recommended Reading which is helpful but not required:
Ruth Milkman, "Women's History and the Sears Case" in _Feminist Studies_ (1986), 395-400.
Joan W. Scott, "Deconstructing Equality-Versus-Difference: Or, The Uses of Poststructuralist Theory for Feminism," in _Feminist Studies_ (1988), 38-48 deal with the Sears case.

Apr. 13 Discussion

Although discussion will focus on the readings through Apr. 8, providing an opportunity for us to pull together all the material in this unit, you may wish to move ahead on the readings assigned for Apr. 15.

II. EXPLORING THE ROLE OF INTEREST GROUPS AND SOCIAL MOVEMENTS IN INFLUENCING POLICY AND BRINGING ABOUT SOCIAL CHANGE

To understand the context within which specific policies can be enacted a number of questions must be considered? What factors make a particular policy option feasible or unfeasible? What role can be played by individual legislators, by interest groups, and by social movements? What is the difference between incremental and comprehensive change? Within our political system, is it possible to achieve both? The following readings, which address these questions, also provide a glimpse of policy-making on women's issues in the 1960s and early 70s.

Apr. 15 Insiders, Interests Groups, and Movements: Women's Issues in the 1960s

Passage of Title VII of the 1964 Civil Rights Act witnessed women's rights advocates efforts to organize into an effective interest group. Significantly, this group included key Congresswomen who helped to secure enactment of important anti-discriminatory legislation before the contemporary feminist movement matured. But such an approach was limited in what could be accomplished and those limits, as Harrison makes clear, dramatized the need for a mass-based social movement which developed with the emergence of the second wave feminism in the late 1960s. Why did the movement emerge? What basic beliefs did feminists share? What were their goals? Did different elements in the movement have different objectives?

Assignment

Cynthia Harrison, On Account of Sex: The Politics of Women's Issues, 1945-1968 (1988), 169-191 211-221.

Jane DeHart, "The New Feminism and the Dynamics of Social Change," in Linda Kerber and Jane DeHart eds., Women's America: Refocusing the Past, (1991) 3rd. ed., 493-521.

no class meeting on Apr. 15

Apr. 20 Social Movements, Interest Groups and Incremental Versus Transformative Change

How do social movements and interest groups differ? Can each affect policy changes? Which element in the feminist movement would find it easiest to function as an interest group? Can interest groups in our system bring about the kind of transformative changes feminism called for. Think about this question carefully and consider Lindblom's argument?

Assignment

Anne Costain, "Representing Women: The Transition from Social Movement to Interest Group," in Ellen Boneparth, ed. Women, Power and Policy, 19-37.

Marion Paley and Joyce Gelb, "Women and Interest Group Politics: A Comparative Analysis of Federal Decision-Making," in Journal of Politics (1979): 362-392.

Charles E. Lindblom, "Still Muddling, Not Yet Through," in Public Administration Review (1979): 517-526.

IV. EXAMINING APPROACHES TO POLICY AND REPRODUCTIVE ISSUES

In order to understand the policy process, we also need a "bare bones" understanding of different approaches to policy analysis. In particular, we need to understand approaches which rely heavily on cost-benefit analysis as well as a very different approach arising out of a hermeneutical tradition which views policy analysis as "the interpretation of beliefs." In this policy framework, the analyst pays as much attention to values, beliefs, and ideology as to empirical evidence. Indeed this framework understands that all policy choices, even the choice of method itself, are values statements. How these approaches compliment and contradict each other -- the strengths and limitations of each -- can be explored as we look at abortion. The abortion issue also how demonstrate how scientists as well as historians can influence policy. It also allow us to explore more

fully why reproductive control is such a fundamental part of a
feminist agenda and why it is so opposed by some women as well as
some men.

Apr. 22 The Abortion Conflict: Policy Approaches and Expertise

Looking at an especially controversial issue allows us to
explore more fully various approaches to policy. Use the articles
simply to get a sense of how policy analysts approaching abortion
policy could proceed. What is Legge's primary concern? What role
does Calahan see for science in the abortion date? Does it
provide us with definitive answers in this instance? What did
historians hope to demonstrate about the relevance of history in
the Webster brief? How does Luker, as a sociologist, approach
the abortion issue and what do her findings about California
abortion activists tell us about the issue itself and the value
of an "interpretive social scientific" approach rather than a
cost-benefits approach? How does Petchevsky, a political
theorist, further illuminate the problems of arriving at a policy
on which both sides will agree?

Assignment
Jerome S. Legge, Jr., Abortion Policy: An Evaluation of the
Consequences for Maternal and Infant Health, 1-15, 44-51, 151-161
Daniel Callahan, "The Role of Science in Moral and Societal
Decision Making: The Human Life Bill as a Case Study," in
Margery W. Shaw and A. Edward Doudera, eds., Defining Human Life:
Medical, Legal and Ethical Implications, 314-325
Brief of Historians as Amiici Curiae Supporting Appelles,
Webster v. Reproductive Health Services (1989), 1-30.
Kristin Luker, Abortion & the Politics of Motherhood, 192-
215.
Rosalind Petchesky, Abortion and Women's Choice: The State,
Sexuality and Reproductive Freedom, 330-367.

Apr. 27 Abortion, the Constitution, and the Court

While experts in the sciences as well as in the social
sciences can contribute to the policy process, the courts play a
major policy-making role, as we have seen in the Sears case.
Rosenburg provides us with a history of Roe v. Wade (1973) that
address some of the constitutional issues involved in abortion
policy. How has the Court dealt with those issues most recently
in Planned Parenthood v. Casey (1992)? Inasmuch as a woman's
freedom of choice is balanced in Roe by the state's right to
protect potential life, how should we deal a different, but
related problem -- the drug dependent pregnant woman?

Assignment
Rosalind Rosenburg, "The Abortion Case" in Jack Garraty,
ed., Quarrels that Shaped the Constitution, 351-78.
"Planned Parenthood v. Casey," The New York Times, June 30,

1992
     Jose A. Gomez-Ibanez, "Cocaine Mothers" in Kenneth Winston
and Mary Jo Bane, eds. Gender and Public Policy: Cases and
Comments (1993), 294-303.

Apr. 29 New Technologies, New Choices, and Old Identities

     Why haven't new technologies such as amniocentesis and the
new "contragestive" pill made reproductive choices less
contested? Are we back to Luker and different views on
motherhood and fetal personhood? Can we expect RU486 to end the
abortion war? What groups have a stake in the drug's control?
Poor women and especially poor women of color have a different
history with respect to the state and fertility control inasmuch
as they have been victims of sterilization abuse. Why might they
approach the issue of reproductive freedom differently from
middle-class white women?

Assignment
     Rayna Rapp, "XYLO: A True Story" in Rita Arditti, Renate
Duelli Klein, and Shelley Minden, eds. Test-Tube Women: What
Future for Motherhood?, 3113-38
     Anna Quindlen, "Life in the 30s," New York Times, May 22,
1988, C2.
     Christopher Sturr, "Fertility and Control: The Case of RU
486," in Kenneth Winston and Mary Jo Bane, eds. Gender and Public
Policy, 52-72.

May 4 Discussion

Assignment
     Paper: Because of the new political climate in Washington,
an American organization concerned with research and population
control has made an arrangement with the European producers of RU
486 for testing in the United States with the goal of obtaining
permission from the FDA for its eventual sale in the U.S. As an
advisor to President Clinton and to his Secretary of Health and
Human Services, it is your job to inform him of all the
ramifications of a favorable decision by the FDA. The President
wishes to be informed about public reaction, especially from
women's groups, as well as the medical community and
pharmaceutical companies. Explain to him in a 3-4 page typed
paper what to expect and why. For example, if you argue that
pro-choice and anti-choice activists will react differently, make
clear to him what is involved for each side.

V. EQUALITY, DIFFERENCE AND GENDER JUSTICE IN THE WORKPLACE

     Gender has long been an important a factor is the workplace
and nowhere has the problem of reconciling sexual difference and

equality been better illustrated than in employment policies.
Exploring first how jobs and wages were gendered historically and
how race and class have affected economic opportunity, we will
move on to specific policies used to promote gender justice in
the workplace: equal pay legislation, affirmative action, and
comparable worth.

Because so many women in the workforce are also mothers or
potential mothers, we must also examine the problem of fetal
protection, pregnacy disability, and parental leave. These
issues also allow us to explore debates among feminist
policymakers whether the better strategy is to maximize or
minimize sexual difference. Whether gender justice demands
equality of opportunity or equality of results, equal (same)
treatment or different (special) is hotly debated among Americans
and a matter of key concern to us as well.

**May 6   Women and Employment in Historical Perspective: Sex
          Stratification an Equal Pay and Equal Access Policies**

What is meant by the term "the gendering of work"? What is
involved? If race and gender defined who did/does a particular
job, what happened to equality of opportunity? Why has it taken
so long to develop policies to cope with the problem?

Assignment

William Chafe, Paradox of Change: American Women in the
Twentieth Century, 79-98.
Jacquelyn Jones, "Crosscurrents of Change: The Divergent
Status of Black Working Women in the 1960 and 1970s" in Labor of
Love, Labor of Sorrow: Black Women, Work and Family, 301-310.
David L. Kirp, Mark G. Yudof, and Marlene Strong Franks,
Gender Justice, 145-167.
"Experts Say Job Bias Persists," New York Times, Jan. 25,
1984.

May 11   Wage Inequities and Equal Worth Policies

Kessler-Harris argues that wages are also gendered and
provides historical evidence to support her argument. Do you
find that argument convincing. How would comparable worth
policies address the problem? What do Evans and Nelson tell us
about the various variable that would help predict whether or not
a particular state is likely to institute comparable worth as a
policy? Why is the policy itself so controversial?

Assignment
Alice Kessler Harris, "The Just Price, The Free Market, and
the Value of Women, " A Woman's Wage: Historical Meanings and
Social Consequences, 113-29.
Sara M. Evans and Barbara J. Nelson, "Feminists, Union
Leaders and Democrats: The Passage of Comparable Worth Laws" in

Evans and Nelson, Wage Justice: Comparable Worth and the Paradox of Technocratic Reform, 69-81.
Barbara R. Bergmann, "Pay Equity - Surprising Answers to Hard Questions," Challenge (1987): 45-51.

May 13   Fetal Protection, Pregnancy Disability and Equality and Difference in the Marketplace

What are the issues involved in this case? Who do fetal protection and pregnacy disability policies generate arguments even among feminist legal strategists?

Assignment
International Union, United Automobile, Aerospace and Africultural Implement Workers of America, UAW, et al. and Local 322, Allied Industrial Workers of America, AFL-CIO v. Johnson Controls, Inc., "Fetal Protection," (1989) (abbreviated version), 208-227

Paper: Taking the role of the judge in this case, prepare a 3-4 page **typed** paper in which you explain the decision you made on the basis of the evidence presented. Be sure to explain which of the arguments of the other side you accept and which you reject and why you find for the plaintiff (or why you find for the defendant).

May 18 Discussion

How would Littleton and Scott have us solve the difference dilemma? (You don't have to understand the section about poststructural theory in order to absorb the basic points of Scott's argument.)

Assignment
Christine A. Littleton, "Equality and Feminist Legal Theory," in Kathryn Kish Sklar and Thomas Dublin, eds., Women, and Power in American History, 276-89.
Joan W. Scott, "Deconstructing Equality-Versus-Difference: Or, the Uses of Poststructuralist Theory for Feminism" in Feminist Studies (1989):34-48. (article # 10 in your coursepack)

IV SEXUAL VIOLENCE: PREVIEWING THE PORNOGRAPHY PROBLEM

Sexual violence is a major social problem and one involving dominance, a topic upon which we touched in the early reading and to which we now return. Because sexual violence and policies to deal with it are also the focus of the proseminar, at least a preview is in order. One of the most intriguing and controversial of the issues we will deal with in the proseminar is the relationship between sexual violence and pornography depicting violence against women. This section provides a brief glimpse of the rich and complex debate about this multifacted problem and whether and how to deal with it in terms of policy. Pay particular attention to the Minneapolis Anti-Pornography Ordinance, the assumption behind it, the specifics of the ordinance itself, and the various objections to it. Why do feminists find this issue to be so divisive?

May 20   Violent Pornography and Violence Against Women: Looking to the State

Assignment
    Susan Gubar and Joan Hoff, "Introduction" in Gubar abd Hoff, eds.,For Adult Users Only: The Dilemma of Violent Pornography, 1-14
    Catherine A. MacKinnon and Andrea Dworkin, "An Ordinance of the City of Minneapolis" and "Memo to the Minneapolis City Council on Proposed Ordinance on Pornography" in Winston and Bane, eds., Gender and Public Policy, 149-59.
    "Foes of Pornography and Bigotry Join Forces," New York Times, March 12, 1993.

May 25   Violating the 1st Amendment and Regulating Sexuality: Beware the Patriarchical State

Assignment

    Lisa Duggan, Nan Hunter, and Carole Vance, "False Promises: Feminist Antipornography Legislation in the U.S.," in Varda Burstyn, ed. Women Against Censorship, 130-51.
    Elizabeth Fox-Genovese, "Pornography and Individual Rights," in Feminism Without Illusions: A Critique of Individualism, 87-111.

May 27   Adjudicating Differences

Assignment
    Martha Minow, "Adjudicating Differences" in Marianne Hirsch and Evelyn Fox Keller, eds. Conflicts in Feminism, 149-63.

June 1/3 Summing Up, Preparing for the Exam and Saying Goodby

Women's Lives, Women's Work:
Female Activism and Engagement in American History
History 119
Fall 1996

Nancy S. Dye, Cox 100
X8400
and
Carol Lasser, Rice 313
X6712

The instructors come to this class having thought much about Oberlin's slogan: "Think one person can change the world? So do we." We invite you to join us as we take the opportunity offered by this class to ponder the strengths and limits of this slogan. We believe that we can better understand ourselves, our beliefs and our orientations if we place them in an historical context, and think about the lives and motives, the choices and possibilities of selected American women who have engaged in activism.

We ask questions about what constitutes activism, and about how possibilities for and enactments of activism are shaped by gender as well as race, class, and historical moment. We seek to understand the individual in her context, appreciating both her specific situation and the historically shaped circumstances in which she found herself. We look into the impact of age, marital status, sexual orientation, and religion to understand individuals; we examine politics and culture to find out more about broad social trends and movements. We hope to learn more about change over time in varieties of women's activism.

Class Expectations

Students are expected to come to class prepared to participate.

Supplemental class meetings will be held on Thursdays, 1-2:45, arranged as small group meetings for discussion and projects. Students are expected to participate

An on line discussion group will be arranged. Students will be expected to participate by posting at least one comment per week, either individually or as part of their small group meeting, and to respond to one other comment.

Assignments:

For October 8: Students will be expected to choose one letter from Soul Mates that they believe would help a student trying to understand Stone, Brown, or the history of Oberlin, or the history of coeducation, and write 2-3 pages about why the letter was chosen.

For October 15: Students will , in consultation with the faculty, propose an activist woman about whom they will read. Choices must be approved in advance by the faculty.

November 19: Students will be expected to prepare a paper and presentation on the activist woman chosen the previous month. Students may work in teams of up to three. Students will be asked to make presentations to the class.

December 10: Final paper due. This will be a synthetic essay.

Schedule of Classes

Students with less familiarity with the narrative and chronology of American women's history are encouraged to refer to Eleanor Flexner, Century of Struggle, as appropriate for background information.

September 3	Video Showing: "The Return of Martin Guerre," parts. A showing of the remainder of the video will be arranged.(Optional)
September 10	A Woman of the Early Republic: Work, Life and Engagement Laurel Thatcher Ulrich, A Midwife's Tale, pp. 3-161 and 346-352; optional: 286-308.
September 17	The Grimke Sisters as Feminist Abolitionists Readings: •Eleanor Flexner, Century of Struggle, Chapters 3, 4, 5; •Shirley Yee, Black Women Abolitionists, Introduction and Chapters 1 and 2; •Catherine Birney, The Grimke Sisters (1885) , Chapters 1-3, 6-15 •Gerda Lerner, The Grimke Sisters From South Carolina (1967), pp. 63-65 (to contrast with Birney, p. 450); also pp. 86-111 and 183-204.
September 24	A Slave Narrative : Captivity and Escape Reading: Harriet Jacobs, Incidents in the Life of a Slave Girl, entire.
October 1	Sojourner Truth: Activist and Legend Readings: Narrative of Sojourner Truth. Jeffrey Stewart, editor (Schomburg Library edition): Read pages 1-126 of the Narrative itself, then pages 131-135 of the "Book of Life" that follows, beginning mid page with "In the year 1851..." Next read Jeffrey Stewart's introduction, which begins on page xxxiii of this edition. Finally, read in "The Book of Life" pp. 137-139, and Harriet Beecher Stowe's "Libyan Sibyl" essay on pages 151-173. Also: •Carleton Mabee, "Why Did She Never Learn to Read," pp. 60-66 in Sojourner Truth, Slave, Prophet, Legend (New York: New York University Press, 1993) •Nell Irvin Painter, "Difference, Slavery, and Memory: Sojourner Truth in Feminist Abolitionism," pp. 139-158 in Jean Fagan Yellin and John C. Van Horne, eds., The Abolitionist Sisterhood (Ithaca: Cornell University Press, 1994).

October 8	Oberlin Women: Coeducation, Women's Rights, and Antislavery
	
	Readings:
	Carol Lasser and Marlene Deahl Merrill, eds., <u>Soulmates: The Oberlin Correspondence of Lucy Stone and Antoinette Brown, 1846-1850</u>, entire. (The book will be provided for you)
	
	Also:
	      •Lucy Stone, "Oberlin and Woman," in <u>The Oberlin Jubilee, 1833-1883</u>, W.G. Ballentine, ed. (Oberlin, 1883), pp. 311-321.
	      •Ronald Hogeland, "Coeducation of the Sexes at Oberlin College: A Study of Social Ideas in Mid-Nineteenth-Century America," <u>Journal of Social History</u> 6 (Winter 1972-3): 160-176.
	      •Lori D. Ginzberg, "The 'Joint Education of the Sexes': Oberlin's Original Vision," in <u>Educating Men and Women Together: Coeducation in a Changing World</u>, Carol Lasser, ed. (Urbana, 1987), pp, 67-80.
	Optional but recommended:
	      Letters written by African American women who were Oberlin students, 1860-1866, in Dorothy Sterling, ed., <u>We Are Your Sisters: Black Women in the Nineteenth Century</u>, pp. 190-213.
	
	Assignment: Students will suggest whether any of the Soulmates Letters should be part of Electronic Oberlin History Project; would think about an assignment that would ask students to nominate a letter and explain why.

October 15	Fissures in the Abolitionist-Feminist Alliance
	
	Reading:
	      •Flexner, <u>Century of Struggle</u>, Chapter 10.
	      •Elizabeth Cady Stanton, Address in Favor of Universal Suffrage (1867), photocopy;
	      •Excerpts from Elizabeth Cady Stanton et al., <u>History of Woman Suffrage</u>, volume II, on speeches and debate at May 1869 meeting of the American Equal Rights Association;
	      •Angela Davis, "Racism in the Woman Suffrage Movement," in <u>Women, Race and Class</u>, pp. 70-86 (on reserve).
	Choice of Activist Woman due

October 22	FALL BREAK
October 29	Maternal Activism Jane Addams, <u>Twenty Years at Hull House</u>, Chapters 1-7, 9-11, 13. Also: Jane Addams, "The Objective Necessity for Social Settlements," photocopy.

November 5	An African American Woman's Activism

	Video: Ida B. Wells: A Passion for Justice
	Reading:
	Ida B. Wells Barnett , Crusade for Justice, Introduction pp. xiii-xxxii and 3-113;
	Also:
	       •Mary Church Terrell, Introduction to Ida B. Wells, photocopy.
	       •Ida B. Wells, "Southern Horrors," photocopy distributed to pairs;
	       •Memphis Diaries of Ida B. Wells, Miriam De Costa-Willis, ed., pp. 109-
	       151 and 184-186.

November 12	White Women's Activism Against Lynching Jacquelyn Dowd Hall, Revolt Against Chivalry: Jessie Daniel Ames and the Women's Crusade Against Lynching, entire
November 19	Papers and Presentations due. Details to be distributed.

November 26	Women's Bodies and Women's Activism
	
	Margaret Sanger , My Fight for Birth Control, pp. 3-199.
	Also:
	       •Linda Gordon "Birth Control and Social Revolution," in Nancy Cott
	       and Elizabeth Peck, eds., A Heritage of Her Own, pp. 445-475 (on
	       reserve).

December 3	Women and Labor Activism
	
	Elizabeth Gurley Flynn, The Rebel Girl .
	Also:
	Selections from Rosalyn Baxandall, ed., Words on Fire: The Life and Writings of Elizabeth Gurley Flynn:
	       •"Women in Industry Should Organize,"pp. 91-96
	       •"Men and Women," PP. 100-104
	       •"Problems Organizing Women," pp. 134-138
	       •"Women in American Socialist Struggles," pp. 169-175.

December 10	Writing Assignment and Presentation Due. Details to be distributed

Grading

Class participation will account for 25% of your final grade. Participation includes: making a weekly posing on our electronic forum; coming to class prepared; and participating appropriately in class discussions.

The first writing assignment, the paper on SoulMates, will account for 20% of your final grade. Please remember that this assignment will be due in class on **October 8.**

The second assignment, your paper on an activist woman and your brief classroom presentation, will account for 25% of your final grade. Please remember that your choice of an activist woman should be approved by **October 15**; you should schedule a time to speak with one of the instructors before this date. Your paper and presentation are due in class on **November 19**.

Your final paper will account for 30% of your final grade. Your final paper is due in class on **December 10.** College regulations require that all written work for a course be submitted by the end of reading period, December 14 unless an official incomplete has been granted.

ED 488: Women and the Professions: A Historical Perspective

Mondays, 7:35-10:00, 160-B Dewey Hall
Professor Lynn Gordon, 1-339 Dewey Hall, 275-7721, 442-7173
Office hours: Tuesdays 2-4 and by appointment

Course Description: "Women and the Professions: A Historical Perspective" deals with the experiences of educated American women in prestigious occupations from the mid-nineteenth century to the present. Among the topics/issues for discussion in this course will be: women's access to higher education and their entry into the professions; the nature of professional/graduate education; changing historical views of educated women and work; tensions between personal and professional lives; the differing experiences of professional women due to racial, class, and ethnic factors; the impact of gender analysis on theories about the professions and professionalization. Although the course employs primarily historical methods and analyses, we will consider the relationship between historical and contemporary themes pertaining to women and the professions.

Course Requirements: Regular attendance and informed participation in discussions will account for 25% of the student's final grade. For the remaining 75% of the grade, students must complete a research paper of between 20-30 pages (not including notes and bibliography). The paper should address some aspect of the history of American women in the professions, and utilize both secondary and primary sources. See class schedule below for deadlines for progress reports, etc.

Course Readings: All books listed below as reading assignments are available in paperback at the campus Barnes and Noble Bookstore, and have been placed on reserve for this class at Rush Rhees Library.

Course Schedule and Assignments

Monday, September 8th

Introduction and Library Class

Monday, September 15th

Women Writers in the Nineteenth Century

Reading: Mary Kelley, <u>Private Woman, Public Stage</u>

Monday, September 22nd

The "Feminization" of Teaching, 1830-1880

Reading: Kathryn Kish Sklar, <u>Catharine Beecher</u>

Monday, September 29th

The "New Woman" and Women's Higher Education, 1865-1900

Due: 1-2 page statement of paper topic and bibliography; conference with instructor required

Monday, October 6th

Professionalization of Social Work, 1890-1940

Reading: Robyn Muncy, Creating a Female Dominion of Reform

Monday, October 13th

Female Academics, 1865-1940

Margaret Rossiter, Women Scientists (selected chapters)

Monday, October 20th

Women and Medicine, 1847-1940

Reading: Regina Morantz-Sanchez, Sympathy and Science

Due: 1-2 page statement—update on paper and bibliography; conference required

Monday, October 27th

Women and Nursing, 1865-1940

Reading: Darlene Clark Hine, Black Women in White

Monday, November 3rd

The Doldrums?: 1920-1960

Reading: Joyce Antler, Lucy Sprague Mitchell: The Making of A Modern Woman

Monday, November 10th

Journalism, 1865-1945

Due: Oral report on paper

Monday, November 17th

Gender and Teaching in the 20th Century, 1880-1945

Reading: Ruth Markowitz, My Daughter the Teacher

Monday, November 24th

Women and the Law, 1880-present

Reading: Mona Harrington, <u>Women Lawyers: Re-writing the Rules</u>

Monday, December 1st

Feminist Movement and Women in the Professions, 1960-present

Reading: Nadya Aisenberg & Mona Harrington, <u>Women of Academe</u>

Note: If you wish me to read a first draft of your paper (typed, including notes and bibliography), you need to turn it in no later than this class. The paper will be returned to you by December 8th.

Monday, December 8th

Discussion of Sinclair Lewis, <u>Arrowsmith</u> and <u>Ann Vickers</u>

Film: "His Girl Friday"

Final versions of papers are due <u>no later than noon on Thursday, December 18th. They should not be shoved under my office door, but placed in an envelope (manila or intramural) and put in my mailbox in the faculty-student lounge. Please be sure to keep a copy of your paper.</u>

History 381
Tuesday 2:30-4:50
Fellows 424
Denison University

Amy Green
Office: Fellows 407
Office Hours: Wed. 3:30-5:00
email: greena   phone x6229

WOMEN, MEN, AND NATURE:
Gender Identity and the American Outdoor Tradition

Overview

This seminar will explore the ways in which women and men have reinforced, expanded, and challenged their gender identities through outdoor experiences and nature writing. We will examine the historical relationship between ideas of the environment--nature, out-of-doors, wilderness, the West--and ideas of gender--manhood, womanhood, girlhood, and boyhood. We will cover such topics as the Transcendental movement, the western survey explorations, nature tourism and outdoor recreation, children's fiction, and the environmental movement. This course is interdisciplinary, bringing together history, art, literature, popular culture, and theory. It will emphasize the analysis of primary sources such as nature essays, adventure narratives, and popular novels to develop the student's understanding of Euro-American attitudes toward nature, gender, and self.

Description of Themes/Explanation of Course Structure

In 1912, Ernest Thompson Seton, nature writer and Boy Scout leader, described the camping and woodcraft tradition as a "school for Manhood." Sixty-five years later, Kathleen Farmer wrote a "just for woman" camping manual, entitled Woman in the Woods (1977). In her chapter on "Retaining Femininity," Farmer asks, if "the rugged outdoors transforms a boy into a man" then "what does it do to a girl?" The purpose of this course is to explore the relationship between outdoor experiences and the changing construction of gender. Throughout the course we will consider what is meant by "manhood" and "womanhood". how have these categories changed over time; how have they shaped our attitudes toward nature; and how has nature itself influenced our conceptions of male and female? How does the nature experience as a rite of passage from childhood to adulthood differ for boys and girls? To what degree has the out-of-doors historically been a male domain where women enter on male terms only? How have both women and men represented different visions of the natural and the wild in their nature writing and photography?

The course will also carefully consider the meanings of nature, out-of-doors, and wilderness. How can we locate these categories in history and culture? Are there qualities intrinsic to natural landscapes which are not contingent upon human attitudes and values? How is the natural landscape an agent in its own right, operating beyond the bounds of culture? How does this "other world" of nature create new possibilities for urban men and women? This course, at times, emphasizes the role of women in nature and the out-of-doors, a subject which has been relatively neglected by historians and literary critics; yet, gender is the primary concern of our investigations. How do both women and men struggle with the categories of maleness and femaleness in their journeys through the psychic and physical landscapes of nature? The course covers a long historical period, beginning with the American romantic tradition of the mid-nineteenth century, and then moving through the back-to-nature movement of the late-nineteenth and early-twentieth century. We will cover different aspects of the twentieth-century environmental movement, and conclude with the camping revival of the 1970s and the Ecofeminist and "Wild Man" movements of the past two decades. This course will isolate and examine recurring themes of nature and gender in United States history, and introduce students to a broad range of primary material as stimulus for further research and exploration.

Requirements

1) Seminar participation includes unfailing class attendance, thoughtful contributions to discussion, and 9 informal weekly journals (40% of your grade).

Journals: This assignment is an opportunity for you to explore issues--raised in class discussion and in the readings--that interest you both intellectually and personally. Journal due dates are included in the syllabus; entries must relate directly to the week's reading. Journals will be evaluated for the quality of thinking they reflect. These are not formal writing assignments; so, you should feel free to explore the issues that interest you the most. NO late journals will be accepted. You are allowed to miss one journal entry without it affecting your grade. I will accept handwritten entries. The journals will be graded on a scale of 1-10.

2) **In-class oral reports**: (20% of your grade)
Beginning with week 5, one or two students will provide the class with some background material on the writers and events covered that week. These reports should be relatively brief (10-15 minutes) and should include biographical and historical information which can be easily gleaned from secondary sources, including American history textbooks. In the interests of making these reports clear and informative, I will require that you hand in an outline or written version of the report. Reading directly from a written report is acceptable, **if** you read **slowly** and **engage** the class through well chosen pauses and eye contact. These reports will be graded on a scale from 1 to 10.

3) **Short Essays** (40% of your grade)
The formal writing component of this class includes **4** short essays (3 pages each). Each essay assignment is designed to engage you in a close analysis of primary and secondary sources. In these essays you will be evaluated on your writing and analytical skills. These essays will be graded on a scale from 1 to 10.

$Readings on reserve in history office; *Readings in course packet
OUTLINE AND READINGS
Week 1 (Sept. 2) Introduction

Week 2 (Sept. 9) Theoretical Overview: Is Gender in Nature?
Readings:
$ "Gender and the New Women's History," in Women's America
$Sherry Ortner, "Is Female to Male as Nature is to Culture," in Woman, Culture and Society
$Carolyn Merchant, "Nature as Disorder," in The Death of Nature
Discussion themes and questions:
Where do we locate gender, in nature, in society? How do we experience ourselves as gendered individuals? Are women more natural than men?
FIRST PAPER DUE!

Week 3 (Sept. 16) Historical Overview: Gender and Nature in Time
Readings:
$Barbara Welter, "The Cult of True Womanhood, 1820-1860," American Quarterly 18 (1966)
$Mark Carnes, "Middle-Class Men and the Solace of Fraternal Ritual," in Meanings for Manhood:
    Construction of Masculinity in the Victorian America
$Roderick Nash, "The Romantic Movement," in Wilderness and the American Mind
$Peter Schmitt, "Introduction," in Back to Nature: The Arcadian Myth in Urban America
Discussion themes and questions:
In this week, we will explore male and female gender roles in the context of Victorian America. We will also explore the shifting attitudes toward nature which characterize this period in history.
JOURNAL 1 DUE

Week 4 (Sept. 23) Romancing the Wilderness: A Room of One's Own
Readings:
Henry David Thoreau, Walden, or Life in the Woods (selections)
Discussion themes and questions:
Walden, the American classic in nature writing, survives today as a literary formula for outdoor experience and reflection. We will look at Thoreau's efforts at Walden to construct a space and an identity beyond the bounds of town and society. Throughout the course we will consider the

continuing influence of the cabin-in-woods narrative on women and men alike.
JOURNAL 2 DUE

Week 5 (Sept. 30) Nineteenth-Century Exploration Narratives: Is the Wilderness a Man's World?
Readings:
*Clarence King, Mountaineering in the Sierra Nevada (excerpts)
$Janet Robertson, "The First Female Mountain Climbers, 1858-1906," in The Magnificent
Mountain women :
$Anne LaBastille, "Changing Times," in Women and Wilderness
Discussion themes and questions:
What is the relationship between the wilderness expedition and the romantic tradition, and how do
male desires and visions inform this experience? Does the wilderness experience facilitate and
legitimize homo-social bonding? How (and why) has the wilderness been constructed historically
as an exclusively male sphere?
JOURNAL 3 DUE

Week 6 (Oct. 7) Nineteenth-Century Recreation and Tourism: The Domestication of Nature
Readings:
*Helen Hunt Jackson, "Ah-wah-ne days; a visit to the Yosemite Valley in 1872."
William H. H. Murray, Adventures in the Wilderness (selections)
Discussion themes and questions:
Nature tourism--facilitated by railroads and hotels--opened the out-of-doors to women and children
and other folks not used to the "rugged" life. Did women's experiences in cabins and camps and
hotels reinforce or expand traditional female gender roles? Similarly, in what way did this popular
phenomenon of outdoor recreation contribute to the urban, middle-class male gender identity?
SECOND PAPER DUE!

Week 7 (Oct. 14) Real Men and Wild Men
Readings:
*Theodore Roosevelt, "The Strenuous Life"
*George S. Evans, "The Wilderness"
*John Muir (to be announced)
$John Higham, "The Reorientation of American Culture in the 1890s"
Discussion themes and questions:
By the turn of the century, many middle-class men feared that urban-industrial life had
"effeminized" them. What were these men searching for; what did they actually fear? Did the
wilderness provide an antidote to their gender anxieties?
JOURNAL 4 DUE

Week 8 (Oct. 21) The Child-in-Nature: Nature Novels as Teacher and Guide
Gene Stratton Porter, Girl of the Limberlost
Porter was one of the most prolific nature writers/novelists at the turn of the century. Some of her
most popular works concerned the education of children in the out-of-doors. We will evaluate
Porter's depiction of the outdoor experience as a personal "rite of passage" for her protagonist
Elnora.
JOURNAL 5 DUE

Week 9 (Oct. 28) The Desert as Muse (Part I)
Readings:
Mary Austin, Land of Little Rain
Discussion themes and questions:
How does the landscape itself--the desert in this instance--determine one's vision of nature and
human nature? How does the projection of female desires/identities on the land, in turn, shape that
vision?

JOURNAL 6 DUE

Week 10 (Nov. 4) The Desert as Muse (Part II)
Readings:
Edward Abbey, Desert Solitaire (selections)
Discussion themes and questions:
In this week, we will compare the desert writings of Edward Abbey with that of Mary Austin.
How are environmental values and aesthetics informed by male and female desires and identities?
What environmental concerns do both of these writers share? Are they environmentalists in the
modern sense of the term?
THIRD PAPER DUE!

Week 11 (Nov. 11) Environmentalism in the Twentieth Century: Nature Comes Home
Readings:
Rachel Carson, Silent Spring
Discussion themes and questions:
Carson's Silent Spring galvanized the environmental movement in the 1960s. In addition, she
played a pioneering role for women in her own struggle to enter the traditionally male realms of
science and environmentalism. We will consider how Carson integrated her unique understanding
and experience of womanhood into her environmental vision.
JOURNAL 7 DUE

Week 12 (Nov. 18) Reclaiming Wilderness: A Room of One's Own
Readings:
Anne Labastille, Woodswoman
Discussion themes and questions:
Like Carson, Anne Labastille has played a pioneering role for women in the environmental
movement, in this instance as a professional and amateur woodswoman. We will explore
Thoreau's influence on Labastille's backwoods retreat in the Adirondacks, and how her identity as
a woman and a scientist altered (or didn't) this traditional romantic communion.
We will also consider Kathleen Farmer's camping manual and the extent to which she uses the
outdoor experience to reaffirm or challenge traditional notions of femininity.
JOURNAL 8 DUE

*************************************BREAK***********************

Week 13 (Dec. 2) Reclaiming the "Wild": Cultural feminism
Readings:
Susan Griffin, Woman and Nature: The Roaring Inside Her
Discussion themes and questions:
During weeks 13 and 14, we will consider how visions of nature serve as metaphors for the inner
landscape of the human psyche, of male and female identity. Why and how do these cultural
movements of the late-twentieth century seek to preserve and reclaim an ideal of a primal, original
connection with the natural and the wild?
JOURNAL 9 DUE!

Week 14 (Dec. 9) Reclaiming the "Wild": The Mythopoeic Men's Movement
Readings:
$Robert Bly, Iron John   FOURTH PAPER DUE!

165

THE HISTORY OF FEMINIST THEORY
G57.2291

Penny Johnson   53 Washington Sq. S.
penny.johnson@nyu.edu   998-8619

Dear Class:
    Constructing this course raises the fundamental question of
whether a course in "feminist theory" should concentrate on
postmodern feminist theory or cover the history of feminist
theory. it is a question I have been unable to answer to my
complete satisfaction, since doing one without the other seems
sadly incomplete, while doing both together in one term is
clearly impossible. In addition, studying theory without "doing"
theory seems to be an inherent difficulty with most courses on
theory. My suggestion, after wrestling with this problem for
several months, is a reconfigured course which will not pretend
to read everything; we will read a sampling of contemporary
theory first, then will read some of the milestones in the
development of that theory, using the theoretical tools already
acquired in the first half for understanding and writing about
the tradition. We will conclude with papers which will allow you
to formulate your own feminist theory.

Introduction
    Valerie Bryson, Feminist Political Theory; An Introduction
(1992).
    *Joan Scott, "Gender: A Useful Category of Historical
Analysis," AHR 91 (1986): 1053-1075, also appears as chap. 2 in
Gender and the Politics of History (1988).
    NB--These should be read before our first meeting.

PART ONE

Framework and Cautions:
    Judith Butler, Gender Trouble: Feminism and the Subversion
of Identity (1990).
    *Maria Lugones and Elizabeth Spelman, "Have we got a theory
for you! Feminist Theory, Cultural Imperialism and the Demand
for 'the Woman's Voice.'" Women's Studies International Forum
(1983): 571-81.
    *Audre Lorde, " An Open Letter to Mary Daly," in This Bridge
Called my Back: Writings by Radical Women of Color, ed. Cherrie
Maraga and Gloria Anzaldrea (1983), 94-7.
    *Chandra T. Mohanty, "Under Western Eyes: Feminist
Scholarship and Colonial Discourses," in Third World Women and
the Politics of Feminism, ed. Chandra T. Mohanty, et. al. (1991):
51-80.

Marxist Theory:
F. Engels, The Origins of the Family, Private Property and the State (1884), intro., 87-170, 217-237.
*Karen Sacks, "Engels Revisited," Woman, Culture and Society ed. Michelle Rosaldo and Louise Lamphere (1974) 207-222.
*Catharine A. MacKinnon, "Feminism, Marxism, Method, and the State: An Agenda for Theory," Signs 7 (1982): 515-544.
FIRST PAPER DUE: 3-4 page informal historical speculation on gender as a category for theory and/or history.

Freudian Theory:
*Sigmund Freud, "Femininity," from New Introductory Lectures on Psychoanalysis (1933): 74-81.
Sigmund Freud, Dora: An Analysis of a Case of Hysteria (1905).
*Maria Ramas, "Freud's Dora, Dora's Hysteria," in In Dora's Case, eds. Charles Bernheimer and Claire Kahane (1985).
*Nancy Chodorow, "What is the Relation between Psychoanalytic Feminism and the Psychoanalytic Psychology of Women?" in Theoretical Perspectives on Sexual Difference ed Deborah L. Rhode (1990).
SECOND PAPER DUE: 3-4 page response to either: MacKinnon, Sacks, Ramas, or Chodorow.

Literary Theory:
Marks and de Courtivron, New French Feminisms Introductions, pp. 90-113; 189-98; 242-264.
*Jonathan Culler, Theory and Criticism after Structuralism (1982), 17-30.
Chris Weedon, Feminist Practice and Poststructuralist Theory (1987).
*Jane P. Tompkins, "An Introduction to Reader-Response Criticism," in Reader-Response Criticism: From Formalism to Post-Structuralism ed. Jane P. Tompkins (1980).

Foucault:
Michel Foucault, The Care of the Self vol. 3 in The History of Sexuality trans. Robert Hurley (1986).
Lois McNay, Foucault and Feminism (1992).
*Cecile Dauphin et al., "Women's Culture and Women's Power: An Attempt at Historiography," Journal of Women's History 1 (1989): 63-88.

PART TWO
Each set of class partners will sign up to prepare a brief background for one class meeting in this part of the course.

Where it all Started: The late Medieval Querelle des Femmes:
Christine de Pizan, The Book of the City of Ladies.

*Joan Kelly, "Early Feminist Theory and the Querelle des Femmes 1400-1789," Signs 8 (1982): 4-28.
   *Susan Schibanoff, "Comment on Kelly's "Early Feminist Theory and the Querelle des Femmes, 1400-1789," Signs 9 (1983): 320-326.
   *Beatrice Gottlieb, "The Problem of Feminism in the Fifteenth Century," in Women of the Medieval World, ed. Julius Kirshner and Suzanne Wemple, pp. 337-364.

Enlightenment and Revolution:
   Mary Wollstonecraft, A Vindication of the Rights of Woman (1792), 7-122.
   *Condorcet, "On the Admission of Women to the Rights of Citizenship," (xerox)
   Mary Wollstonecraft in The Feminist Papers, ed. Alice Rossi (1973), 25-40.
   Zillah Eisenstein, The Radical Future of Liberal Feminism (1992) chap. 4-5, pp. 55-112.
   THIRD PAPER DUE: 3-5 page analysis of Christine de Pizan or Wollstonecraft using a feminist theoretical approach.

Suffrage, Activism, and Theory:
   Elizabeth Cady Stanton and Susan B. Anthony in The Feminist Papers, 378-470.
   Emma Goldman in The Feminist Papers, 506-516.
   Zillah Eisenstein, The Radical Future of Liberal Feminism (1991), chap. 6-7, pp. 113-173.

Woolf and de Beauvoir:
   Virginia Woolf, A Room of One's Own (1927).
   Simone de Beauvoir, The Second Sex (1949), 3-67, 74-91, 109-155, 755-814 are required. Try to read the entire book if possible.
   Woolf and de Beauvoir in The Feminist Papers pp. 622-6, 672-4.
   FOURTH PAPER DUE: 3-5 page comparison of Woolf and de Beauvoir using a feminist theoretical approach.

The American "Second Wave":
(four weeks of reading)
   Betty Friedan, The Feminine Mystique (1963).
   Zillah Eisenstein, The Radical Future of Liberal Feminism (1991), chap. 8, pp. 175-200.

cont:
   Kate Millett, Sexual Politics (1969).
   *Robin Morgan (ed.), Sisterhood is Powerful (1970)
"Introduction" xii-xli.

*Audre Lorde, "Uses of the Erotic," in Weaving the Visions: New Patterns in Feminist Spirituality ed. Judith Plaskow and Carol Christ (1989), 208-213.

cont:
Carol Gilligan, In a Different Voice (1982).
*bell hooks, "Writing Autobiography," in Feminisms: An Anthology of Literary Theory and Criticism ed. Robyn R. Warhol and Diane Herndl (1991), 1036-9.
*Linda Alcoff, "Cultural Feminism," Signs 13 (1988): 399-416.

cont:
bell hooks, Feminist Theory: From Margin to Center (1984).

Last class:
dinner and
FINAL PAPER DUE: 8-10 page paper which presents your own framework for a feminist theory with which to do historical analysis.
Note: There will be _no_ extensions for this paper.

Course Requirements:
Careful preparation, attendance, and class participation are essential, since this is a colloquium. The reading is arranged so that it is heavy at the beginning of the term and lightens as the term progresses. You will write four short papers and one final longer paper.
You will have a class partner whose work you will read and with whom you will plan a brief background presentation for one class in Part Two of the course.

Grading:
Equal weight will be given to: class participation
4 short papers
class presentation
final paper.

*Indicates articles are both available in a packet at Unique Copy Center on Greene St. and also on reserve under my name in Bobst Library.

WOMEN'S STUDIES 431
Childbirth in the United States
Spring Semester, 1995

Judith Walzer Leavitt, Ph.D.   Office Hours: 9:30-11:00 TR
1419 Medical Science Center   and by appt.
263-4560 or 262-1460

COURSE MEETS: Tuesdays and Thursdays 11:00 - 12:15; Room 5295 MSC

This course examines women's childbirth experiences in the
United States from the colonial period to the twentieth century.
It addresses throughout questions of authority and decision
making that remain central in women's health policy debates
today. Physiology of childbirth, interactions between birthing
women and their attendants, changes in experiences, and evolving
ideas about "choices" are major themes addressed during the
semester.

COURSE REQUIREMENTS:

The enrollment for this course is kept as low as possible so
that the class can be run primarily as a seminar-discussion. All
students are expected to complete the assigned readings before
coming to class and to participate regularly, actively, and
constructively in the class discussion. Graduate students must
attend an additional seminar, the time to be arranged on the
first day of class.

        Undergraduate Students: Group project   20%
                                 In-class Exam   25%
                                 Final Exam   35%
                                 Class participation &   20%
                                   Worksheets

        Graduate Students: Research paper   70%
                                 Seminar work   30%

Course Readings: (ordered at Room of One's Own)

Laurel Thatcher Ulrich, A Midwife's Tale: The Life of Martha
Ballard, Based on Her Diary, 1785-1812 (New York: Vintage, 1991).
Judith Walzer Leavitt, Brought to Bed: Childbearing in
America 1750-1950 (New York: Oxford University Press, 1986).
Barbara Katz Rothman, Recreating Motherhood: Ideology and
Technology in a Patriarchal Society (Norton, 1989, paper).

431 Reader, available at Agricultural Journalism Copy
Center, Room B25, Agricultural Engineering Building.

For Graduate Students Only:
    Emily Martin, _The Women in the Body: A Cultural Analysis of Reproduction_ (Boston: Beacon, 1992).
    Robbie Davis-Floyd, _Birth as an American Rite of Passage_ (University of California Press, 1992).

431 Class Schedule

January	24	Introduction
	26	Procreation and Women's Lives
January	31	Community of Women
February	2	Traditional Midwives
February	7	Birthing Women, Midwives, Physicians
	9	Traditional Home Delivery
February	14	Anatomy and Physiology of Birth
	16	Anatomy and Physiology of Birth
February	21	In-class Exam
	23	"All My Babies"
February	28	Shadow of Maternity
March	2	Physician Interventions/forceps
March	7	Anesthesia
	9	Scrupulous Cleanliness/Surgery
March	14	Spring Recess
	16	Spring Recess
March	21	Gender and Differences in the Birthing Room
	23	Shadow of Maternity & the Federal Government
March	28	Social Childbirth/Group Projects
	30	Social Childbirth/Group Projects
April	4	Social Childbirth/Group Projects
	6	Social Childbirth/Group Projects
April	11	Birth Moves to the Hospital
	13	Childbirth in the Hospital
April	18	Early 20th Century Attack on Midwifery
	20	Lay Midwives and Nurse-Midwives
April	25	"Natural Childbirth," Lamaze, etc.
	27	Home or Hospital? Decision Making and Change
May	2	Recreating Motherhood
	4	Recreating Motherhood
May	9	Recreating Motherhood
	11	Summary and Review

FINAL EXAM: MAY 18, 199? at 2:45 p.m.

431 Group Projects
Spring, 1995

The purpose of the group project assignment is to allow
students the opportunity to research and present in oral and
written form childbirth experiences of specific groups of women.
The main question to be addressed in the project is how group
identity and experience change or affect women's childbirths.
The presentations can focus on historical or contemporary
experiences. Suggested groups of women whose birth experiences
can be studied include (but are not limited to) Lesbian, Single,
Teen-age, Urban, Rural, African-American, Hispanic, US ethnic,
American Indian, Religious, Communal. More than one group can
explore the experiences of the same group of women, but we should
aim for as much diversity as possible.

The project has two components: an oral presentation to the
class, and a written version to be handed in. All students in
the group (which can range from two to six) will be assigned the
same grade for the project. The group project accounts for 20%
of the grade for the course. Class presentations should focus on
raising issues of common interest to the group, and may use tape
recordings or other visual and audio props. Class time allowed
will depend on the number of groups organized and will be clearly
announced in class. The written version must include specific
documentation, bibliography, and methodology, like a research
paper would. It should not be longer than 10 pages of text, but
can include appendices.

Please consult the Writing Lab guidelines for research
papers and note especially definitions of plagiarism. It is
expected that students will do their own work for this project
and when adopting and using ideas and writings of others will
give clear credit to originators.

The project must be soundly based in written and/or oral
sources. Students may conduct oral interviews, use library
sources, observe in community or family settings, etc. Whatever
conclusions are reached must be backed up in the evidence
collected and presented with a solid base of documented evidence.
It would also be advisable to connect to the class readings and
common issues.

Some questions/themes that could be addressed in the project
include:
1. Description of women's practices: culture of childbirth
2. Uniqueness/differences of practices and experiences
3. Changes over time
4. Controversies about experiences or interpretations
5. Importance of social and political context
6. Roles of other women; hospitals; physicians; midwives

Women's Studies 431
Required Readings

January 26: Procreation and Women's Lives

*Paula A. Treichler, "Feminism, Medicine, and the Meaning of
Childbirth," in Mary Jacobus, Evelyn Fox Keller, and Sally
Shuttleworth, eds., Body/Politics: Women and the Discourses of
Science (Routledge University Press, 1990), pp. 113-138.

January 31-February 9: Childbirth & Traditional Midwifery

Laurel Thatcher Ulrich, A Midwife's Tale: The Life of Martha
Ballard, Based on Her Diary, 1785-1812 (New York: Vintage,
1991).
1/31/95: pp. 3-101
2/02/95: pp. 102-203
2/07/95: pp. 204-285
2/09/95: pp. 286-364

February 14-16: Anatomy and Physiology of Birth

Pregnancy and Birth pamphlets, available in class
*PDR Family Guide to Women's Health and Prescription Drugs,
miscellaneous diagrams.
*Alice Hoffman, "Fortune's Daughter" excerpts.

February 23: "All My Babies"

*George Stoney, "All My Babies, Research"

February 28-March 9: Maternity & Physicians

Judith Walzer Leavitt, Brought to Bed: Childbearing in
America, 1750-1950 (New York: Oxford, 1986).
2/28/95: pp. 3-35
3/02/95: pp. 36-63
3/07/95: pp. 116-141
3/09/95: pp. 142-170

*H.B. Willard, Obstetrical Journal, 1849-1856 (3/2)
*McCormick letters, 1890 (3/2).
*Fanny Longfellow, Diary and Letters, 1844-1853 (3/7)
*Joseph B. DeLee, "Prophylactic Forceps Operation," American
Journal of Obstetrics and Gynecology 1 (1920): 34-44; 77-80.
(3/9)

*J. Whitridge Williams, "A Criticism of Certain Tendencies
in American Obstetrics," New York State Journal of Medicine 22
(1922): 493-499. (3/9)

March 21: Gender & Difference in the Birthing Room

Leavitt, Brought to Bed, pp. 64-115

March 23: Shadow of Maternity & the Federal Government

*Molly Ladd-Taylor, Raising a Baby the Government Way: Mothers' Letters to the Children's Bureau, 1915-1932 (1986): 47-65.
*Grace Meigs, "Maternal Mortality from All Conditions Connected with Childbirth in the United States," Children's Bureau Publication No. 19 (1917): 7-8, 24-27.
*Excerpts from the Congressional Debate on the Sheppard-Towner Bill, 1921.
*An Act for the Promotion of the Welfare and Hygiene of Maternity and Infancy, (Sheppard-Towner Act), 1921.
*Illinois Medical Journal 39 (1921): 143; JAMA 78 (1922): 1709.

April 11: Birth Moves to the Hospital

Leavitt, Brought to Bed, pp. 171-195.

April 13: Childbirth in the Hospital

*Gustav Zinke, "The Mortality and Morbidity of Child-Bearing Could be Reduced to a Minimum if Maternity Hospitals were more in Favor with the Profession and Laity," The Lancet-Clinic (1908): 71-80.
*Gladys Denny Shultz, "Journal Mothers Report on Cruelty in Maternity Wards," Ladies' Home Journal 75 (May, 1958): 44-45; 153-54; (December, 1958): 58-59; 137-39.
*Letter in Response to JWL Author's Query, 1983.
*Anais Nin, "Birth" from Under a Glass Bell.

April 18: Early 20th Century Attack on Midwifery

*S. Josephine Baker, "Schools for Midwives," American Journal of Obstetrics and Diseases of Women & Children 65 (1912): 256-270.
*Joseph B. DeLee, "Progress Toward Ideal Obstetrics," American Journal of Obstetrics and Diseases of Women & Children 73 (1916): 407-415.
*Dorothy Reed Mendenhall, "Prenatal and Natal Conditions in Wisconsin," Wisconsin Medical Journal 15 (1917): 353-369.

April 20: Lay and Nurse-Midwives

*Nancy Schrom Dye, "Mary Breckinridge, The Frontier Nursing Service, and the Introduction of Nurse-Midwifery in the United States," in Women & Health, pp. 327-344.
*Linda Janet Holmes, "African American Midwives in the South," in The American Way of Birth, ed. Pamela Eakins (1986): 273-291.
*Holly F. Mathews, "Killing the Self-Help Tradition Among African Americans: The Case of Lay Midwifery in North Carolina, 1912-1983," in African-Americans in the South: Issues of Race, Class and Gender, ed. Hans Baer and Yvonne Jones (1992): 60-78.
*Eugene R. Declercq, "The Transformation of American Midwifery: 1975-1988," American Journal of Public Health 82 (1992): 680-684.

April 25: "Natural Childbirth," Lamaze, etc.

*Marjorie Karmel, Thank You Dr. Lamaze: A Mother's Experiences in Painless Childbirth (1959): 69-85; 87-89.
*Margot Edwards & Mary Waldorf, Reclaiming Birth: History and Heroines of American Childbirth Reform (1984): 29-48.
*Toi Derricotte, "Natural Birth" excerpts.

April 27: Home or Hospital? Decision Making and Change

Leavitt, Brought to Bed, pp. 196-218.
*Alice Gilgoff, "Home Birth," in Encyclopedia of Childbearing ed. Barbara Katz Rothman (1993), pp. 175-177.
*Robbie Davis-Floyd, "Hospital Birth," Ibid, pp. 178-181.

May 2-9: Recreating Motherhood

Barbara Katz Rothman, Recreating Motherhood: Ideology and Technology in a Patriarchal Society (1989).
5/2/95: pp. 17-81
5/4/95: pp. 85-184
5/9/95: pp. 196-260.

WOMEN'S STUDIES 431
TABLE OF CONTENTS

16. Gladys Denny Schultz, "Journal Mothers Report on Cruelty in Maternity Wards," Ladies' Home Journal 75 (May, 1958): 44-45; 153-4; (December, 1958): 58-59; 135; 137-139.

17. Letter in response to Author's Query, 1983.

18. Anais Nin, "Birth," excerpts in Cradle and All: Women Writers on Pregnancy and Birth ed. Laura Chester (Faber and Faber, 1989), pp. 152-155.

19. S. Josephine Baker, "Schools for Midwives," American Journal of Obstetrics and Diseases of Women and Children 65 (1912): 256-270.

20. Joseph B. DeLee, "Progress Toward Ideal Obstetrics," American Journal of Obstetrics and Diseases of Women and Children 73 (1916): 407-415

21. Dorothy Reed Mendenhall, "Prenatal and Natal Conditions in Wisconsin," Wisconsin Medical Journal 15 (1917): 353-369.

22. Nancy Schrom Dye, "Mary Breckinridge, The Frontier Nursing Service, and the Introduction of Nurse-Midwifery in the United States, in Women and Health, pp. 327-344.

23. Linda Janet Holmes, "African American Midwives in the South," in The American Way of Birth, ed. Pamela Eakins (1986), pp. 273-291.

24. Holly F. Mathews, "Killing the Self-Help Tradition Among African Americans: The Case of Lay Midwifery in North Carolina, 1912-1983," in African Americans in the South: Issues of Race, Class, and Gender, ed Hans Baer and Yvonne Jones (University of Georgia Press, 1992), pp. 60-78.

25. Eugene R. Declercq, "The Transformation of American Midwifery: 1975-1988," American Journal of Public Health 82 (1992): 680-684.

26. Marjorie Karmel, Thank You Dr. Lamaze: A Mother's Experience in Painless Childbirth (1959), pp. 69-85; 87-89.

27. Margot Edwards and Mary Waldorf, Reclaiming Birth: History and Heroines of American Childbirth Reform (Crossing Press), pp. 29-48.

28. Toi Derricotte, "Natural Birth," excerpts in Cradle and All: Women Writers on Pregnancy and Birth ed. Laura Chester (Faber and Faber, 1989), pp. 108-115.

29. Alice Gilgoff, "Home Birth," in Encyclopedia of Childbearing ed. Barbara Katz Rothman (1993), pp. 175-177.

30. Robbie Davis-Floyd, "Hospital Birth," Ibid, pp. 178-181.

Professor Vicki L. Ruiz
Office: Women's Studies Program
Office Hours: T 3-5/W 1-3
or by appointment
965-3656
vruiz@asuvm.inre.asu.edu

WOMEN'S STUDIES/HISTORY 498/598

AMERICAN WOMEN AND WORK

This advanced undergraduate/graduate readings course explores historical perspectives on women and work in the United States from the colonial era to the present. Focusing on theory, methodology, and resources, it will examine the ways in which historians (and two anthropologists) have embodied issues of race, class, culture, and region in formulating new interpretations of women's work experiences. As in all of my classes, I have selected monographs which engage students to the extent that they feel they are "curling up with a good book" rather than drudging through the required readings. Course requirements involve weekly book precés, in-class oral presentations, and one 20 to 25 page historiographical essay.

REQUIRED READINGS:

Mary Beth Norton and Carol Groneman, "To Toil the Livelong Day": America's Women at Work, 1780-1980

Laurel Ulrich, A Midwife's Tale

Deborah Gray White, Arn't I A Woman? Female Slaves in the Plantation South

Jacqueline Jones, Labor of Love, Labor of Sorrow: Black Women, Work, and the Family, From Slavery to the Present

Peggy Pascoe, Relations of Rescue: The Search for Female Moral Authority in the American West, 1874-1939

Judy Yung, Unbound Feet: A Social History of Chinese Women in San Francisco

Anneliese Orleck, Common Sense and a Little Fire

Jacquelyn Dowd Hall et. al, Like a Family

Joanne Meyerowitz, Not June Cleaver: Women and Gender in Postwar America, 1945-1960

Patricia Zavella, Women's Work and Chicano Families: Cannery Workers of the Santa Clara Valley

Karen Sacks, <u>Caring By The Hour: Women, Work, and Organizing at the Duke Medical Center</u>

Rosalyn Baxandall and Linda Gordon, <u>America's Working Women: A Documentary History</u>

COURSE OUTLINE

Week 1
8/28   Introduction
            Film: <u>Indians, Outlaws, and Angie Debo</u>

Week 2
9/4   A Patchwork Quilt
            Reading assignment: <u>To Toil the Livelong Day</u>

Week 3
9/11   Women and Colonial Life
            Reading assignment: <u>A Midwife's Tale</u>

Week 4
9/18   Resiliency and Resistance
            Reading assignment: <u>Arn't I A Woman</u>

Week 5
9/25   Synthesis and African American Women's History
            Reading assignment: <u>Labor of Love, Labor of Sorrow</u>

Week 6
10/2   Gender, Religion, and Work
            Reading assignment: <u>Relations of Rescue</u>

Week 7
10/9   Making Their Own Paths
            Reading assignment: <u>Unbound Feet</u>

Week 8
10/16   "Organizing the Unorganizable"
            Reading assignment: <u>Common Sense and a Little Fire</u>

Week 9
10/23   Family, Community, and Class
            Reading assignment: <u>Like A Family</u>

Week 10
10/30   Research Day

Week 11
11/6   Beyond the Feminine Mystique
            Reading assignment: <u>Not June Cleaver</u>

Week 12
11/13   "I'm Not Exactly In Love With My Job"
         Reading assignment: Women's Work and Chicano Families

Week 13
11/20   The Politics of Race, Class, and Gender
         Reading assignment: Caring By The Hour

Week 14
11/27   Representations of Wage Earning Women
         Bring copies of print ads, magazines articles, video
         clips to discuss media gazes of women's work.
         Prepare a brief five to ten minute talk.
         Film: Killing Us Softly

Week 15
12/4   Building Community Through Work, Family, and
         Neighborhood

Week 16
12/11   Voicing The Past
         Reading assignment: America's Working Women
         Potluck at Professor Ruiz's home

COURSE EXPECTATIONS

The Readings

Each student will be expected to give an in-class presentation of
one monograph in which she or he discusses the author's thesis,
narrative line, evidence, and interpretation. The presentation
should not be a rehash of the book, but a thoughtful review of its
contributions to our understanding of women and work. For every
monograph, students will prepare a one page synopsis or precís
summarizing the author's major points. Also, bring to class one
scholarly review of the monograph under discussion.

Historiographical Essay

The major portion of the student's grade will be based on a 20-25
page historiographical essay which draws upon the books selected
for this course. In addition to discussing the comparative merits
and limitations of particular approaches, students will be expected
to address and interpret specific conceptualizations of women's
work experiences across time, region, class, and ethnicity. In
particular, they are to access the applicability of popular
paradigms (e.g. public/private spheres and work place cultures) in
elucidating women's dreams and routines. Furthermore, students
will ascertain relations of power as they influence women's
decision making with regard to work and family. Paper is due
Monday, December 16th at 4 p.m.

Attendance
Given the time constraints of this course, attendance at every class is mandatory.

Grading

30% Monograph Presentation
20% Class Participation
50% Historiographical Essay

Syllabus: History of Women's Education in the U.S.   Maxine S. Seller Fall 1997

Texts:

Sara Evans, Born for Liberty
David Tyack and Elisabeth Hansot, Learning Together
Packet of articles-- at University Bookstore, North Campus

Requirements:

1. Weekly reading assignments and short writing assignments. When you have a choice between two or more readings, these readings will be on Lockwood Reserve.
2. Presentation of one "option" in class. Summarize book, tell how it relates to topic of the week. Hand in written book summary and questions by the Friday preceding presentation.
Grading: ½ on general class participation, 1/4 on short written assignments, 1/4 on   oral oral presentations.

Sept 2 Introduction

Sept 9 Historiography / Colonial Beginnings
Mary Leach, "Toward Writing Feminist Scholarship into History of Education," Educational Theory 40:4 (Feb,1990), 453-461
M. Seller "Transplanting Inequality: Women's Education in Western Europe and Early Colonial America" [unpublished manuscript]
Evans, 1-33
OPTIONS See next week options-- Ulrich, Axtell, Gutierrez, or Fraser.

Sept 16 The Eighteenth Century
Evans 33-43
M. Seller, "The Widening Gap,"[unpublished manuscript]
Tyack and Hansot 13-27.
Julia Spruill, Women's Life and Work in the Southern Colonies ch 9 and 10
Susan Dion, "Women in the Boston Gazette 1755-1775" Historical Journal of Massachusetts 14:2 June 1986, 87-102

OPTIONS: Laurel Thatcher Ulrich, Good Wives: Image and Reality in the Lives of Women in Northern New England 1650-1750; James Axtell,The School upon a Hill: Education and Society in Colonial New England; Ramon Gutierrez, When Jesus Came, the Corn Mothers Went Away;   Mary Benson Sumner Women in Eighteenth Century America: Study of Opinion and Social Usage; Carol Karlsen and Laurie Crumpacker, eds. The Journal of Esther Edwards Burr;, Antonia Fraser The Weaker Vessel (women in England 17th and 18th c)

Sept 23 Revolutionary Generations 1776-1840 Write 1-2 pages on : Why did serious education for women in U.S. begin at this time?

183

Evans 45-66

Tyack and Hansot 28-55

Sharon Harris, ed. American Women Writers to 1800 #4 Priscilla Mason's graduation address at the Young Ladies Academy of Philadelphia, and #5 Judith Sargent Murray on women's education.

Ruth Bloch, "American Feminine Ideals in Transition, Feminist Studies 4:2, June 1978, 100-126"

ONE of the following:

Mary Johnson, "Madame Rivardi's Seminary in the Gothic Mansion," The Pennsylvania Magazine of History and Biography, 104:1 Jan 1980, 3-38.

Catherine Clinton: "Equally Their Due," The Education of the Planter Daughter in the Early Republic." Journal of the Early Republic2 spring 1982

Joan M. Jensen, "'Not Only Ours But Others:' The Teaching Daughters of the Mid Atlantic 1760-1850," History of Education Quarterly spr 1984, 3-19.

OPTIONS Mary Beth Norton, Liberty's Daughers; Janet Wilson James, Changing Ideas about Women in the United States 1776-1825; Nancy Cott, The Bonds of Womanhood; Jane Rendall, The Origins of Modern Feminism: Women in Britain, France and the United States 1780-1860

Sept 30 Expanding Education I

Evans 67-92

Tyack and Hansot 46-77, 114-145

Helen Lefkowitz Horowitz "Plain But Very Neat"Alma Mater 9-27

John Rury and Glenn Harper, "The Trouble with Coeducation," History of Education Quarterly 26:4 winter 1986, 81-102

OPTIONS: Katherine Kish Sklar, Catherine Beecher: A Study in American Domesticity, Susan McIntosh Lloyd, A Singular School: The Abbott Academy 1828-1973; Barbara Brenzel, Daughters of the State: A Social Portrait of the First Reform School for Girls in North America, 1856-1905 Women Teachers on the Frontier, Elizabeth Fox-Genovese, Within the Plantation Household: Black and White Women of the Old South, ; Catherine Hobbs, Nineteenth Century Women Learn to Write Pollu Kaufman, Women Teachers on the Frontier

Oct 7 Expanding Education II-- "Marginalized" Women

Evans, 93-124

Linda Perkins "The Impact of the "Cult of True Womanhood" on the Education of Black Women" Nancy Cott The History of Women in the US 12, 145-155

Robert Trennert, "Educating Indian Girls at Nonreservation Boarding Schools, in Nancy Cott, The History of Women in the US 12, 1878-1920.

Ron Butchart, "Perspectives on Gender, Race, Calling, and Commitment in 19th c America," Vitae Scholasticae spring 1994, 15-32

M Seller, Women Educators in the US F.M. Perko "Sister Blandina Segale"438-445.

OPTIONS Eileen Mary Brewer, Nuns and the Education of American Catholic Women; Ellen

McKenzee Lawson. The Three Sarahs: Documents of Black Antebellum College Women: Linda Perkins. Frances Coppin Jackson: Gretchen M. Bataille and Kathleen Mullen Sands. American Indian Women Telling Their Lives: Carolyn Niethammer. Daughters of the Earth: Patricia Albers and Beatrice Medicine. The Hidden Half: Studies of Plains Indian Women: Richard Griswold del Castillo, La Familia: Chicana Families in the Urban Southwest 1848 to the Present. Sarah Deutsch. No Separate Refuge.

Oct 14 Informal Education in the Nineteenth Century.
Evans. 125-143
Ronald E. Butchart. "Lydia Maria Child" in Seller. Women Educators in the United States
Nina Baym. Women's Fiction 22-50
Nancy Walker and Zita Dresner. Redressing the Balance 46-50. 98-106
Lucy Forsyth Townsend, "Jane Addams Abroad: Travei as Educational Finish" Vitae Scholasticae 6 (spring 1987). 225-246
David Gerber et all. Identity, Community, and Pluralism in America pp. 139-145

OPTIONS: Barbara Leslie Epstein. The Politics of Domesticity: Women, Evangelists, and Temperance in the Ninteenth Century; Susan Conrad, Perish the Thought: Intellectual Women in Romantic America 1830-1860: Karen Blair, The Clubwoman as Feminist; Nancy Walker. A Very Serious Thing: Women's Humor and American Culture, Jean Boydston, Mary Kelley, and Ann Margolis. The Limits of Sisterhood: The Beecher Sisters on Women's Rights and Women's Sphere Gerda Lerner. The Grimke Sisters ; Thompson, Eleanor Wolf. Education for Ladies 1830-1860: Ideas on education in magazines for women

Oct 21 Higher Education
Evans 145-173
Rosalind Rosenberg. "The Academic Prism," in Berkin and Norton Women in America 319-341
Helen Lefkovitz Horowitz. Alma Mater "The Life." 147-178
Anzia Yezierska Bread Givers 209-234
Sarah L. Delany and Elizabeth Delany, Having Our Say: The Delany Sisters' First Hundred Years ch 16-18.
Seller. Women Educators in the United States One of the following biographies:
   Mary McLeod Bethune. Sophonisba Breckinridge. Ellen Swallow Richards,or M Carey Thomas
OPTIONS: Marjorie Dobkin. The Making of a Feminist: Early Journals and Letters of M Carey Thomas; Charlotte Conable, Women at Cornell, Lynn D. Gordon, Gender and Higher Education in the Progressive Era; Mary J. Oates, Higher Education for Catholic Women; Chase Woodhouse, ed., After College--What? A Study of 6665 land-grant college women...

Oct 28 Women in the Professions Read one book about the history of women in the professions
in the nineteenth an early twentieth century. We will develop questions about earliy women in the

professions in class on Oct 21. Write 1-2 pages explaining how your book addresses at least three of these questions. Suggested books (there are many others): Mary Roth Walsh , Doctors Wanted, No Women Need Apply; Regina Morantz-Sanchez, Sympathy and Science: Women Physicians in America; Susan Reverby Ordered to Care: The Dilemma of American Nursing 1850-1945; Twentieth century; Barbara Clark Hine, Black Women in White; Karen Berger Morello, The Invisible Bar: The Woman Lawyer in America 1638 to the Present; Margaret Rossiter, Women Scientists in America; Geraldine Clifford, Lone Voyagers: Academic Women in Coeducational Institutions 1870-1937; Joyce Antler, The Educated Woman and Professionalization:The Struggle for a New Professional Identity 1890-1920

Nov 4 Urban America: Women and Progressive Education

Tyack and Hanot. 165--242

M. Seller, "The Education of the Immigrant Women," Journal of Urban History 4 (1978) 307-330

Thomas McCluskey, "We Specialize in the Wholly Impossible," Signs winter 1997 v22:2 403- 427

Options: Marjorie East, Home economics: Past, Present, and Future; Margaret Davies, Woman's Place Is at the Typewriter; Ellen Lagemann, A Generation of Women: Education in the Lives of Progressive Reformers; Margaret Haley, Autobiography of Margaret Haley; Sarah Deutsch, No Separate Refuge

Nov 11 Losses and Gains 1920-1960

Evans 173-241

Patricia Hummer, The Decade of Illusive Promise.1-19, 131-138

Mary J. Oates, "The Development of Catholic Colleges for Women 1895-1960" US Catholic Historian 7 (Fall 1988) 413-28

Beverly Guy-Sheftall, "Black Women and Higher Education: Spelman and Bennett Colleges Revisited" in Nancy Cott. ed. History of Women in the United States vol 11, 389-398.

OPTIONS: William Chafe, The American Woman: Her Changing Social, Economic,and Political Roles 1920-1979; Lois Scharf To Work and to Wed; Dorothy Brown, Setting a Course: American Women in the 1920s; Nancy Cott, The Grounding of Modern Feminism (the 1920s) Susan M. Hartmann, The Home Front and Beyond:American Women in 1940s; Eugenia Kaledin, Mothers and More: American Women in the 1950s. Marion V. Cuthbert, Education and Marginality: A Study of the Negro College Woman Graduate (done in 1930s)

Nov 18 Informal Education in the 20th Century

Evans 243-262

Barbara Gittings, "Looking for My People" in Jonathon Katz, ed. Gay American History 421-423.

Vicki Ruiz, "Star Struck," in Building with Our Hands Adela De La Torre and Beatriz Pesquera, 109-129.

Laurie Coyle, Gail Hershatter, and Emily Honig, "Why Did I Put Up With It All These Years? In M. Seller, ed. Immigrant Women 287-296.

Gracie Tyon. "The Way of My Grandmother, My Mother, and Me" Frontiers 6:3. 1992, 51-2 (class handout)

"Black Women on TV Still Stereotyped" USA Today Magazine July 1993, v. 12 n2578, p.7 (class handout)

OPTION: Barbara Ehrinreich and Deidre English, For Her Own Good

Write 1-2 pages describing a form of informal education that you have experienced.

Dec 2 Social change and Educational Reform 1965-1985

Evans 263-307

David Tyack and Elisabeth Hansot, Learning Together 243- 292

M. Chamberlain, "Enriching the Curriculum" NEA Higher Education Journal, 4:2 fall 1988, 21-40

Public Law 92-318-- Title IX

OPTIONS Barbara Bergmann, The Econommic Emergence of Women; Ellen Dubois et al, Feminist Scholarship; Judith Stacy, And Jill Came Tumbling After; L.H. Fox et al, Women and Mathematics, Carol Gilligan, In a Different Voice; Carol Pearson et al. Educating the Majority; Kathryn Clarenbach, Educational Needs of Rural Women and Girls; Sari Knopp Biklen and Diane Pollard, Gender and Education; Myra Sadker, Failing at Fairness: How America's Schools Cheat Girls; Frances Maher and Mary Tetreault, The Feminist Classroom; AAUW Survey researched by Harris/Scholastic Research. Hostile Hallways; Shelly Bergum, Alice Imazi, Judith Heumann, Educational Needs of Disabled Women (Unpublishesd report. See me for copy)

Dec 9 Unfinished Business Bring in one recent article on a current problem relating to women's education. Write 1-2 pages explaining the problem and relating it to what you have learned about the history of women's education this semester.

Evans 309-332

Deborah Woo, "The Gap Between Striving and Achieving: The Case of Asian American Women" in Making Waves Asian Women United of California, 184-194

Didi Khayatt, "Surviving School as a Lesbian Student," Gender and Education v 6:1, 1994

Susan Klein et al, "Continuing the Journey Toward Gender Equity," Educational Researcher Nov 1994, 13-21

History, Women's Studies   Dr. L. L. Stevenson
SPRING 1996   Stager 301, 291 4048

<h2 style="text-align:center">U.S. National Discourse</h2>

Throughout U.S. history women have shaped the national discourse on key issues including the environment, democracy and freedom, immigration, race, slavery, and war and peace. We will study how women academics, essayists, novelists, journalists, social workers and teachers have influenced national debates. In addition, we will learn what stances women have taken to enter into public life, how gender conventions shaped their participation, and what ideas they have offered.

The class will meet weekly and attendance at all sessions is required. Class participation is expected and will count 30% of the final grade. For another 30% of the grade, students will present at least 3 oral reports and hand in summaries and bibliographies of their presentations. From one of their oral reports, students will develop term papers of 12 to 15 pages due no later than May 2 (40%).

You may contact me by phone at home (daytimes and 8:00-9:15) or school. You may also email me questions and comments (L_Stevenson). Please see me in person Wednesday, 10-12, Thursday 1:30-3:00, after classes, and by appointment.

Books available for purchase, in order of assignment.
> Kathleen Hall Jamieson, <u>Beyond the Double Bind</u>.
> Joan Hedrick, <u>Harriet Beecher Stowe</u>.
> Harriet Beecher Stowe, <u>Uncle Tom's Cabin</u>.
> Ida Wells Barnett, <u>Crusader for Justice</u>.
> Evelyn Fox Keller, <u>A Feeling for the Organism</u>.
> Susan Douglas, <u>Where the Girls Are</u>.

<h3 style="text-align:center">Reading Schedule</h3>

Jan. 23   Introduction

Contemporary Observers Speak Out

Jan. 25   Kathleen Hall Jamieson, <u>Beyond the Double Bind</u>, chs. 1, 3.
Jan. 30   Jamieson, chs. 4-6.
           Nina Baym, <u>American Women Writers</u>, chs. 1-2.
           Stevenson, "Little Women?," in <u>History Today</u> (4 Mar. 1995), 26-31.
           Mary Kelley, "The Literary Domestics: Private Women on a Public Stage," in <u>America's Cultures</u>, ed. Hamilton Cravens, ch. 5
Feb. 1   Presentation and Critique of Summary Papers.

188

Victorian Intellectuals

Feb. 6   Joan Hedrick, <u>Harriet Beecher Stowe</u>, chs. 1-8.
Feb. 8   Hedrick, <u>Stowe</u>, chs. 9-20.
Feb. 13   Hedrick, <u>Stowe</u>, chs. 21-26 & Summary statement on the antislavery message.
Feb. 15   Harriet Beecher Stowe, <u>Uncle Tom's Cabin</u>, chs. 1-9.
Feb. 20   Conferences
Feb. 22   Stowe, <u>Uncle Tom's Cabin</u>, finish.

Case Studies

Feb. 27   Summary statements on HBS as author. Lydia Maria Child, Frances Wright, Angelina and Sarah Grimké.
Feb. 29   Sarah Josepha Hale, Sara Willis Parton, Margaret Fuller.
Mar. 5   Amended Summary Statements.

African American Women Intellectuals

Mar. 5   Ida Wells Barnett, <u>Crusader for Justice</u>, foreword, introduction, preface, chs. 1-7.
Mar. 7   Barnett, <u>Crusader for Justice</u>, chs. 7-24.
Mar. 19   Barnett, <u>Crusader for Justice</u>, finish.
Mar. 21   Summary statements and reports: Phillis Wheatley, Linda Brent and/or Charlotte Forten, Zora Neal Hurston, Ntozake Shange, Alice Walker, Toni Morison, Bell Hooks.
Mar. 26   Amended Summary Statements and Critiques.

Pre-1960s

Mar. 26   Evelyn Fox Keller, <u>A Feeling for the Organism</u>.
Mar. 28   Evelyn Fox Keller, <u>A Feeling for the Organism</u>.
Apr. 2   Reports: Margaret Mead, Hannah Arendt, Ayn Rand, Rachel Carson
Apr. 4   Summary statements and critique.

Contemporary Women

Apr. 4   Susan Douglas, <u>Where the Girls Are</u>, Part 1.
Apr. 9   Douglas, <u>Where the Girls Are</u>, Part 2. Jamieson, <u>Double Bind</u>, ch. 2.

Apr. 11   Conferences

Apr. 16   Conferences

Apr. 18   Work on your papers

Apr. 23   Report Presentations

5. Graduate and Undergraduate Courses and Seminars on Gender and Sexuality

Hist 495 06
Fall, 1997
120 O'Shag
M W 1:30-2:45

Professor Gail Bederman
255 Decio
E-Mail   Gail.Bederman.1@nd.edu
Office Hours: Wednesdays 3-4
or by appointment
Office Phone 631-7789

RESEARCH SEMINAR: GENDER IN THE U.S., 1941-1986

READINGS:

Sara M. Evans, *Born For Liberty* (1997), is available for purchase in the bookstore. (It is also on reserve at the Hesburgh Library.) Note: if you can find a used copy, the previous edition is almost exactly the same as the new edition, with one additional chapter, and expanded footnotes..

Students are required to read a large packet of xeroxed articles, which is available for purchase at the Copy Center in **O'Shaughnessy Hall,** as well as certain readings on reserve in the library.

Optional Readings:

Three other valuable women's history textbooks are also on reserve at the Hesburgh Library: Mary Ryan's *Womanhood in America*, 3rd edition (1983) Rosalind Rosenberg, *Divided Lives: American Women in the Twentieth Century* (1992), and Mary Beth Norton, and Ruth M. Alexander, *Major Problems in American Women's History* (1996) These books are fine supplementary texts, especially for students with little background in American women's history.

Kate L. Turabian's *Student's Guide for Writing College Papers* 3rd ed. (1976) is also available in the bookstore and on reserve, and is highly recommended. It includes both a style guide, and helpful hints in writing research papers. Students usually find the sections on what to footnote and footnote styles especially helpful.

SYLLABUS

Week 1:
Wed. Aug. 27 Organizational Meeting

Week 2:
Mon. Sept. 1: What is Women's History? What are Primary Sources?
1997 Primary Sources--handouts. Also bring in a primary source on gender in the 1990s.
*Joan Wallach Scott, "Women's History"(1983, rev. 1989) in *Gender and the Politics of History* 15-27
Sara M Evans, *Born for Liberty*, 1-6; 197-218. (Optional: 175-196.) As you read, concentrate on analyzing whether, and in what ways, Evans writes the sort of history Scott and Kerber & DeHart describe.

Wed. Sept. 3 World War II *MEET IN CCE ETS (IN BASEMENT IN CCE)*
Film: *Rosie the Riveter*
Evans, *Born for Liberty*, 219-241
* Leisa D. Meyer, "Creating G.I. Jane: The Regulation of Sexuality and Sexual Behavior in the Women's Army Corps during World War II." *Feminist Studies* 18, no. 3 (September 1992): 581-601.

* Maureen Honey, "The Working Class Woman and Recruitment Propaganda during World War II: Class Differences in the Portrayal of War Work" *Signs* 8, no 4, (1983) 672-687.
Note: There's a lot of reading next week. You might be wise to begin it now!
You should also begin working at the library, looking for research topics, and locating a primary source document to write about, due Sept 15.

Week 3:
Mon. Sept. 8 Motherhood and "The Feminine Mystique" in Post-War America
Evans, *Born for Liberty*, 243-262
*Betty Friedan, *The Feminine Mystique* (1963), pages 15-18, 33-68
* Joanne Meyerowitz, "Beyond the Feminine Mystique: A Reassessment of Postwar Mass Culture, 1946-1958," *Journal of American History* 79 (March, 1993)1455-1483.
* Rickie Solinger, "Race and 'Value': Black and White Illegitimate Babies, in the USA, 1945-1965." *Gender & History* 4, no. 3 (1992): 343-363.
* Primary source excerpts in Ruth Barnes Moynihan, et. al., *Second to None: A Documentary History of American Women* (1994), 236-245

Wed,. Sept. 10 Women in the Civil Rights Movement

*Jo Ann Gibson Robinson, *The Montgomery Bus Boycott and the Women Who Started It: The Memoir of Jo Ann Gibson Robinson* ed, David J. Garrow (1987) 9-11; 19-52.
*Sara Evans, *Personal Politics: The Roots of Women's Liberation in the Civil Rights Movement and the New Left* (1979) ix-xi, 60-82.
*Cynthia Griggs Fleming, "Black Women Activists and the Student Nonviolent Coordinating Committee: The Case of Ruby Doris Smith Robinson" *Journal of Women's History:* 4 (Winter 1993) 64-82

Week 4
Mon. Sept. 15 **PROGRESS REPORT AND DOCUMENT ANALYSIS DUE IN CLASS.**
Library Day. MEET AT HESBURGH LIBRARY. COME IN PREPARED TO DISCUSS YOUR RESEARCH ON TOPIC SO FAR AND WITH AT LEAST ONE, WRITTEN, SPECIFIC QUESTION TO ASK ABOUT RESEARCH STRATEGIES OR RESOURCES.

Wed. Sept. 17 Women and Roman Catholicism in the Post-war Era
* James J. Kenneally, *The History of American Catholic Women* (1990) 176-201
* Robert A. Orsi, "Chapter 3: Imagining Women" *Thank You Saint Jude: Women's Devotion to the Patron Saint of Hopeless Causes* (1996) 70-94
* M. Madeleva Wolff, CSC, "Educating Our Daughters as Women" *My First Seventy Years* (1959) 125-130
*Clare Ansberry, "Sisterly Love: Seven Women, Sharing Secrets for Fifty Years, Remain the Dreamers'" *Wall Street Journal* July 27, 1994, 1 & 6 .

Week 5
Mon. Sept. 22 Gays and Lesbians before Stonewall
* Margaret Cruikshank, *The Gay and Lesbian Liberation Movement* Routledge (1992) xv (Preface), 25-36 & 57-77.
* Nancy Adair and Casey Adair, *Word Is Out: Stories of Some of Our Lives,* (1978) 3-13; 55-65.
* Allan Bérubé, "Marching to a Different Drummer: Lesbian and Gay GIs in World War II," *Powers of Desire,* Ann Snitow et. al. eds. (1983), 88-99.
* Penn, Donna. "The Meanings of Lesbianism in Post-War America." *Gender and History* 3, no. 2 (June 1991): 190-203.

Wed. Sept. 24 Women's Liberation and the Rebirth of Feminism
   Evans, *Born for Liberty* 263-301
   * Susan Ware, *Modern American Women: A Documentary History*, 334-349
   * Robin Morgan, *Sisterhood is Powerful: An Anthology of Writings from the Women's Liberation Movement* (1970; hard cover edition) xiii-xxxvi,
   * Barrie Thorne, "Women in the Draft Resistance Movement: A Case Study of Sex Roles and Social Movements," *Sex Roles* 1 (1975) 179-195.

Week 6
 Mon. Sept. 29 Debates over the ERA.
   Evans, *Born for Liberty* 301-14
   * Equal Rights Amendment
   * "A Primer on ERA: Back to Basics," *Ms. Magazine* January 1977, 74-76.
   * Ruth Bader Ginsburg, "Let's Have ERA as a Signal," *American Bar Association Journal* 63, (January 1977), 70-73.
   * Phyllis Schlafly, Chapter 1, *The Power of the Positive Woman* (1977) 11-28
   * Donald G. Mathews & Jane Sherron De Hart, *Sex, Gender, and the Politics of ERA* (1990) 152-180.
   * Jane Sherron De Hart, "Oral Sources and Contemporary History: Dispelling Old Assumptions," *Journal of American History* 80, September 1993, 582-95.

   Wed. Oct. 1 Independent Research.

Week 7
   Mon. Oct. 6 **Proposal & Bibliography Due; come prepared to discuss it in class.**

   Wed. Oct. 8 Independent Research.

Week 8:
   Mon. Oct. 13 Independent Research.

   Wed. Oct. 15 **Progress report, including annotated bibliography, due.**

Mid Semester Break, Oct. 18-26

Week 9:
   Mon. Oct. 27 Independent Research.

   Wed. Oct. 29 Class meets: Discuss how to write an introduction.

Week 10
   Mon. Nov. 3 Independent Research. **A detailed outline and draft of introduction is due a minimum of one week before your first draft is due.**

   Wed. Nov. 5 Independent Research

Week 11
   Mon. Nov. 10 Independent Research and Writing

   Wed. Nov. 12 Independent Writing **First Drafts Due Mon. or Wed. - First Half of Class** (Especially for perfectionists who like to revise slowly and carefully)

Week 12
   Mon. Nov. 17 Independent Writing

Wed. Nov. 19 **First Draft Due - Second Half of Class** (For students who like to work round the clock under great pressure.)

Week 13 *Thanksgiving Week*
Mon. Nov. 24. Work on Revisions

Wed. Nov. 26 Work on Revisions

Week 14
Mon. Dec. 1 Work on Revisions

Wed. Dec. 3 Work on Revisions

Week 15
Mon. Dec. 8 Class meeting to fill out TCE's. Work on Revisions

Wed. Dec. 10 Work on Revisions

The final paper will be due on or before the time of the scheduled final exam.

CLASS OBJECTIVES

This course emphasizes research and writing. The object, as in all History Department research seminars, is for each student to produce a twenty-five page paper, based on original research and interpretation of primary sources. There are abundant sources in the library for such work, although some students may want to go farther afield to locate sources. As the course progresses we will discuss the research and writing process in more detail.

During the first part of the semester, we will spend a great deal of time reading and discussing recent journal articles, excerpts from books, and primary sources. The aim is to introduce students to women's history--both the methodology and some of the topics on which historians have focused their attention.

During this first half of the semester, students' attention should be split: On the one hand, students should focus on the assigned reading, paying particular attention to the methodology and context. This will help deepen your analysis in your own research paper. On the other hand, even in the very early weeks of the semester, students should be actively working in the library to identify a research topic that interests them and to locate the necessary primary sources. In this research process, the assigned class reading can be extremely helpful. Pay particular attention to footnotes. What sorts of sources have other historians used, that might be available to you, here? Be creative!

During the second half of the semester, students will focus all their energies on independent research and writing. Classes will meet irregularly, as scheduled.

SEMINAR MECHANICS

Seminars only work well when everybody in class is willing to share their thoughts on the subject and readings. Thus, three things are required: First, everybody must do the assigned readings. Second, everybody must think **critically** about the assigned readings, and be willing to share their thoughts on what they found interesting, boring, persuasive, or problematic. Finally, an interest in and respect for other students' opinions is essential! Listen to what your colleagues are saying, and take their opinions seriously.

Active participation at all discussions **by all students** is mandatory and will be **graded**. Miserliness in sharing your opinions will not be tolerated!

To encourage active participation, **each student must bring three written questions on the readings for discussion to each class where there is assigned reading.** In addition, please bring the assigned readings with you to class.

ATTENDANCE

Attendance at all regularly scheduled class meetings is mandatory. Students with more than two unexcused absences will be penalized a fraction of their final grade. Students with more than four unexcused absences will be penalized a full grade. Additional unexcused absences will be penalized proportionately. (Students are not required to attend any classes explicitly designated "informal" or "optional," of course.)

SUMMARY OF WRITTEN REQUIREMENTS AND GRADING

--Informed participation in and leadership of discussion	20%
--Progress Report and Document Analysis (Due Mon. Sept. 15)	10%
--Proposal and Bibliography (Due Mon. Oct. 6)	10%
--Detailed outline and introduction	
(Due minimum of 1 week before first draft due)	*
--First draft	
(Due Wed. Nov. 12 for half the class; Wed. Nov. 19 for half the class)	*
--Research Paper (Due Final Exam week)	60%

Late assignments: All assignments are due in class at 1:30. After that instant, unless accompanied by a verified excuse from the Office of Residence Life, they will be downgraded a fraction of a grade for each day (24 hours) late. Late papers should be placed in my mailbox in 219 O'Shaughnessy. This inflexible policy is designed to insure fairness.

Early assignments: Any assignment may be turned in early. I will try to return any early papers to you within a week after you submit it to me. It is probably an excellent idea to turn in all assignments except the document analysis as early in the semester as possible, to allow yourself the most time to revise.

* The outline and first drafts are tools to help me help you produce a top-quality paper. The grades I assign them will not count toward the final grade, but will give you a sense of what quality I think your work has, at the moment. However, even though they don't count toward the final grade, they must be turned in in a timely fashion! Students who neglect to turn in the outline assignment will be penalized 5% of their final grade. Students who neglect to turn in a first draft of their research paper will not be allowed to turn in their final paper, and will receive an "F" on their research paper. Students who turn in these assignments late will have their final grades penalized, as they would if these papers were graded. (See above paragraph.)

INFORMAL CONFERENCES

All students are required to come to my office hours , or to set up an appointment, to discuss your research topic at least once before October 6, when the proposal is due; and again, at least once before you turn in your outline & introduction (i.e. before November 5 or November 12).

But please don't wait for those required occasions to come to my office hours! Feel free to stop by to let me know how things are going, to discuss any questions (specific or amorphous) that have been raised by the course, to discuss any frustrations, or excitement about your research, or just to check in and say hello. I really enjoy getting to know my students, so please--come see me during my office hours!

SEXUAL IDENTITIES IN AMERICAN HISTORY

Fall 1996

Jeanne Boydston   Office Hours:
5120 Humanities   2:30-3:30 MW
boydston@facstaff.wisc.edu   & by appt.

You will be responsible for:

1. coming to class each week prepared to engage in critical discussion of the
   assigned readings;
2. co-leading a class discussion;
3. writing 3 3-page essays on some aspect of the assigned readings--and revisions
   of essays 1 and 2 as noted. (The final grade for revised essays will reflect
   the level of work and engagement in both drafts.)
4. writing an 8-10 page out-of-class final exam, due by 12:25 Friday, December 20.

Class Schedule

Wednesday, September 4: *Introductions*

Wednesday, September 11: *Backgrounds*
   Reading Assignment: Robert Padgug, "Sexual Matters: Rethinking Sexuality in History"
                         in Hidden from History, 54-64
                         Michel Foucault, "The Repressive Hypothesis" in The History of
                         Sexuality

Wednesday, September 18: *Colonial Sexualities and Heterosexual Enlightenments*
   Reading Assignment: Michel Foucault, "Scientia Sexualis" in The History of Sexuality
                         Winthrop Jordan, "Fruits of Passion" from The White Man's Burden
                         (Reserve)
                         "Moll Placket-Hole" from Root of Bitterness (Reserve)
                         Ann Laura Stoler, "Colonial Studies" in Race and the Education of
                         Desire (Reserve)

198

Wednesday, September 25: *Separate Spheres and the Construction of Homoeroticism*
    Reading Assignment: Nancy Cott, "Passionlessness: An Interpretation of Victorian
                Sexual Ideology" in <u>A Heritage of Her Own</u> (Reserve)
                Carroll Smith Rosenberg, "The Female World of Love and Ritual"
                <u>Signs</u> (Reserve)
                Christine Stansell, "The Uses of the Streets" from <u>City of Women</u>
                (Reserve)
                Linda Gordon, "Voluntary Motherhood" from <u>Woman's Body, Woman's
                Right</u> (Reserve)
                Nell Irvin Painter, "Soul Murder and Slavery: Toward a Fully
                Loaded Cost Accounting" in <u>U.S. History as Women's History</u>
                (Reserve)

Wednesday, October 2: *Passing*
    Reading Assignment: Lauren Cook Burgess, ed., <u>An Uncommon Soldier: The Civil War
                Letters of Sarah Rosetta Wakeman</u>
                San Francisco Lesbian and Gay History Project, "'She Even Chewed
                Tobacco': A Pictorial Narrative of Passing Women in America
                in <u>Hidden from History</u>
                Nancy Sahli, "Smashing" <u>Chrysalis</u> (Reserve)
    Writing Assignment: Paper 1 due

Wednesday, October 9: *Manliness in Mid-Nineteenth-Century America*
    Reading Assignment: Martin Duberman, "'Writhing Bedfellows' in Antebellum South
                Carolina: Historical Interpretations and the Politics of
                Evidence" in <u>Hidden from History</u>, 153-168
                Robert Martin, "Knights Errant and Gothic Seducers: The
                Representation of Male Friendship in Mid-Nineteenth-Century
                America" in <u>Hidden from History</u>, 169-82.
                Herman Melville, <u>Billy Budd, Sailor</u> (Reserve)

Wednesday, October 16: *Dislocation and the Crossing of Boundaries*
    Reading Assignment: Kathy Peiss, "'Charity Girls' and City Pleasures: Historical
                Notes on Working-Class Sexuality, 1880-1920" in <u>Powers of
                Desire: The Politics of Sexuality</u> (Reserve)
                Ida Wells, Barnett, <u>A Red Record</u>
                Charlotte Perkins Gilman, <u>The Yellow Wallpaper</u> (Reserve)
    Writing Assignment: Paper 1 re-write due

Wednesday, October 23: *Race, Gender, Sex, and Nationalism*
    Reading assignment: Gail Biederman, <u>Manliness and Civilization</u>

Wednesday, October 30: *Twentieth-Century Exoticisms: The New Woman*
    Reading Assignment: Carroll Smith-Rosenberg, "Discourses of Sexuality and
                Subjectivity: The New Woman, 1870-1936" in <u>Hidden from
                History</u>
                George Chauncey, Jr., "From Sexual Inversion to Homosexuality:

                --continued on next page--

                        199

Medicine and the Changing Conceptualization of Female
Deviance." Salmagundi 58-9 (Fall-Winter 1983) (Reserve)
Siobhan Simerville. "Scientific Racism and the Invention of the
Homosexual Body" in Queer Studies: A Lesbian, Gay, Bisexual
and Transgender Anthology (Reserve)
Writing Assignment: Paper 2 due

Wednesday, November 6: *Twentieth-Century Exoticisms: Harlem*
Reading Assignment: Eric Garber. "A Spectacle in Color: The Lesbian and Gay Subculture
of Jazz Age Harlem" in Hidden from History. 318-31.
Esther Newton. "The Mythic. Mannish. Lesbian: Radclyffe Hall and
the New Woman" in Hidden from History. 281-93
Gloria T. Hull. "Introduction" and "Angelina Weld Grimke" in
Color, Sex, and Poetry: Three Women Writers of the Harlem
Renaissance (Reserve)

Wednesday, November 13: *The Politics of Defining Communities*
Reading Assignment: George Chauncey. Gay New York
Writing Assignment: Paper 2 re-write due

Wednesday, November 20: *War and Sexual Control*
Reading Assignment: Allan Berube. Coming Out Under Fire
Leisa Meyers. "GI Jane" Feminist Studies (Reserve)

Wednesday, November 27: CLASS CANCELED

Wednesday, December 4: *Pre-Political?*
Reading Assignment: Elizabeth Lapovsky Kennedy and Madeline D. Davis. Boots of
Leather, Slippers of Gold
Writing Assignment: Paper 3 due

Wednesday, December 11: *Conclusions (or not)*

HISTORY 610

Fall 1997

Gender in Southern History

Sheldon Hackney   Tuesdays, 3:30-5:30
Drew Faust

9/9 INTRODUCTION

9/16 GENDER AND THE MEANING AND PERSISTENCE OF HISTORY; VMI
AND THE CITADEL

        Joan Scott, "Gender: A Useful Category of
Historical Analysis," AHR 91 (December 1986) 1053-75.
(Bulk Pack)

        Evelyn Brooks Higginbotham, "African American
Women's History and the Metalanguage of Race," in We
Specialize in the Wholly Impossible: A Reader in Black
Women's History ed. Darlene Clark Hine et al. (Bulk Pack)

        Elsa Barkley Brown, "'What Has Happened Here,'
The Politics of Difference in Women's History and Feminist
Politics," in We Specialize (Bulk Pack)

        Susan Faludi, "The Naked Citadel," The New Yorker,
September 5, 1994 (Bulk Pack)

        The VMI Case (Selected materials from the case to
be provided)

9/23 COLONIAL BEGINNINGS OF A RACE AND GENDER SYSTEM

        Kathleen Brown, Good Wives, Nasty Wenches and
Anxious Patriarchs: Gender, Race and Power in Colonial
Virginia*

Report Books:

Kenneth Lockridge, On the Sources of Patriarchal Rage:
The Commonplace Books of William Byrd and Thomas Jefferson
and teh Gendering of Power in the 18th Century

Julia Cherry Spruill, Women's Life and Labor in the
Southern Colonies

Catherine Clinton and Michelle Gillespie, eds. The
Devil's Lane: Sex and Race in the Early South

9/30 MASCULINITY IN THE OLD SOUTH

        Bertram Wyatt-Brown, Southern Honor: Ethics and
Behavior in the Old South*

Report Books:
    W.J. Cash, The Mind of the South
    John Hope Franklin, The Militant South
    Christine Heyrman, Southern Cross: The Beginnings of the
Bible Belt
    Drew Gilpin Faust, James Henry Hammond and the Old
South: A Design for Mastery

10/7 GENDER AND POWER IN THE OLD SOUTH

        Stephanie McCurry, Masters of Small Worlds: Yeoman
Households, Gender Relations, and the Political Culture of
Antebellum South Carolina*
        Elliot Gorn, "Gouge and Bite, Pull Hair and
Scratch: The Social Significance of Fighting in the Southern
Back Country," AHR 90(February 1985) 18-43 (Bulk Pack)

Report Books:
    Kenneth Greenberg, Honor and Slavery: Lies, Duels,
Noses, Masks, Dressing Like a Woman, Gifts . . . .etc.
    Steven Stowe, Intimacy and Power in the Old South:
Ritual in the Lives of the Planters
    Jane Turner Censer, North Carolina Planters and Their
Children
    Joan Cashin, A Family Venture
    _Anne Firor Scott, The Southern Lady: From Pedestal to
Politics

10/21 MEN, WOMEN AND SLAVERY

        David Barry Gaspar and Darlene Clark Hine, More
Than Chattel: Black Women and Slavery in the Americas*
        Deborah Gray White, "Female Slaves: Sex Roles and
Status in the Antebellum Plantation South," in Unequal
Sisters, ed. Vicki Ruiz and Ellen DuBois (Bulk Pack)
        Bertram Wyatt-Brown, "The Mask of Obedience: Male
Slave Psychology in the Antebellum South," AHR 93 (December
1988) 1228-52 (Bulk Pack)

Report Books:
         Deborah Gray White, <u>Ar'n't I a Woman: Female</u>
<u>Slaves in the Plantation South</u>
         Stanley Elkins, <u>Slavery: A Problem in American</u>
<u>Institutional and Intellectual Life</u>
         Patricia Morton, ed. <u>Discovering the Women in</u>
<u>Slavery: Emancipating Perspectives on the American Past</u>
         Brenda Stevenson, <u>Life in Black and White:</u>
<u>Family and Community in the Slave South</u>
         Marli Wiener, <u>Mistresses and Slaves:</u>
<u>Plantation Women in South Carolina, 1830-1880</u>
         Suzanne Lebsock, <u>Free Women of Petersburg:</u>
<u>Status and Culture in a Southern Town, 1784-1869</u>
         Elizabeth Fox-Genovese, <u>Within the Plantation</u>
<u>Household: Black and White Women of the Old South</u>
         Ann Patton Malone, <u>Sweet Chariot: Slave Family</u>
<u>and Household Structure in Nineteenth Century Louisiana</u>
         John Blassingame, <u>The Slave Community</u>

10/28 GENDER AND THE CIVIL WAR

         Drew Gilpin Faust, <u>Mothers of Invention: Women</u>
<u>of the Slaveholding South in the American Civil War</u>*
         Jim Cullen, "I's a Man Now: Gender and African
American Men," in <u>Divided Houses</u>, ed. Catherine Clinton and
Nina Silber (Bulk Pack)
         W.E.B. Du Bois, "Robert E. Lee," <u>The Crisis</u>,
March 1928 (Bulk Pack)

Report Books:
         LeeAnn Whites, <u>The Civil War as a Crisis in Gender:</u>
<u>Augusta, Georgia, 1860-1890</u>
         George Rable, <u>Civil Wars: Women and the Crisis of</u>
<u>Southern Nationalism</u>
         Catherine Clinton and Nina Silber, <u>Divided Houses</u>:
<u>Gender and the Civil War</u>
         Kym Rice and Edward D.C. Campbell, eds. <u>A Woman's War</u>:
<u>Southern Women, Civil War, and the Confederate Legacy</u>

11/4 GENDER AND RECONSTRUCTION

         Laura Edwards, <u>Gendered Strife and Confusion: The</u>
<u>Political Culture of Reconstruction</u>*

Report Books:
         Leslie A. Schwalm, <u>A Hard Fight for We: Women's</u>
<u>Transition from Slavery to Freedom in South Carolina</u>
         Nina Silber, <u>The Romance of Reunion: Northerners and</u>
<u>the South</u>

11/11 AFRICAN AMERICAN WOMEN IN FREEDOM

Evelyn Brooks Higginbotham, Righteous Discontent: The Women's Movement in the Black Baptist Church, 1880-1920*

Report Books:

Tera Hunter: To Joy My Freedom: Southern Black Women's Lives and Labors After the Civil War
Jacqueline Jones, Labor of Love, Labor of Sorrow: Black Women, Work and the Family from Slavery to the Present

11/18 GENDER AND JIM CROW

Glenda Elizabeth Gilmore, Gender and Jim Crow: Women and the Politics of White Supremacy in North Carolina 1896-1920*
Suzanne Lebsock, "Woman Suffrage and White Supremacy: A Virginia Case Study," in Visible Women, ed. Nancy A. Hewitt and Suzanne Lebsock, eds. (Bulk Pack)

Report Books:
Marjorie Spruill Wheeler, New Women of the New South: Leaders of the Woman Suffrage Movement in the Southern States, 1890-1920
Ted Ownby, Subduing Satan: Religion, Recreation and Manhood in the Rural South, 1865-1920
Dolores Janiewski, Sisterhood Denied: Race, Gender and Class in a New South Community
Mary Martha Thomas, The New Woman in Alabama: Social Reforms and Suffrage, 1890-1920

11/25   LYNCHING, RACE AND GENDER

Jacqueline Dowd Hall, Revolt Against Chivalry: Jesse Daniel Ames and the Women's Campaign Against Lynching*
Lynching Forum in the Journal of American History, March 1997 (Bulk Pack)
Nancy MacLean, "Gender, Sexuality and the Politics of Lynching: The Leo Frank Case Revisited," in W. Fitzhugh Brundage, ed., Under Sentence of Death: Lynching in the South (Bulk Pack)
Gail Bederman, "Civilization, the Decline of Middle Class Manliness, and Ida B. Wells' Anti Lynching Campaign," in We Specialize in the Wholly Impossible: A Reader in Black Women's History, ed. Darlene Clark Hine et al. (Bulk Pack)

Report Books: James Goodman, Scottsboro Stories
W. Fitzhugh Brundage, ed., Under Sentence of Death: Lynching in the South
W. Fitzhugh Brundage, Lynching in the New South: Georgia and Virginia, 1880-1930

Arthur Raper, The Tragedy of Lynching(1933)
Trudier Harris, Exorcising Blackness:
Historical and Literary Lynchings and Burning Rituals
Nancy MacLean, Behind the Mask of Chivalry:
The Making of the Second Ku Klux Klan

12/2 UPPITY WOMEN IN THE TWENTIETH CENTURY

Virginia Foster Durr, Outside the Magic
Circle: The Autobiography of Virginia Foster Durr*
Hazel Carby, 'It Jus be's Dat Way
Sometime,': The Sexual Politics of Black Women's Blues," in
Unequal Sisters (Bulk Pack)
Jacquelyn Dowd Hall, "Disorderly Women:
Gender and Labor Militancy in the Appalachian South," in
Unequal Sisters (Bulk Pack)
"The Waveland Statement, 1964" in Mary King,
Freedom Song, 567-9 (Bulk Pack)
Bernice Johnson Reagon, "Women as Culture
Carriers in the Civil Rights Movement," in Women in the
Civil Rights Movement, ed. Vicki Crawford (Bulk Pack)

Report Books:
Lillian Smith, Killers of the Dream
Donald G. Mathews and Jane Sherron DeHart, Sex, Gender and
the Politics of ERA: A State and the Nation
James T. Sears, Lonely Hunters: An Oral History of Lesbian
and Gay Southern Life
John Howard, ed., Carryin' On in the Lesbian and Gay South
John Berendt, Midnight in the Garden of Good and Evil
Belinda Robnett, How Long? How Long?: African American Women
in the Struggle for Civil Rights

* Available for purchase at the Pennsylvania Book Center,
37th and Walnut Streets

Course Requirements: Four short (3-4 pages) reading response
papers.
    Reading questions to the listserve on weeks without
response papers.
    Two oral book reports(5-10 minutes) on supplementary
readings.
    A 10-15 page paper due at the end of the semester. This
assignment will ask you to take a classic of southern
history and evaluate it in light of the new gender
scholarship.

LESBIAN AND GAY HISTORY

Lori Ginzberg
410 Weaver
863-8947

His/WS 497C
Fall 1996
email: LDG1@psu.edu

Office hours: Wednesday 9-11

This course will explore some of the most recent and innovative
writings on the history of sexuality, focusing on the experiences,
ideas, and conflicts that have shapedd conflicts that have shaped the
emergence of modern gay and lesbian identities. It will explore such
questions as: What is the gay and lesbian past? How have historians
recovered the stories of lesbians and gay men who lived in societies
and eras vastly different from our own? What can we learn from
history about gender and sexuality, repression and resistance,
deviance and acceptance, identity and community? We will use films,
primary and secondary readings, discussions, and written assignments
to explore a range of topics that should help us begin to answer
these and other questions.

The success of this course depends on everyone's participation.
Therefore, class attendance and active participation will be a major
part of your grade. In addition, students will do research projects
on a specific field of gay/lesbian history. That project will
require at least one meeting with the professor, a written proposal
and bibliography, a rough draft, and a final paper of 15-25 pages.

The following books are available at the bookstore and are on
reserve. There will also be a packet of readings (marked with an
asterisk* in the syllabus) which is available for purchase.

> Allan Berube, Coming Out Under Fire
> George Chauncey, Gay New York
> Martin Duberman, Martha Vicinus, George Chauncey,
> Hidden From History
> Lillian Faderman, Odd Girls and Twilight Lovers
> Leslie Feinberg, Stone Butch Blues
> Radclyffe Hall, The Well of Loneliness

<u>Written Requirements</u>:

In addition to expanding our knowledge of lesbian and gay history, this course will stress reading, research, and writing skills. Students will be required to develop a research goal, do research, and write and revise a paper. The following schedule will be <u>strictly</u> observed:

1. <u>Consultation</u> with the professor on the research idea during the week of September 24 (no class that week).
2. A typed project <u>proposal</u>, which will include a summary of the relevant questions, a realistic plan for research, and a preliminary bibliography (due October 8).
3. A <u>rough draft</u> of the paper (due November 12).
4. A <u>final draft</u> of the paper (due during finals week).

<u>Grading</u>:

Grades will be based half on class participation and half on the research project. You must complete all the work to pass the course. Late assignments (without an appropriate excuse) will be graded down.

P.S. It is impossible in one course to cover all issues, not to mention the variety of perspectives on any given subject. Also, since I am an American historian, you will quickly notice that the course leans heavily toward scholarship about the United States. Students are encouraged to become familiar with gay, lesbian, and feminist publications, such as <u>Gay Community News</u>, <u>off our backs</u>, <u>Out/Look</u>, <u>Philadelphia Gay News</u>, <u>The Advocate</u>, <u>Bridges: A Journal for Jewish Feminists and Our Friends</u> (and others, including many cities' gay/lesbian publications.) In addition, I can steer you toward anthologies of fiction, theory, "coming out" stories, and activist memoirs which you may want to consult on given topics. As for journals that include articles on gay/lesbian history, I recommend <u>Signs</u>, <u>Feminist Studies</u>, <u>Quest</u>, <u>Journal of the History of Sexuality</u>, <u>The Journal of Homosexuality</u>, and <u>Women's Studies Quarterly</u>. Anyone wishing to read an overview of the history of sexuality in the United States should consult John D'Emilio and Estelle Freedman, <u>Intimate Matters</u>. Finally, I am more than happy to lend my set of bibliographies compiled by the Committee on Lesbian and Gay History of the American Historical Association if anyone wants to become completely overwhelmed!

SCHEDULE OF READINGS AND CLASSES:

August 27:   INTRODUCTION TO THE COURSE

Sept. 3:   HISTORICAL PERSPECTIVES

Reading:

*Jonathan Ned Katz, Introduction to <u>Gay American</u>
<u>History</u> (1976) (1-9)
"Introduction," <u>Hidden from History</u> (1-13)
Leila Rupp, "'Imagine My Surprise': Women's
Relationships in Mid-Twentieth Century America,"
in <u>Hidden from History</u> (395-410)
*Jonathan Ned Katz, "The Invention of
Heterosexuality," <u>Socialist Review</u> 90/1 (7-34)
*Gayle Rubin, "Thinking Sex: Notes for a Radical
Theory of the Politics of Sexuality," <u>The Lesbian</u>
<u>and Gay Studies Reader</u> (3-44)

September 10:   FINDING A GAY PAST

Reading:

John Boswell, "Revolutions, Universals, and Sexual
Categories," <u>Hidden from History</u> (17-36)
David Halperin, "Sex Before Sexuality: Pederasty,
Politics, and Power in Ancient Athens," <u>Hidden</u>
<u>from History</u> (37-53)
Paula Gunn Allen, "Lesbians in American Indian
Culture," <u>Hidden from History</u> (106-117)
*Ramon A. Gutierrez, "Must we Deracinate Indians to
Find Gay Roots? <u>Out/Look</u>, winter 1989

September 17:   PREINDUSTRIAL SOCIETIES

Reading:

Randolph Trumbach, "The Birth of the Queen," <u>Hidden</u>
<u>from History</u> (129-140)

AND ANY TWO OF THE FOLLOWING ARTICLES:

Judith Brown, "Lesbian Sexuality in Medieval and Early
Modern Europe," <u>Hidden from History</u> (67-75)
Vivien Ng, "Homosexuality and the State in Late
Imperial China," <u>Hidden from History</u> (76-89)
James M. Saslow, "Homosexuality in the Renaissance,"
<u>Hidden from History</u> (90-105)
Paul Schalow, "Male Love in Early Modern Japan,"
<u>Hidden from History</u> (118-128)

September 24:   NO CLASS: consultations about research projects

October 1:   THE NINETEENTH CENTURY: SEX AND DOMESTICITY

                Reading:

                *Nancy Cott, "Passionlessness," in Cott & Elizabeth
                    Pleck, A Heritage of her Own (162-81)
                *Carroll Smith-Rosenberg, "The Female World of Love
                    and Ritual," Disorderly Conduct (53-76)
                Martin Duberman, "'Writhing Bedfellows," Hidden from
                    History (153-168)

October 8:   THE NINETEENTH CENTURY: REDEFINITIONS

PAPER PROPOSALS DUE!

                Reading:

                *George Chauncey, "From Sexual Inversion to
                    Homosexuality," in Salmagundi (1982-83) (114-46)
                Martha Vicinus, "Distance and Desire," Hidden from
                    History (212-229)
                Carroll Smith-Rosenberg, "Discourses of Sexuality and
                    Subjectivity," Hidden from History (264-80)
                SF Lesbian/Gay History Project, "'She Even Chewed
                    Tobacco'," Hidden from History (183-194)

October 15:   THE MAKING OF THE GAY MALE WORLD

                Reading:

                George Chauncey, Gay New York: Gender, Urban Culture,
                    and the Making of the Gay Male World, 1890-1940
                Jeffrey Weeks, "Inverts, Perverts, and Mary-Annes,"
                    Hidden from History (195-211)
                James D. Steakley, "Iconography of a Scandal," Hidden
                    from History (233-263)

October 22:   "WILLFUL WOMEN": ROLES, REPRESSION, AND REBELLION

                Reading:

                Radclyffe Hall, The Well of Loneliness
                Esther Newton, "The Mythic Mannish Lesbian," Hidden
                    from History (281-293)

October 29:   ODD GIRLS AND TWILIGHT LOVERS

               Reading:

               Lillian Faderman, Odd Girls and Twilight Lovers: A
                  History of Lesbian Life in the Twentieth Century
                  (to page 117)
               Eric Garber, "A Spectacle in Color," Hidden from
                  History (318-331)

November 5:   WORLD WAR II AND ITS AFTERMATH

               Film: "Before Stonewall"

               Reading:

               Allan Berube, Coming Out Under Fire
               Faderman, Odd Girls and Twilight Lovers (118-187)
               Erwin Haeberle, "Swastika, Pink Triangle, and Yellow
                  Star," Hidden from History (365-382)

November 12:   WOMEN'S LIBERATION, GAY LIBERATION, AND IDENTITY

PAPER DRAFTS DUE!

               Reading:

               Leslie Feinberg, Stone Butch Blues
               Faderman, Odd Girls and Twilight Lovers (188-245)
               Madeline Davis and Elizabeth Lapovsky Kennedy, "Oral
                  History and the Study of Sexuality in the Lesbian
                  Community," Hidden from History (426-440)

November 19:   GAY COMMUNITIES, GAY POLITICS

               Film: "The Times of Harvey Milk"

               Reading:

               John D'Emilio, "Gay Politics and Community in San
                  Francisco Since WW 2," Hidden from History (456-
                  476)

November 26:   THE REAGAN ERA AND "SEXUAL MINORITIES"

                Reading:

                Faderman, Odd Girls and Twilight Lovers (246-302)
                *Eric Rofes, "Gay Lib vs. Aids: Averting Civil War in
                    the 1990s," Out/Look, spr 1990 (8-17)
                *Marlon Riggs, "Ruminations of a Snap Queen,"
                    Out/Look, spr 1991 (12-19)
                *Allan Berube, et al., "Queer Nation," Out/Look,
                    winter 1991 (14-23)

December 3:   DISCUSSION OF RESEARCH PROJECTS

HISTORY 661

SEXUALITIES
HISTORIES/THEORIES

FALL, 1997

Carroll Smith-Rosenberg
G 415 Mason Hall
Office Hours. Th 2-5, Fri 2-5
    call for appointment -- 763-1460
email address: csmithro@umich.edu

Sexuality pervades the modern world. It is central to our definitions of pleasure and pain, central to our self-image, central as well to the production and deployment of power and knowledge. It dominates both popular culture and high theory. In its more violent forms, rape, for example, or castration, sexuality plays a critical role in the creation of modern nation states and national identities. (The bodies of raped women guard the borders of modern India and Pakistan, Serbia, Croatia and Bosnia.) Sexualized rhetoric legitimated Europe's domination of the world. The sexual exploitation of Native American and African women has characterized European/African/American relations from the 15th to the 20th century. On the domestic front, for the past 30 years, sexual issues have dominated Congressional debates, Supreme Court decisions, national and Local elections. They have cloaked the New Right and extended governmental power into the most private spheres.

This course explores the modern construction of sexuality, beginning with the Renaissance. We will explore examples drawn from Europe, the Americas and South Asia. We will examine the central role sexuality plays in the production of modern knowledge/power grids, the embodiment of modern republican states, nationalist and colonizing projects. Our focus will be multi-disciplinary and cross cultural. We will work to locate sexual beliefs and practices within specific cultures, times and social groups. The impact of class, race and gender will be central to our analyses. The course will begin with Sigmund Freud and Michel Foucault, move on to an exploration of French psychoanalytic feminism with works by Julia Kristeva, Luce Irigaray, and Rosi Braidotti, explore the suggestions of symbolic anthropologist Mary Douglas, critical legal theorist Drucilla Cornell, feminist post-structuralists Sue Ellen Case and Judith Butler, political scientist Carole Pateman. We will read novels and short stories, watch movies, read histories. We will examine aspects of homosexuality and heterosexuality, incest, slavery, abortion, prostitution, pornography, transvestism -- and still other aspects of everyday sexuality.

This course is a colloquium -- not a research seminar. Focus will be on the weekly readings and on class discussions. Consequently, there will be no research paper. Rather class members will be responsible for writing a 1-2 page paper each week analyzing the week's readings. These papers must be handed in at the beginning of each class meeting. If you have not read the assignments and do not have a paper, please do not come to class. Class discussions only work if all members of the class are fully prepared and ready to enter into analysis and debate. Remember there are never any right or wrong answers. The only error is silence.

* indicates books ordered at Shaman Drum Book Store

** indicates articles and chapters xeroxed and placed in the History Graduate lounge, First Floor, Connector Building. and in the American Culture Library, G410 Mason

All books are also on reserve in the Undergraduate Library.

Sept. 9.

I. INTRODUCTION.

A discussion of various aspects of sexuality and approaches to its study.

II. COMPILING AN ANALYTIC TOOL CHEST

Sept. 16. SEXING THE KNOWLEDGE/POWER GRID

Readings:
* Michel Foucault, History of Sexuality, v. I.
* Rosi Braidotti, Patterns of Dissonance, Introduction, ch 3-4.

Sept. 23. ENGENDERING THE SEXUAL UNCONSCIOUS

Readings:
* Sigmund Freud, Dora
** _____, "The Aetiology of Hysteria" (1896)
** Judith Herman, MD, excerpts from Trauma and Recovery

Sept. 30 PERMEABLE BOUNDARIES: PHYSICAL/SOCIAL BODIES

Readings:
** Douglas, Mary, Natural Symbols, ch
** Peter Stallybrass and Allon White, Politics and Poetics

of Transgression, Introduction, ch 1 & 4.

Oct. 7 **REFUSING THE LAW OF THE SAME.**
FEMINIST PSYCHOANALYTIC VISIONS/VOICES

Visiting Lecturer -- Professor Domna Stanton, Romance Language
Department and Women's Studies Program

Readings:
*   Braidotti, _Patterns_, ch 1,5,8,
** Braidotti, _Nomadic Subjects_, "Introduction"

additional essays to be announced

III. **HISTORICAL APPLICATIONS: CONSTITUTING THE BODY POLITIC**

Oct. 14. **EMBODYING THE EMERGENT BRITISH BOURGEOISIE**

Readings:
*   Daniel Defoe, _Moll Flanders_

Oct. 21 **CORPOREALLY MAPPING OF THE MODERN METROPOLIS.**

Readings:
*   Judith Walkowitz. _The City of Dreadful Delights_

Oct. 28 **PASSING THROUGH THE BODY OF MODERNITY**

Readings:
** Martha Vicinus, "Turn-of-the Century Male Impersonation
        Rewriting the Romance Plot," in _Sexualities in
        Victorian Britain_, eds, Andrew H. Miller and
        James Eli Adams, ch 10.

**   Judith Butler, _Gender Trouble_, 1, "Subjects of
        Sex/Gender/Desire," pp. 1-34
        and 3,iv "Bodily Inscriptions, Performative
        Subversions," pp. 128-49

____, ch.4, "Paris is Burning," in _Bodies that Matter_
        pp. 121-40

** Joan Riviera, "Masquerade..."

** Sue Ellen Case, "The Butch Femme Aesthetic,"

and the film "Paris is Burning"

214

IV. POLITICIZING SEXUALITY/SEXUALIZING POWER

Nov 4.   BY-PASSING THE KNOWLEDGE/POWER GRID

Readings:
*   Nella Larsen , Passing in Quicksand and Passing

      Deborah McDowall, "Introduction" in Quicksand and
      Passing

** Earl Lewis and Heidi Ardizzone, " A Modern Cinderella:
      Race, Sexuality, and Social Class in the Rhonelander
      Case," International Labor and Working-Class History, no.
      51 (Spring, 1997), pp. 129-147.

** "The Rhinelander Case," documents 1924-1925

** J. Butler, ch 6, "Passing, Queering: Nella Larsen's
      Psychoanalytic Challenge," in Bodies that
      Matter, pp. 167-186.

and the film: "Pinky"

Nov. 11.   INSCRIBING SEXUAL POWER: THE OTHER BODY AND THE MAPPING
           OF POWER.

Readings:
*   James Baldwin, "Going to the Man," in Going to the Man

      Ida Wells Barnett, Southern Horrors and Other Writings.
      The Anti-Lynching Campaign of Ida B. Wells,
      1892-1900

Nov. 14.   EMBODYING THE NATION STATE:
           NATIONALISM AND ENGENDERED VIOLENCE.

Guest lecturer Professor Sumathi Ramaswamy, University of
Pennsylvania

will discuss engendering the maps of national consciousness

Readings: to be announced

NOTE THE CHANGE OF CLASS DATE. WE WILL MEET TWICE THE WEEK OF NOV
10TH   ON TUES NOV 11 AND FRI NOV 14TH
      there will be no class meeting Tues Nov. 25th, the Tues before
      Thanksgiving!!!

Nov. 18 SEXUALIZING EMPIRES/FRACTURING RACE

Readings:

* Ann Stoller, Race and the Education of Desire. Foucault's History of Sexuality and the Colonial Order of Things.

** Sandor Gilman. "The Hottentot and the Prostitute," & "Black Sexuality and Modern Consciousness" in Henry Lewis Gates, Race, Writing and
** Gayatri Chakravorty Spivak. "Three Women's Texts and a Critique of Imperialism" ibid.

Dec. 2 EMBODYING THE LIBERAL REPUBLIC

Readings:

* Carole Pateman, Sexual Contract

** Lynn Hunt, "The Imagery of Radicalism" and "The Many Bodies of Marie Antoinette"

** Lucienne Frappier-Mazur, "The Social Body: Disorder and Ritual in Sade's Story of Juliette

** Peggy Watson, "Civil Society and the Politicisation of Difference in Eastern Europe," in press.

** Carroll Smith-Rosenberg, "Violently Excluding Women: The First Contract with America."

ADDITIONAL SUGGESTED READINGS:

** Mona Harrington, "What Exactly is Wrong with the Liberal State as an Agent of Change?"

** Anne Phillips "Universal Pretensions in Political Thought"

Dec. 9 RE-FORMING THE LIBERAL STATE:
       FEMINIST CRITICAL LEGAL THEORY

Readings:
* Drucilla Cornell, The Imaginary Domain. Abortion, Pornography & Sexual Harassment

additional readings to be announced

BODIES:

PERFORMED and REPRESENTED, CONSTITUTED and CORPOREAL

WOMEN'S STUDIES 698/HISTORY 760

Carroll Smith-Rosenberg

University of Michigan
Fall, 1996

READING ASSIGNMENTS

September 4 INTRODUCTION: MANY BODIES FORM HUMANITY

September 11 THE TWO BODIES OF SYMBOLIC ANTHROPOLOGY:
THE PHYSICAL AND THE SOCIAL

Readings:

Mary Douglas, Natural Symbols,
Introduction and chs.2,4,5,6,7,8,9,10

Victor Turner, The Ritual Process, Forward
and chs 3-4.

September 18 HISTORICAL AND POLITICAL APPLICATIONS --
REVOLUTIONARY FRANCE

Readings:

Lucienne Frappier-Mazur, Writing the Orgy,
Power and Parody in Sade

Marquis de Sade, Philosophy in the Bedroom

September 25 OTHER POLITICAL BODIES. FEMINISM AND ABORTION,
PORNOGRAPHY AND THE LAW

Readings:
Drucilla Cornell, The Imaginary Domain

Rosi Braidotti, Nomadic Subjects,
"Mothers, Monsters and Machines"

October 2 SEXUALIZING SCIENCE/POLITICIZING DIFFERENCES

217

Readings:

Donna Haraway, <u>Simians, Cyborgs and Women.</u>
<u>The Reinvention of Nature</u>

Braidotti, <u>Nomadic Subjects,</u>   Intro and
   chs 1,4

October 9   **COLONIZED BODIES: ANTHROPOLOGY REVISITED**

Readings:
Ann Laura Stoler, <u>Race and the Education</u>
<u>of Desire.   Foucault's History of</u>
<u>Sexuality and the Colonial Order of</u>
<u>Things.</u>

October 16   **PASSING CREOLE: SHADOWING BRITANNIA. RACE AND**
IDENTITY IN THE CARIBBEAN

Readings:
Mary Prince, <u>The Autobiography of Mary</u>
<u>Prince</u>

October 23   **E-RACING SCIENCE**

Readings:
James Jones, <u>Bad Blood</u>

October 30   **THE STORIES THE LAW TELLS**

Readings:

November 6   **THE RETURN OF THE FRENCH -- OR QUEER PERFORMING**

Readings:

"More Gender Trouble: Feminism Meets Queer
Theory." Judith Butler, ed. <u>Differences.</u>
<u>A Journal of Feminist Cultural Studies</u>,
v.6,   Summer-Fall, 1994

Class will recess to proceed on their individual research project,
They will continue to meet individually with me -- on a weekly or
bi-weekly basis.   The last two sessions of the class, we will
regather to read and discuss the research papers.

Spring 1994

Women's History/ Women's Voices:
Identity, Authority and Power in American History

Carroll Smith-Rosenberg

WOMEN'S VOICES.
WOMEN AS AUTHORS.
FEMALE AUTHORITY.
THE WORLD ACCORDING TO WOMEN.

How would America's past appear if we saw it only through women's eyes, women's words?

How would women's lives appear, if we saw them only in women's writings?

What new light does the phenomenon of women writers shed on the relation of authorship and authority?

This course examines the diverse writings of America's many different women. We will explore women's narratives (slave narratives, Euro-American women's narratives of Indian captivity, American Indian women's narratives of colonial oppression); women's personal letters and journals (the teenage letters of young Quaker and Episcopal girls in 18th-century Philadelphia, the teenage diary of education pioneer and Bryn Mawr College president, M. Carey Thomas, the letters of sophisticated women artists and Kansas farm wives); women's autobiographies -- and women's fiction. The course will examine great American novels SUCH as Toni Morrison's Beloved ,novels of protest, Kate Chopin's The Awakening and Charlotte Perkins Gilman's, Yellow Wallpaper, novels about America's forgotten women, Hurston's Their Eyes Were Watching God, Leslie Silko's Storyteller, or Yezierska's The Bread Givers.

The course has three specific goals:

(1)   To examine American society and America's history.

America's historians have most commonly been men, whose histories, only naturally, have reflected their authors' experiences and perspectives. This course will engage in an experiment. Will a different image of America emerge if, rather than reading male historians, we read the writings of women commenting on the times in which they lived? We will examine the writings of rich and poor women, of women who attended elite colleges and of those who lived in slave quarters, of those who chronicled New York's elite during the Gilded Age and Florida sharecroppers in the age of lynching, of white women who helped invent American racism and of black and American Indian women who reflected on its burdens.

(2) The course is concerned not only about American history in general, but about the history of America's women, in particular. It will seek to reconstruct women's experiences, world views, presumptions and resentments -- as much as possible as women lived them, as little as possible as men constructed them. And we will bear always in mind that there is not a normative American woman, but many American women -- American Indian, Hispanic American, African American, Asian American and Euro-American women; Protestant, Jewish, Catholic and atheist women; urban and rural; rich, poor and middle class. This course will seek out the multiple, contested and contesting voices of America's women.

(3) It is not enough to examine women's experiences. The course will also explore the concept and the practices of authorship and of reading. Authority underwrites authorship; it is essential to the act of writing. Yet throughout much of American history, significant social and legal barriers operated to limit women's access to the public prints. Throughout the colonial period the majority of women, even of white women, were illiterate. Until Reconstruction, southern state laws had made it illegal to teach African American women to read or write. After that de facto peonage, deprived poor African American women of access to education. American Indian women were systematically denied any claim to a legitimate voice. Far into the nineteenth century, legal codes deprived married women -- even white married women -- of legal and economic subjectivity. Immigrant women, sent to factories or sweated in home industries as children, married early, beset with children, oppressed by poverty, rarely achieved much education. Few women could claim what Virginia Woolf considered necessary to write - - 500 pounds and a room of their own.

Yet as Nathaniel Hawthorne complained, women were damned scribblers. African American women, American Indian women, immigrant girls, depressed housewives, divorced and abandoned women who struggled to support themselves and their children, educated and privileged women -- all these different women wrote about themselves, the worlds that shaped them and which their presence transformed. The course will examine the kinds of SELF-hood women writers asserted and the ways their books encouraged a sense of Self and of SELF-respect (SELFhood) in their women readers. How did women gain the ability to challenge, invert, subvert the culture that would have had them remain silent? How did that world form and inform their sense of SELF? What do women writers tell us not only about America and America's women, about sex and ambition, work and men, but even more importantly about writing, authorship and author-ity -- about the construction of self in a world that would repress that self or brand it mad, hysterical, foolish -- or aggressive?

Writers require readers -- as do publishers. Reading, like writing, is a socially constructed practice. Social, political, economic, demographic and cultural practices shape readers, determining who can read, what they read and how they read. The course will also address the production of the American woman reader and the complex interaction that existed between authors, their imagined readers, actual readers and the world that framed them all.

The class crosses disciplinary boundaries. Examining the history of America's varied women, the material, ideological and political forces affecting their lives, silencing or encouraging them to develop a public voice, it draws heavily upon recent feminist literary criticism and, more broadly, on post-structuralist and material-cultural approaches to the analysis of authorship, autobiography and authority, of subjectivity and ideology. Nor will it ignore the contributions folklorists and anthropologists have made to the analysis of these subjects.

CLASS REQUIREMENTS.

1. Class members will be expected to read every assignment.

2. A one to two page paper (not a paragraph longer!) addressing questions asked of each week's reading must be submitted at the beginning of each class.

3. Teams of two students will take responsibility for additional research and leading class discussion for one of the classes beginning February 15.

4. These will be the only research and written assignments for the class. There will be no final exam.

5. **I DO NOT GIVE INCOMPLETES!**

January 11	Introductory meeting -- discussing the course's theoretical premises
January 18	The Woman Writer: Engendering Selfhood and Subjectivity, Author-ity and Ideology.

January 18

READINGS:
(bulk pack)
Roland Barthes, "Death of the Author," from Images, Music,
Paul Smith, "Preface" & "Note on Terminology" in Addressing the Subject.
Catherine Belsey, Critical Practice, ch. 3-4-5.
Annette Kollodny, "A Map for Misreading: or, Gender and the Interpretation of Literary Texts," from New Literary History v. 11, 1979-80.
New York Times Magazine, January   1994.
New York Times, January 6, 1994.

Class will begin by watching a video of Virginia's Woolf's "A Room of One's Own."

January 25

White women write colonialism and racism.
The American Indian as negative other...

READINGS:
(bulk pack)
Mary Rowlandson's Captivity Narrative
read first:
Theda Purdue, "Cherokee Women and the Trail of Tears," Journal of Women's History, v. 1, Spring, 1989.
Richard Slotkin, "Introduction"
Gayatri Spivak, "Three Women's Texts and a Critique of Imperialism."
Raman Gutierrez, "When Padre Jesus Came the Corn Mothers went away."

February 1

Life, Liberty and Property. Novels of Seduction, the American Revolution and Empowering Women as Subjects.

READINGS:
Hannah Foster, The Coquette
    House of our Own (HOOO)

Cathi Davidson, "Privileging the _Feme Covert_: The Sociology of Sentimental Fiction," (ch. 6) in Davidson, Revolution and the Word.

February 8   Life, Liberty and Property. Slavery, Racism and Women's resistance. African American Women Write Back. The voice of the 1860s.

READINGS.
Harriet Jacobs, Incidents in the Life of a Slave Girl (HOO)
Jean Yellin, "Introduction," to Jacobs.
Valerie Smith, "Form and Ideology in Three Slave Narratives," in Smith Self-Discovery and Authority in Afro-American Narrative. (bulk pack)

February 15   History, Memory and Responsibility.
African American women rewrite Racism and Slavery, The voice of the 1980s.

Beginnings of class presentations

READINGS.
Toni Morrison. Beloved (HOO)

Class will watch video of Toni Morrison.

February 22   Rural women in the North. Women rewrite the country

Sarah Orne Jewett. Country of the Pointed Firs (HOO)

March 1   White middle-class Women rewrite Ambition and Education
Feminism in the 1870s

READINGS.
Marjorie Dobkin, The Making of a Feminist. (HOO)
Smith-Rosenberg, "The Female World of Love and Ritual"; "New Woman as Androgen" (bulk pack)

223

March 15	White American Women rewrite Self and Marriage. Feminism in the 1890s

READINGS.
(HOO)
Kate Chopin, The Awakening
Charlotte Perkins Gilman, Yellow Wallpaper |
| March 22 | The New Immigrant Woman Re-views Class and Self Feminism in the 1920s

READINGS.
(HOO)
Anya Yezierska, The Bread Givers |
| March 29 | African American Women rewrite Self and Marriage, Sex and Gender Feminism in the 1930s

READINGS.
(HOO)
Zora Neal Hurston, Their Eyes Were Watching God |
| April 5 | American Indian Women rewrite America Feminism in the 1970s.

READINGS.
Leslie Marion Silko, Storyteller |
| April 12 | Speaking with Different Voices in a Multi-Cultural American.

Gloria   Anzaldua,   Borderlands/La   Frontera
      (HOOO)
bulk pack:
Adrienne Rich, "Compulsory Heterosexuality,"
Barbara Smith, "Black Lesbians -- Who will Fight for Our Lives But Us?" in Barbara Smith, Home Girls

Video: "Oranges Are Not the Only Fruit" |

April 19   The New Feminists -- the New Backlash -- the New
            State
            Feminism in the 1980s.

            READINGS.
            Margaret Atwood. Handmaids Tale.

Reading materials for the course can be purchased at:

Bulkpack. Campus Copy   3907 Walnut Street

BOOKS have been ordered at **A HOUSE OF OUR OWN,** 3920 Spruce Street

Harriet Jacobs, Incidents in the Live of a Slave Girl (Harvard
                University Press edition, Jean Yellen editor)
Hannah Foster, The Coquette
Toni Morrison. Beloved
Sarah Orne Jewett. Country of the Pointed Firs
Marjorie Dobkin, The Making of a Feminist.
Kate Chopin, The Awakening
Charlotte Perkins Gilman, Yellow Wallpaper
Anya Yezierska, The Bread Givers
Zora Neal Hurston, Their Eyes Were Watching God
Leslie Marion Silko, Storyteller
Gloria Anzaldua, Borderlands/La Frontera
Margaret Atwood, Handmaid's Tale

If members of the class prefer, books can also be put on reserve at
Rosengarten Library.   Please discuss this matter with the
professor.

PRINCETON UNIVERSITY
Department of History

GENDER IN AMERICA: COLONIAL, REVOLUTIONARY, AND VICTORIAN SOCIET

HISTORY 384

Fall Term 1996-97

Professor C. Stansell
Dr. Allyn

Books are available for purchase in the University Store. In addition, there is a small course packet of articles which can be purchased at Print-It, 12 Witherspoon Street, Princeton.

Required:
Cott, Bonds of Womanhood
Cott, Root of Bitterness
Dubois, Feminism and Suffrage
Fox-Genovese, The Plantation Household
Gates, Six Women's Slave Narratives
Johnson and Wilentz, Kingdom of Matthias
Karlsen, Devil in the Shape of a Woman
Kerber, Women of the Republic
Schneir, Feminism: The Essential Historical Writings
Sklar and Dublin, Women and Power in American History
Smith-Rosenberg, Disorderly Conduct
Stansell, City of Women
Ulrich, Goodwives

Course Requirements:

a)   Four short (2 - 3) page papers, to be discussed in precept (papers must be ready for class to b graded -- no exceptions or extensions.)
b)   One midterm paper: an analysis of a woman's slave narrative (7 - 9 pgs.)
c)   Final Exam (take home)
d)   Precept attendance. Please note: IF YOU MISS MORE THAN TWO PRECEPTS, YOU WILL FAIL THIS COURSE.

Introduction: September 12

Week One: Making a New World: Power, Conquest and Sexual Difference
September 16, 19

Guttierez, "The Pueblo World" and Brown, "the Anglo-Algonquian Gender Frontier" (packet)
"Carolina Women Observed" in Root of Bitterness

226

Week Two: Divisions of Labor and Family Government in the Colonies
September 24, 26

Ulrich, Goodwives
"Statutes on Slave Descent," "Diary of Mary Cooper" in Root of Bitterness
* **Short paper due in class**

Week Three: Disorders of Gender
October 1, 3

Karlsen, Devil in the Shape of a Woman, chapts. 1-6
"Church Trial of Ann Hibbens," Root of Bitterness

Week Four: Revolution
October 8, 10

Kerber, Women of the Republic
Abigail Adams letter and Wollstonecraft, "Vindications of the Rights of Women" in Schneir, Feminism
Eliza Southgate letters, Root of Bitterness
* **Short paper due in class**

Week Five: Slavery and the Powers of Gender
October 15, 17

Fox-Genovese, The Plantation Household, chapts. 2-3, 6-7
Louisa McCord on the enfranchisement of women, Root of Bitterness

Choose one of these narratives in Six Women's Slave Narratives:

       The Story of Mattie Jackson
       The History of Mary Prince or
       Lucy Delaney, From the Darkness Cometh the Light
* **Drafts of papers due to be discussed in class.**

Week Six: Northern Households: Changing "The Home"
October 22, 24

Cott, Bonds of Womanhood, chapts. 1-4
Catherine Beecher, "Peculiar Responsibilities of American Women;" "A New York Woman on a North Carolina Plantation," Root of Bitterness
* **Paper (7 - 9 pages) due by 3 p.m., Friday, October 25, History Department Office.**

FALL RECESS

Week Seven: Evangelical Religion
November 5, 7

Johnson and Wilentz, The Kingdom of Matthias
Smith-Rosenberg, "Beauty, the Beast and the Militant Woman," in Disorderly Conduct

Truth, "Ain't I a Woman" in Schneir, Feminism, p. 93 / alternative text (handout)

Week Eight: Work, Poverty and the Industrial Revolution
November 12, 14

Dublin\Sklar, Women and Power, articles by Blewett, Dublin, Lasser
"Petition for a 10 Hour Day," Root of Bitterness

Week Nine: Anti-slavery and the "Woman Movement"
November 19, 21

Dubois, Feminism and Suffrage, chapt. 1
In Schneir, Feminism

       Grimke, Letters on the Equality of the Sexes, p. 35
       Declaration of Sentiments, Seneca Falls, p. 76
       Truth, "What Time of Night It Is," p. 96 and "Keeping the Thing Going...", p. 128
       Stone, "Marriage of Lucy Stone Under Protest" and "Disappointment is the Lot of
           Woman," pp. 103 ff.
* **Short paper due in class**

Week Ten: Women and Men in the Cities
November 26

Stansell, City of Women, chapts. 1-3
"Margaret McCarthy Writes Home" and "Working Girls of Boston," Root of Bitterness
Smith-Rosenberg, "Davy Crocket as Trickster," Disorderly Conduct

Week Eleven: Disorderly Women Revisited: Sexuality
December 3, 5

Stansell, City of Women, finish
in Schneir, Feminism, Woodhull and Claflin, selections, pp. 143-54
"Abortion in New York," Root of Bitterness
Smith-Rosenberg, "The Abortion Movement and the AMA," Disorderly Conduct
* **Short paper due in class**

Week Twelve: The Civil War, Reconstruction and the Question of Equal Rights
December 10, 12

Dubois, Feminism and Suffrage, 2-3, 6
"A Freedwoman Before the Southern Claim's Commission," Root of Bitterness
Hodes, "The Sexualization of Reconstruction Politics" (packet)
*Short paper due in class

6. Graduate and Undergraduate Courses and Seminars on Race and Ethnicity

HISTORY 506:402 RESEARCH ON BLACK WOMEN

Professor Mia Bay
Office: Van Dyck 002D, Tel. 932-6695
Office Hours: Thurs 4-5, and by appointment
email: bay@zodiac.rutgers.edu

COURSE DESCRIPTION

This seminar is an introduction to research in African-American women's history. This history is a relatively new field: the story of black women has been largely omitted from our historical literature until quite recently. Historians have tended to study either women's history or African-American history, obscuring the historical experience of African-American women. The experiences of black women have also been overlooked because they are poorly documented. A long history of racial oppression and poverty has meant that black women have had few opportunities to record their experiences. Nonetheless, there are a variety historical sources that document the historical experience of black women, ranging from novels and diaries to court testimony. In recent years, historians have begun to use these sources to explore the history of black women.

The course will teach students how to do research in this new field. We will examine the historical sources that can be used to study African-American women and the historical problems involved in reconstructing the history of black women. During the first half of the course our readings and discussions will survey the black female experience from slavery to the civil rights movement. We will read a variety of autobiographies, novels, and historical works, and view several films. Drawing on the readings and class discussions, students will also chose topics and begin to plan their research papers. During the second half of the course students will draft and revise these papers, working together in small groups, and individually with me.

Course Requirements

The weekly reading in this course usually ranges between 100 and 150 pages. Students are expected to do all the reading and will be asked to submit brief comments or questions on each week's reading. Students will also be asked to give a series of presentations on their research topics; and present a 3-5 page paper proposal outlining their project. The final assignment, which you will work on throughout the course, will a 20-page research paper. The course grade will be divided as follows. The paper proposal will count for 15%, participation, presentations and the comment assignments will comprise 35%, and the final paper will be worth 50%.

Required Reading

We will read four books in this course, which will be supplemented by a course packet of xeroxed readings. The packet is available at ABC Duplicating and Design, 308 George St., New Brunswick (just south of the Crossroads Theater, the telephone number is 249-3703). The readings in the packet are not optional and not easily available elsewhere, so be sure to pick up a packet. The following books can be purchased at the Rutgers University Bookstore, and are also available at New Jersey

233

books: Deborah Gray White, Ar'n't I a Woman; Harriet Jacobs, Incidents in the Life of a Slave Girl; [Buy this or , Melton McLaurin, Celia]; Evelyn Brooks Higginbotham, Righteous Discontent, and Melva Beals, Warriors Don't Cry. All readings should also be available on reserve at Alexander library. One copy of the packet will be place on closed reserve.

Research on Black Women - COURSE SCHEDULE

Week 1 (January 17) Introduction

Week 2 (January 24) Enslaved Women

Deborah Gray White, Ar'n't I a Woman 13-160

Week 3 (January 31) Struggle and Survival

Harriet Jacobs, Incidents in the Life of a Slave Girl
                    OR Celia

Week 4 (February 7) Freedom

Deborah Gray White, Ar'n't I a Woman 161-167
Frances Harper, "We Are All Bound Up in this Together" (1866)
Elsa Barclay Brown, "Negotiating and Transforming the Public Sphere: African-American Political Life From Slavery to Freedom"

PAPER TOPICS DUE

Week 5 (February 14) Black Women in the Church

Evelyn Brooks Higginbotham, Righteous Discontent

Week 6 (February 21) Black Women's Activism

Anna Julia Cooper, A Voice From the South, Part 1; Gail Bederman "'Civilization' the Decline of of Middle Class Manliness, and Ida B. Well's Antilynching Campaign; Tera Hunter, "Domination and Resistance: The Politics of Wage Household Labor in New South Atlanta"

FILM: Ida B. Wells

234

Week 7 (February 28) The Harlem Renaissance

Nella Larson, <u>Passing</u>; Elise MacDougal "The Task of Negro Womanhood" in <u>The New Negro</u>, Alain Locke ed.; Hazel Carby, "It Just Be's Dat Way Sometime: The Sexual Politics of Women's Blues," PACKET

Week 8 (March 6) Migration and Depression

Jacqueline Jones, Labor of Love Labor of Sorrow, selections; Darlene Clark Hine, "Rape and the Inner Lives of Black Women in the Middle West: Preliminary Thoughts on a Culture of Dissemblence", "Black Migration to the Urban Midwest, The Gender Dimension"

RECESS

Week 9 (March 20) The Civil Rights Movement

Melva Beals, <u>Warriors Don't Cry</u>

Week 10 (March 27) DRAFTS DUE

Week 11 (April 3) Drafts

Week 12 (April 10) Drafts

Week 13 (April 17) Drafts

Week 14 (April 24) FINAL PAPER DUE

History 335/435; Women's Studies 335
Gender and Ethnicity in American History
Spring Semester 1995
Mondays, 1:40-4:40, Lattimore 431

Professor Lynn Gordon
Rush Rhees 420, 5-9360; Dewey 1-339, 5-7721 (messages)
Home phone: 442-7173 (evenings 8:30-11 and weekends)
Office Hours: Thursday 2-4 in Dewey or by appointment

Course Description: In this seminar we will examine the intersection between two bodies of historical literature--American women's history, and the study of immigration and ethnicity. Among the issues to be considered are: how does gender analysis affect the historiography of American ethnicity, and how does knowledge about immigration and ethnicity affect the study of American women?

Course Requirements: Each class session will be devoted to the analysis and discussion of at least two of the readings and to student reports. To allow students sufficient time for preparation, the class will normally meet every two weeks.

Grades will be determined as follows:
a) attendance and class participation, including submission of at least two discussion questions to the instructor no later than 10 A.M. Monday morning before class. Questions should be left in my mailbox outside the History Department office on the third floor of Rush Rhees Library (1/3 of grade).
b) writing assignment for students registered for 6-8 credits: two papers, 8-10 pages each, one analyzing the work of a particular historian/sociologist of immigration/ethnicity (including a bibliography of his/her work--possible subjects include Oscar Handlin, John Higham, W.E.B. DuBois, Robert Park, Marcus Hansen, Nathan Glazer, Ronald Takaki, John Hope Franklin) and one bibliographic essay on women of a particular ethnic group, relating the literature to general themes in women's history (2/3 of grade) Students with a special interest in writing a research paper as an alternative to these assignments should consult the instructor during the first two weeks of the semester.
c) writing assignment for students registered for 3-4 credits: one of the short papers described above, and a take-home final essay. (2/3 of grade).

All students will be asked to report on their research to the class.

Course Readings (books are on sale at the Barnes and Noble Bookstore and on reserve at Rush Rhees Library)

Bodnar, John, The Transplanted
Deutsch, Sarah, No Separate Refuge (Hispanic women)
Diner, Hasia, Erin's Daughters (Irish women)
Ewen, Elizabeth, Immigrant Women in the Land of Dollars
Gabaccia, Donna, From the Other Side
Glenn, Evelyn Nakano, Issei, Nisei, War Bride (Japanese women)
Glenn, Susan, Daughters of the Shtetl (Eastern European Jewish women)
Gutierrez, Ramon, When Jesus Came, The Corn Mothers Went Away
Handlin, Oscar, The Uprooted
Jones, Jacqueline, Labor of Love, Labor of Sorrow (African American women)
Osofsky, Gilbert, Harlem: Making of A Ghetto
Weinberg, Sydney, World of Our Mothers (Jewish women)
Yans-McLaughlin, Virginia, ed., Immigration Reconsidered
Nancy Hewitt, "Beyond the Search for Sisterhood: American Women's History in the 1980s" (reserve)
Evelyn Brooks-Higginbotham, "African American Women's History and the Metalanguage of Race" (reserve)

Schedule of Classes and Assignments:

January 23rd: Introduction

January 30th: Discussion of essays by Virginia Yans-McLaughlin and Charles Tilly in Immigration Reconsidered; essays by Nancy Hewitt and Evelyn Brooks-Higginbotham; library tour

February 6th: Discussion of Handlin and Bodnar

February 13th: No formal class-- written description of paper topics due; conference with instructor required during normal class time

February 20th: Discussion of Deutsch and Gutierrez

February 27th

March 6th: Discussion of Diner and Evelyn Glenn

March 13th--No class, spring break

March 20th: Discussion of Jones and Osofsky

March 27th--First paper due

April 10th--Discussion of Weinberg and Susan Glenn

April 17th--may be used for presentation of reports

April 24th--Discussion of Ewen and Gabaccia

May 1st--may be used for presentation of reports

May 8th--Student Reports; final papers due from all students

HISTORY OF AFRICAN AMERICAN WOMEN
History 384, Fall 1996
Tuesdays and Thursdays 10:50 a.m. - 12:05 p.m.

Professor Darlene Clark Hine	Office Hours:
Harold Washington Visiting Professor	Tuesdays and Thursdays 12:15-1:15 p.m.
Roosevelt University	and by Appointment
Chicago, Illinois	Room 642

Course Description:

This course surveys the history of African American women from the African background to the present. Readings highlight and explore major themes including Black women's uses of multiple strategies of resistance to exploitation and oppression in an effort to secure survival of themselves and their people and to preserve their humanity. Specific themes include slavery, institution building, migration, organization of clubs, and Black women's roles in the suffrage and civil rights movements. Attendance is mandatory as class participation is a vital part of the course.

Required Reading Texts:

1. Crawford, Vicki, Jacqueline Rouse, and Barbara Woods, editors, *Women and the Civil Rights Movement: Trailblazers and Torchbearers* (Bloomington: Indiana University Press, 1993).

2. Hine, Darlene Clark, *Hine Sight: Black Women and the Re-Construction of American History* (Brooklyn, NY: Carlson Publishing, 1994).

3. Hine, Darlene, Wilma King, and Linda Reed, editors *"We Specialize in the Wholly Impossible": A Reader in Black Women's History* (Brooklyn, NY: Carlson Publishing, 1995).

4. Shaw, Stephanie, *What a Woman Ought to Be and to Do: Black Professional Women Workers During the Jim Crow Era* (Chicago: University of Chicago Press, 1995).

For Graduate Students (Available at RU bookstore and on reserve in library):

5. Gaspar, David Barry and Darlene Clark Hine, *More Than Chattel: Black Women and Slavery in the Americas* (Bloomington: Indiana University Press, 1996).

6. Guy-Sheftall, Beverly, editor, *Words of Fire: An Anthology of African-American Feminist Thought* (NY: The New Press, 1995).

7. Richardson, Marilyn, *Maria W. Stewart: America's First Black Women Political Writer* (Bloomington: Indiana University Press, 1987).

Optional (Available at RU bookstore and on reserve in library):

8. Hine, Darlene Clark, Elsa Barkley Brown, and Rosalyn Terborg-Penn, editors, *Black Women in America: An Historical Encyclopedia* (Brooklyn, NY: Carlson Publishing, Inc., 1993).

COURSE MECHANICS

Undergraduate Students:

1. 40% of Grade:
    Each student will take one examination mid-way through the semester.

2. 40% of Grade:
    Each student will prepare a final paper not to exceed 15 pages due on the last day of classes. The paper must be typed, double-spaced, properly footnoted and proofread.

    The paper should begin with a brief introductory statement in which you indicate your central thesis and comments upon the sources, both primary and secondary, consulted.

    The body of the paper should be coherently organized and the data thoughtfully analyzed. Please make sure that you use quotation marks to indicate information and insights derived from specific books and sources. It is always good form to credit or acknowledge your debt to other scholars. The last three or four pages should include your personal reflections and the conclusions you have drawn from conducting this research. Yes, you may use lectures and class discussions as sources or as a framework for your paper.

    The topic is of your choosing, but you should clear it with me as early as possible. The topic must elaborate on or relate in some meaningful way to the material covered in the course.

3. 20% of Grade:
    Each student is required to attend every class session and to participate actively in the discussions of the assigned readings. All readings must be completed before the day of the discussion. There may be one (or more) unannounced quiz concerning the reading assignments so be prepared.

Graduate Students:

Graduate students are expected to prepare a longer research paper that integrates all of the readings assigned and in addition must reflect original research in primary sources (including manuscript collections, newspapers, oral interviews, or public documents). The paper should not exceed 25 pages and must have a bibliography attached.

The paper is due the last day of class. Students are urged to consult with me concerning the topic prior to October 1st.

Graduate students have the option of taking the midterm examination and having it count for 25% of the final grade. Otherwise the paper and class participation will comprise the final grade for the course.

READING ASSIGNMENTS

August 29   Introduction to Black Women's History

Sept. 3-5   OVERVIEW

Hine, "Lifting the Veil, Shattering the Silence: Black Women's History in Slavery and Freedom," in *Hine Sight*, pp. 3-26.

Higginbotham, "African-American Women's History and the Metalanguge of Race," in *"Wholly Impossible,"* pp. 3-24.

Robertson, "Africa into the Americas? Slavery and Woman, the Family, and the Gender Division of Labor," in *More than Chattel*, pp. 3-40.

Hine, "Rape and the Inner Lives of Black Women: Thoughts on the Culture of Dissemblance," in *Hine Sight*, pp. 37-47.

Brown, "'What Has Happened Here': The Politics of Difference in Women's History and Feminist Politics," in *"Wholly Impossible,"* pp. 39-54.

Sept. 10-12   AFRICAN BACKGROUND

Thornton, "Sexual Demography: The Impact of the Slave Trade on Family Structure," in *Wholly Impossible*, pp. 57-65.

Klein, "African Women in the Atlantic Slave Trace," in *"Wholly Impossible,"* pp. 67-75.

Lovejoy, "Concubinage and the Status of Women Slaves in Early Colonial Northern Nigera," in *"Wholly Impossible,"* pp. 77-101.

Sept. 17-19   SLAVERY IN THE U.S. I

Steckel, "Women, Work, and Health Under Plantation Slavery in the U.S.," in *More Than Chattel*, pp. 43-60.

Gundersen, Joan, "The Double Bonds of Race and Sex: Black and White Women in a Colonial Virginia Parish," in *"Wholly Impossible,"* pp. 189-209.

Cody, "Cycles of Work and of Childbearing: Seasonality in Women's's Lives on Low Country Plantations," in *More Than Chattel*, pp. 61-78.

Sept. 24-26 SLAVERY IN THE U.S. II

Hine, "Female Slave Resistance: The Economics of Sex," in *Hine Sight*, pp. 27-36.

King, "'Suffer with Them Till Death': Slave Women and Their Children in Nineteenth-Century America," in *More Than Chattel*, pp. 147-168.

Stevenson, "Gender Convention, Ideals, and Identity Among Antebellum Virginia Slave Women," in *More Than Chattel*, pp. 169-190.

Gould, "Urban Slavery-Urban Freedom: The Manumission of Jacqueline Lemelle," in *More Than Chattel*, pp. 298-314.

Oct. 1 FREE BLACK WOMEN
No class
on Oct.3 Newman, "Black Women in the Era of the American Revolution in Pennsylvania," in *Wholly Impossible,* pp. 211-224.

Locke, "From Three-Fifths to Zero: Implications of the Constitution for African-American Women, 1787-1870," in *Wholly Impossible,* pp. 225-234.

Johnson, "Free African-American Women in Savannah, 1800-1860: Affluence and Autonomy Amid Diversity," in *Wholly Impossible,* pp. 237-252.

Schweinger, "Property Owning Free African-American Women in the South, 1800-1870," in *Wholly Impossible,* pp. 253-279.

Oct. 8-10 BLACK WOMEN AND EMANCIPATION?

Frankel, "The Southern Side of 'Glory': Mississippi African-American Women During the Civil War," in *Wholly Impossible,* pp. 335-341.

Butler, "Still in Chains: Black Women in Western Prisons, 1865-1910," in *Wholly Impossible,* pp. 321-334.

Mann, "Slavery, Sharecropping, and Sexual Inequality," in *Wholly Impossible,* pp. 281-302.

Oct. 15-17 BLACK WOMEN'S ERA I

Hine, "Black Women in the Middle West: The Michigan Experience," in *Hine Sight*, pp. 59-85.

Reid, "'A Career to Build, a People to Serve, a Purpose to Accomplish': Race, Class, Gender, and Detroit's First Black Women Teachers, 1865-1916," in *Wholly Impossible,* pp. 303-320.

BLACK WOMEN'S ERA I, continued

Hunter, "Domination and Resistance: The Politics of Wage Household Labor in New South Alabama,: in *Wholly Impossible,* "pp. 343-357.

Hunt, "Clothing as an Expression of History: The Dress of African-American Women in Georgia, 1880-1915," in *Wholly Impossible,* "pp. 393-404.

Oct. 22-24   BLACK WOMEN'S ERA II

Shaw, *What a Woman Ought to Be and to Do* (entire book).

Shaw, "Black Club Women and the Creation of the National Association of Colored Women," in *Wholly Impossible,* "pp. 433-447.

Bederman, "'Civilization' the Decline of Middle-Class Manliness, and Ida B. Well's Antilynching Campaign (1892-94)," in *Wholly Impossible,* "pp. 407-432.

MIDTERM EXAMINATION WEEK OCTOBER 29-31

Nov. 5-7   MIGRATION, REFORM, AND URBANIZATION

Hine, "Black Migration to the Urban Midwest: The Gender Dimension, 1915-1945," in *Hine Sight,* 87-107.

_____, "'We Specialize in the Wholly Impossible': The Philanthropic Work of Black Women," in *Hine sight,* pp. 109-128.

Williams, "And Still I Rise: Black Women and Reform, Buffalo, New York, 1900-1940," in *Wholly Impossible,* "pp. 521-541.

Gordon, "Black and White Visions of Welfare: Women's Welfare Activism, 1890-1945," in *Wholly Impossible,* "pp. 449-485.

Rodrique, "The Black Community and the Birth Control Movement," in *Wholly Impossible,* "pp. 505-520.

Nov. 12-14   PROTEST, WORK, AND CLASS CONSCIOUSNESS

Terborg-Penn, "Discontented Black Feminists: Prelude and Postscript to the Passage of the Nineteenth Amendment," in *Wholly Impossible,* "pp. 487-503.

Harley, "When Your Work Is Not Who You Are: The Development of a Working Class Consciousness Among Afro-American Women," in *Wholly Impossible,* "pp. 25-37.

Hine, "The Housewives' League of Detroit: Black Women and Economic Nationalism," in *Hine Sight,* pp. 129-145

PROTEST, WORK, AND CLASS CONSCIOUSNESS, continued

_____, "Mabel K. Staupers and the Integration of Black Nurses into the Armed Forces during World War II," in *Hine Sight*, pp. 183-201.

Nov. 19-21   CIVIL RIGHTS AND THE MODERN ERA

Fleming, "Black Women Activists and the Student Nonviolent Coordinating Committee: The Case of Ruby Doris Smith Robinson," in *"Wholly Impossible,"* pp. 561-577.

Hine, "The Black Studies Movement: Afrocentric-Traditionalist-Feminist Paradigm for the Next Stage," in *Hine Sight*, pp. 235-250.

Nov. 26   REVIEW

Nov. 28   Thanksgiving

Dec. 3   ALL PAPERS ARE DUE
NO EXCUSES, PLEASE -- LATE PAPERS SEVERELY PENALIZED.

BLACK WOMEN'S HISTORY AND AUTOBIOGRAPHY

Darlene Clark Hine	*Northwestern University*
Avalon Professor	*Evanston, Illinois*
Spring Term 1997	*Fisk Hall, 217*

LECTURES AND RECOMMENDED READINGS

Required Text:
Black Women in America: An Historical Encyclopedia edited by, Darlene Clark Hine, Elsa Barkley Brown, and Rosalyn Terborg-Penn (Bloomington: Indiana University Press, 1995).

APRIL 8, 1997

1. Overview of Black Women's Studies: History, Literary Criticism, and Autobiography

Readings:
Autobiography •Association for the Study of African American Life and History • Association of Black Women Historians • Black Studies

Biographical Entries:
Mary Frances Berry • Letitia Woods Brown • Helen Gray Edmonds • Drusilla Dunjee

APRIL 15, 1997

2. First Voices: In Slavery and Freedom

Readings:
Abolition Movement • Colored Female Free Produce Society • Civil War and Reconstruction • Federal Writers Project • Slave Narratives • Free Black Women in Antebellum North • Free Black Women in Antebellum South • Slave Narratives • Slavery

Biographical Entries:
Mary Ann Shadd • Frances Ellen Watkin Harper • Harriet Jacobs • Sojourner Truth • Harriet Ross Tubman • Elizabeth Keckley • Susie Baker King Taylor • Charlotte L. Forten Grimke

APRIL 22, 1997

3. Definitions and Meanings of Black Womanhood: Images and Struggles

Readings:
Aunt Jemima • Sapphire • Mammy • Memorabilia • Beauty Culture • Kansas Federation of
Colored Women's Clubs • National Association of Colored Women • Neighborhood Union •
Atlanta • New Era Club • North Carolina Federation of Colored Women's Clubs •
Southeastern Association of Colored Women's Clubs • Temperance Work in the Nineteenth
Century • Woman's Improvement Club, Indianapolis

Biographical Entries:
Janie Porter Barrett • Elizabeth Lindsay Davis • Josephine St. Pierre Ruffin • Mary Eliza
Church Terrell • Fannie Barrier Williams • Josephine Silone Yates • Mary Morris Burnett
Talbert • Madame C. J. Walker • Maggie Lena Walker

APRIL 29, 1997

4. Work Patterns, Political Agenda, Black Women's Agency

Readings:
Alpha Suffrage Club • Anti-lynching Movement • Domestic Workers in the North • Domestic
Workers in the South • Physicians-Nineteenth Century • Education • International Council of
Women of the Darker Races • Law: Oppression and Resistance • Suffrage • World War I •
National Association of Colored Graduate Nurses • National Council of Negro Women

Biographical Entries:
Mary McLeod Bethune • Charlotte Hawkins Brown • Victoria Earle Matthews • Adella Hunt
Logan • Rollins Sisters (Ruffin, Terrell, Wells-Barnett, Nannie Hellen Burroughs) • Amy
Euphemia Jacque Garvey • Amy Ashwood Garvey • Anna Julia Haywood Cooper • Mary
Eliza Mahoney • Anna De Costa Banks

MAY 6, 1997

5. Race, Gender and Class in the Social Construction of Black Women's Identity: Migrations

Readings:
The Middle Class • Alpha Kappa Alpha Sorority • Associations for the Protection of Negro
Women • The Depression • The Housewives League of Detroit • Hartshorn Memorial College
• Spelman College • National Urban League • National Urban League Guild • National
Association for the Advancement of Colored People • Universal Negro Improvement
Association • National Council of Negro Women • Birth Control Movement • Black
Nationalism

6. In the Kingdom of Culture: Resistance, Language, and Silence

Readings:
Blues and Jazz • Rhythm and Blues • Harlem Renaissance • Vaudeville and Musical Theater • Composers • Dance Companies • Artistic Directors • Radio • Theater • Sweet Honey in the Rock

Biographical Entries:
Dorothy Dandridge • Hattie McDaniel • Butterfly McQueen • Katherine Dunham • Judith Jameson • Pearl Primus • Ma Rainey • Bessie Smith • Alberta Hunter • Lena Horne •Jackie "Moms" Mabley • Philippa Duke Schuyler • Marian Anderson • Josephine Baker • Nina Simone • Zora Neale Hurston • Era Bell Thompson • Ella Fitzgerald • Billie Holiday • Sarah Vaughan • Margaret Taylor Gross Burroughs • Margaret Walker Alexander • Faith Ringgold • Lois Mailou Jones • Elizabeth Catlett

May 20, 1997

7. Multiple Consciousness: Community Making and Social Change

Readings:
Baptist Church • Black Panther Party • Civil Rights Movement • Highlander Folk School • Labor Movement • International Ladies' Auxiliary • Brotherhood of Sleeping Car Porters • League of Women for Community Service • The Left • Little Rock Nine • Mississippi Freedom Democratic Party • Montgomery Bus Boycott • *Sipuel* v. *Board of Regents* • Women's Political Council, Montgomery, AL • World War II • Student Nonviolent Coordinating Committee

Biographical Entries:
Anna Arnold Hedgeman • Dorothy Height • Pauli Murray • Anne E. Moody • Constance Baker Motley • Daisy Lee Gaston Bates • Mary Fair Burks • Amelia Boynton • Kathleen Neal Cleaver • Fannie Lou Hamer • Coretta Scott King • Rosa Parks • Angela Davis • Diane Nash • Georgia Montgomery Davis Powers • Mary Modjeska Simkins • Septima Poinsette Clark • JoAnn Gibson Robinson • Barbara Jordan • Hajj Bahiyah Betty Shabazz

May 27, 1997

8. Disclosures and Disruptions: Being and Becoming Black

Readings:
Combahee River Collective • Feminism in the Twentieth Century • Sexual Harassment • National Black Sister's Conference • National Welfare Rights Movement • National Political Congress of Black Women • Physicians • Twentieth Century • Social Welfare Movement • Womanist Theology

Biographical Entries:

Johnnetta Betsch Cole • Niara Sudarkasa • Barbara Harris • Byllye Y. Avery • Jewell Jackson McCabe • Faye Wattleton • Marian Wright Edelman • Marva N. Collins • Julie Dash • Koko Taylor • Flo Kennedy ● Writers: Maya Angelou • Toni Cade Bambara • Gwendolyn Brooks • Lorraine Vivian Hansberry • Audre Lorde • June Jordan • Gayle Jones • Toni Morrison • Terry McMillan • Gloria Naylor • Sonia Sanchez • Ntozake Shange • Alice Walker

JUNE 3, 1997

9. Contemporary Narratives in Light of the Past

Readings: Black Studies • Essence Magazine • Fashion Industry • Rap Musicians • Sports • Television

Biographical Entries:
Leanita McClain • Barbara Brandon • Patrice Rushen • Florence Griffith Joyner • Jackie Joyner-Kersee • Betye Saar • Debbie Allen • Barbara Ann Teer • Oprah Winfrey • Vanessa Lynn Williams • Terry McMillan

29.344/644 Topics in Jewish History:
American Jewish Women's History

Required texts:

1. *American Jewish History* vol 83, no. 2 (June 1995). Special issue on American Jewish women.
2. Rose Cohen. *Out of the Shadow: A Russian Jewish Girlhood on the Lower East Side.*
3. Sara Evans, *Born for Liberty.*
4. Paula E. Hyman. *Gender and Assimilation in Modern Jewish History: The Roles and Representation of Women.*
5. Susan A. Glenn, *Daughters of the Shtetl: Life and Labor in the Immigrant Generation.*
6. Sylvia Barack Fishman, *A Breath of Life: Feminism in the American Jewish Community.*
7. Ruth Markowitz, *My Daughter, the Teacher*

Undergraduate Student responsibilities:

1. Class attendance and participation, 10% of final grade. More than three absences may be grounds for failure.
2. One mid-term examination, tentatively scheduled for October 16, 25% of the final grade.
3. One paper, 30% of the final grade, due December 11.
4. Final examination, 35% of the final grade, December 18, 2:10-4:50.

Graduate Student responsibilities:
    The above plus critiques of the readings and additional class meetings.

OFFICE HOURS: 205 McCabe; Monday 11:15-12:30; Wednesday 1:15-2:00, 5:00-7:00.

PHONE and VOICE MAIL: 202-885-2425.   **E-mail:** pnadell@american.edu

General Sources:

American Jewish History, Vol. 70, September 1980 (special issue on American Jewish women's history)
C. Baum, Paula Hyman, & Sonya Michel, *The Jewish Woman in America*
Rudolf Glanz, *The Jewish Woman in America: Two Female Immigrant Generations, 1820-1919*, 2 vols.
The Jewish People in America, 5 volumes published by the American Jewish Historical Society and Johns Hopkins University Press, 1993.
Linda Gordon Kuzmack, *Woman's Cause: The Jewish Woman's Movement in England and the United States, 1881-1933*
Dianne Licthenstein, *Writing their Nations: The Tradition of Nineteenth-Century American Jewish Women Writers*

Lilith: The Jewish Women's Magazine
Jacob Marcus, ed. *The American Jewish Woman: A Documentary History*
June Sochen, *Consecrate Every Day: The Public Lives of Jewish American Women,*
    1880-1980

SYLLABUS

9-4   Introduction
        Jewish Women in Colonial America and The Early Republic
        Sara Evans, *Born for Liberty*, 21-66

9-11   "German" Jewish Women Experience America

        1. Migration and Settlement
           Evans, *Born for Liberty*, 67-118; Paula Hyman, *Gender and
           Assimilation in Modern Jewish History*, 3-49

        2. "Mothers in Israel": Jewish Domesticity
           Evans, *Born for Liberty*, 119-44.

9-18   3. Religion
           a. The *Mitzvah* of good deeds
              Dianne Ashton, "Crossing Boundaries: The career of
              Mary M. Cohen," *American Jewish History* 83 (June
              1995): 153-76.
9-25   b. Changing role of women in the American Reform synagogue
           c. National Council of Jewish Women
              Seth Korelitz, "'A Magnificent Piece of Work': The
              Americanization Work of the National Council of Jewish
              Women," *American Jewish History* 83 (June 1995): 176-
              203.

        East European Immigrant Women and their Daughters

10-2   1. In the world that is no more
           Hyman, *Gender and Assimilation*, 50-93; Susan Glenn,
           Daughters of the Shtetl, 8-49
10-9   2. Migration and settlement
           Glenn, *Daughters of the Shtetl*, 50-89; Rose Cohen. *Out of
           the Shadow*, ix-65

10-16   **MIDTERM**

10-23   3. Family life: negotiating the adaptation to abundance
           Cohen, *Out of the Shadow*, 69-313, Hyman, *Gender and
           Assimilation*, 93-133.

10-30   4. Work and the Unions
           Glenn, *Daughters of the Shtetl*, 90-242

11-6   5. Making a New and Better World
           a. Neighborhood politics
           b. Suffrage

        c. The Left
           Ruth Markowitz, *My Daughter, The Teacher*, all

11-13   6. Religious Life
          Shuly Rubin Schwartz, "'We Married What We Wanted to Be:'
          The *Rebbetzin* in Twentieth-Century America;" Norma Baumel
          Joseph, "Jewish Education for Women: Rabbi Moshe Feinstein's
          Map of America," *American Jewish History* 83 (June 1995):
          205-46.

        At Home in America

11-20   1. Middle-Class Domesticity and the Sexual Politics of Jewish
        Identity
          Hyman, *Gender and Assimilation*, 134-49; Evans, *Born for
          Liberty*, 243-86
11-27   2. Feminism
        a. Impact upon the Jewish Community
          Sylvia Barack Fishman, *A Breath of Life*, 1-120;
          Susanne Klingenstein, "'But My Daughters Can Read the
          Torah': Careers of Jewish Women in Literary Academe,"
          American Jewish History 83 (June 1995): 247-86.
12-4   b. Jewish Feminism and Feminist Judaism
          Fishman, *A Breath of Life*, 121-29

12-11   Catch-up day

12-18   **FINAL EXAMINATION** 2:10-4:40

Professor Vicki L. Ruiz
Office: Women's Studies Program
Office Hours: M/T 1-3
or by appointment
965-3656
vruiz@asuvm.inre.asu.edu

WOMEN'S STUDIES 494/HISTORY 494

CONQUESTS AND MIGRATIONS: MEXICAN WOMEN IN THE UNITED STATES

This class offers an overview of Chicana history from Mesoamerican
origins to the present, focusing on the contributions of Mexican
women to the development of the region now known as the American
West. Decades, even centuries, before the famed covered wagons
rolled across the prairies and deserts, mestizo peoples, citizens
of New Spain (and later Mexico) ventured north. They established
presidios, missions, pueblos, and ranchos. This course relates the
history of these mestizo pioneers, their interaction with American
Indians and EuroAmerican newcomers, as well as the transformation
of their society following the Texas Revolution and the U.S.-
Mexican War. By 1900 one hundred thousand Mexican Americans lived
in the Southwest. By 1930, over one million Mexicanos (one-eighth
of Mexico's population) migrated northward. They settled into
existing barrios and created new communities in the Southwest and
Midwest. For the twentieth century, specific topics to be
explored include immigration, folklore, labor, gender roles,
community organizations, and politics. This class examines Mexican
women as historical actors in the economic and cultural development
of the southwestern United States as well as an examination of the
distinctive regional and generational variations within the
nation's second largest group of color.

I believe in atmosphere of discovery and discussion. This course
should be akin to an archeological dig where teacher and students
together excavate a forgotten, buried past. In addition to
dispelling prevalent myths and misconceptions concerning Mexican
Americans and their history, I attempt to establish an environment
for critical thinking, challenging students to grapple with the
complexities of history and to recover the rich legacy of Mexicans
in the United States. I emphasize a public history approach in
which students learn oral history techniques and make a site visit
to the Heard Museum.

REQUIRED READINGS

David Weber, <u>Foreigners In Their Native Land: Historical Roots of Mexican Americans</u>

Arnoldo De León, <u>Mexican Americans in Texas: A Brief History</u>

Adela de la Torre and Beatríz Pesquera, <u>Building With Our Hands: New Directions in Chicana Studies</u>

Tey Diana Rebolledo and Eliana S. Rivero, eds. <u>Infinite Divisions: An Anthology of Chicana Literature</u>

Patricia Preciado Martin, <u>Songs My Mother Sang For Me: An Oral History of Mexican American Women</u>

Vicki L. Ruiz, <u>Cannery Women, Cannery Lives</u>

Albert Camarillo, <u>Chicanos in California</u>

ON RESERVE:
Ramón Ruiz, ed., <u>The Mexican War: Was It Manifest Destiny?</u>

MEDIA PRESENTATIONS

<u>Seguin</u>
<u>Ballad of an Unsung Hero</u>
<u>Lemon Grove Incident</u>
<u>Huelga</u>
<u>Adelante Mujeres</u>

Week 1
1/16   Introduction
        Instructions for "Representations" Assignment
        Mesoamerican Society

1/18   Colonial Mexico/Expeditions North
        Reading assignment: Weber, 23-50
                            De León, pp. 5-18

Week 2
1/23   Indio/Genízaro/Mestizo
        Reading assignment: Weber, 88-137
                            de la Torre y Pesquera, 15-33

Week 3
1/30   Missions, Mines, and Myth
        "Representations" Assignment Due

2/1   Frontier Mexican Society
        Reading assignment: Weber, 52-86
                            de la Torre y Pesquera, 91-108,
                                                    217-231
Week 4
2/4   Field Trip to the Heard Museum, 1 p.m.
2/6   The Black Legend/The Frontier Dilemma
        Reading assignment: Weber, 52-86
                            de la Torre y Pesquera, 75-90

2/8   The Texas Revolution and U.S.-Mexican War
        Film: Seguin
        Reading assignment: Ramón Ruiz, 1-61
                            Weber, 140-182
                            De León, 19-33
Week 5
2/13   The Gold Rush and Beyond
        Reading assignment: Ramón Ruiz, 62-118

2/15   The Development of the Southwest
        Reading assignment: Weber, 204-240
                            De León, 34-49

Week 6
2/20   The 19th Century Mexican American Family
        Instructions for Folklore Project
        Reading assignment: Rebolledo and Rivero, 1-41

2/22   Midterm Examination

254

```
Week 7
2/27      Oral History Methodology
          Film: Ballad of an Unsung Hero
          Instructions for Oral History Project
          Reading assignment: Begin Songs My Mother Sang For Me

2/29      Border Journeys
          Reading assignment: De León, 50-94

Week 8
3/5       Americanization and the Mexican Immigrant
          Reading assignment: de la Torre y Pesquera, 109-129

3/7       Rural Life in New Mexico and Arizona
          Reading assignment: Conclude Songs My Mother Sang For Me

                        SPRING BREAK
Week 9
3/19      Cultural Traditions
          Folklore Project Due
          Reading assignment: Rebolledo and Rivero, 41-74, 195-271,
                                                           307-340
3/21      The Mexican American Generation
          Reading assignment: Vicki Ruiz, 3-39

Week 10
3/26      Nativism and The Great Depression
          Reading assignment: De León, 95-107
                              Camarillo, California, 32-57

3/28      Women, Children and Civil Rights
          Film: The Lemon Grove Incident
          Reading assignment: Vicki Ruiz, 40-57

Week 11
4/2       Zoot Suits and Finger Tip Coats
          Reading assignment: Camarillo, California, 58-84

4/4       Unions and Community Politics
          Film: Huelga
          Reading assignment: Vicki Ruiz, 69-123
                              De León, 108-121

Week 12
4/9       The Chicano Movement
          Reading assignment: Camarillo, California, 85-103
                              De León, 108-121

4/11      La Nueva Chicana
          Reading assignment: Rebolledo and Rivero, 78-156, 276-304
                              de la Torre y Pesquera, 34-56
```

Week 13
4/16   The Politics of Work and Family
            Film: Adelante Mujeres
            Reading assignment: de la Torre y Pesquera, 168-216

4/18   Building Community Through Work, Church, and Neighborhood
            Reading assignment: Camarillo, 104-113

Week 14
4/23   The U.S.-Mexican Border: A View From El Paso
            Reading assignment: De León, 136-145

4/25   Memories, Media, and Maquildadoras
            Reading assignment: "Cuca" (class hand-out)

Week 15
4/30   American Dreams/Economic Realities
            Oral History Project Due

COURSE EXPECTATIONS

I will not grade on the curve. Each assignment will be evaluated
on its own merits, using the scale outlined below:

90-100 A
80-89   B
70-79   C
60-69   D
0-59   F

The final course grade will be based on the following:

20% Midterm
20% Final
25% Oral History Project
10% Representations Paper
15% Folklore Essay and Presentation
10% Class Participation (includes in-class discussions
                         and writing projects)

Midterm Examination

The in-class midterm examination will contain both short answer and
essay sections. Questions will be drawn from lectures, readings,
films, and class discussions. No make-up tests will be given
unless I receive prior notification.

Final Examination

The take-home final will consist of comprehensive essay questions, the answers must reflect original thought, not simply a regurgitation of lectures and readings. It will be due by Noon on the day of the final examination scheduled for Thursday, May 9th.

Oral History Project

Mexican culture has been essentially an oral culture with corridos y cuentos transmitted verbally from generation to generation. Oral history provides a window to another person's experiences and emotions not only in terms of family history but also in relation to community and international events. Studs Terkel recently won a Pulitzer Prize for his book, The Good War: An Oral History of World War Two, an honor which represents the coming of age for tape-recorded interviews as legitimate historical sources. Recovering "voices" enriches our understanding of Mexican American history and helps us separate realities from stereotypes. For this course, the student will be required to conduct a one hour life history interview with a Mexican American woman over the age of forty and to turn in the tape, edited transcript, and a contextual essay. The interviewee may have been born in the United States or Mexico. The only criterion is that she has lived in the United States for more than five years. Two students may interview a single person as a team. Guides on interview techniques and strategies will be distributed on February 27th. This assignment will be graded on the quality of the interview and the contextual essay. The essay (six to eight pages) should produce a portrait of the interviewee--age, nativity, religion, education, family life, and work experience. More importantly, it should relate the person's life to events and themes in twentieth century Mexican American history. Students who choose to interview as a team may collaborate on the transcript, but turn in separate, individual essays. The combined length of the transcript and essay range from 20 to 25 pages. An analytical research paper of similar length may be substituted for this assignment in consultation with the instructor. It will be due on the last day of class, April 30th.

Representations Paper

Each student will be assigned a particular book or article housed at Hayden Library. She/He will be asked to examine the representations of Mexicans in the text and to write a three page report summarizing her/his findings. This evaluation must contain three basic components: 1) author's interpretation, 2) types of evidence, and 3) student evaluation. Complete instructions will be given on January 16th. Project is due January 30th.

Folklore Essay and Presentation

Mexicans in the United States have rich cultural traditions encompassing both public celebrations and private beliefs. From the commercialized Cinco de Mayo fiestas to home altars, folkways

frequently reinforce ethnic identity and provide insight into
cultural values and world views. For this assignment, you will
select an example of Mexican or Mexican American folklore. You may
utilize materials at the Hayden Library. If you have difficulty
locating a document, please see me during office hours so I can
direct you to the appropriate resources. You also have the option
of interviewing relatives and friends for this project. The essay
should be three pages in length and you should prepare a brief (5-
10 minute) oral presentation. Audio-visual aids, such as posters
and slides, may be used to highlight written materials for display
during in-class discussion. Complete instructions will be given on
February 20th. Project is due March 19th.

In-Class Writing Projects

The in-class writing assignments will be short "think" pieces in
which students have the opportunity to form their own
interpretations of materials presented. It is _very_ important to
complete the assigned readings before coming to class. Do not fall
behind or plan to catch up on the required reading the week before
the midterm or the final.

Attendance Policy

Regular attendance is mandatory.

Bibliography

Mexican American History To 1900

Rodolfo Acuña, Occupied America: A History of Chicanos, 3rd ed.
Tomás Almaguer, Racial Fault Lines
John Bannon, The Spanish Borderlands Frontier, 1513-1821
Richard Bauman and Roger Abrahams, eds. And Other Neighborly Names:
Social Process and Cultural Image in Texas Folklore
Albert Camarillo and Pedro Castillo, eds., Furia y Muerte
Carlos Castañeda, The Mexican Side of the Texas Revolution
John Walton Caughey, The California Gold Rush
Inga Clendinnen, Ambivalent Conquests: Maya and Spaniard in the
Yucatan
Hernando Cortés, Five Letters of Cortés to the Emperor
Rupert Costo and Jeannette Henry Costo, The Missions of California
Rebecca Craver, The Impact of Intimacy: Mexican-Anglo Intermarriage
in New Mexico, 1821-1846
Arnoldo De León, The Tejano Community
Arnoldo De León, They Called them Greasers: Anglo American
Attitudes Toward Mexicans in Texas, 1821-1900
Sarah Deutsch, No Separate Refuge: Culture, Class, and Gender on
the Anglo-Hispanic Frontier in the American Southwest, 1880-1940
Bernal Diaz, The Conquest of New Spain
Nancie González, The Spanish Americans of New Mexico
Richard Griswold del Castillo, The Los Angeles Barrio: A Social
History

258

Richard Griswold del Castillo, La Familia
Ramón Gutiérrez, When Jesus Came, the Corn Mothers Went Away
Neal Harlow, California Conquered
Robert Heizer and Alan Almquist, eds., The Other Californians
Gilberto Hinojosa, A Borderlands Town in Transition: Laredo, 1755-1870
Joan Jensen and Darlis Miller, eds., New Mexico Women: Intercultural Perspectives
Robert Johanssen, From The Halls of Moctezuma
Pat Kelley, Rivers of Lost Dreams: Navigation on the Rio Grande
David Langum, Law and Community on the Mexican California Frontier
Jacqueline Phillips Lathrop, Ancient Mexico
Miguel León-Portilla, Aztec Thought and Culture
Miguel León-Portilla, The Broken Spears
Patricia Limerick, Legacy of Conquest
Walter Lord, A Time to Stand
Carey McWilliams, North From Mexico
D.W. Meinig, Southwest: Three Peoples in Geographical Change
Frederick Merk, Manifest Destiny and Mission in American History
Alfredo Mirandé and Evangelina Enríquez, La Chicana
Eduardo Matos Moctezuma, The Great Temples of the Aztecs
Jay Monaghan, Chile, Peru, and the California Gold Rush of 1849
Douglas Monroy, Thrown Among Strangers
Roxanne Dunbar Ortiz, Roots of Resistance
James Officer, Hispanic Arizona
Michael Ornelas, Between The Conquests: Readings in Early Chicano History
Americo Paredes, With Pistol In His Hand
Octavio Paz, Sor Juana
Leonard Pitt, Decline of the Californios
Glenn Price, Origins of the War with Mexico
Antonio Ríos-Bustamante, An Illustrated History of Mexican Los Angeles, 1781-1985
George Lockhart Rives, The United States and Mexico, 1821-1848
Cecil Robinson, With Ears of Strangers--the Mexican in American Literature
Robert Rosenbaum, History of Mexican Americans in Texas
Robert Rosenbaum, Mexicano Resistance in the Southwest
Lillian Schlissel, Vicki L. Ruiz, and Janice Monk, eds., Western Women: Their Land, Their Lives
Thomas Sheridan, Los Tucsonenses
Jacques Soustelle, Daily Life of the Aztecs
Edward Spicer, Cycles of Conquest. The Impact of Spain, Mexico, and the Untied States on Indians of the Southwest
Frances Swadesh, Los Primeros Pobladores
James Diego Vigil, From Indians to Chicanos
David Weber, ed., Spain's Northern Frontier
Eric Wolf, Sons of the Shaking Earth

Mexican American History Since 1900

David Abalos, Latinos in the United States: The Sacred and the Political
Rudy Acuña, A Community Under Siege: A Chronicle of Chicanos East of the Los Angeles River
Robert Alvarez, Familia: Migration and Adaptation in Baja and Alta California, 1800-1975
Gloria Anzaldúa and Cherrie Moraga, This Bridge Called My Back
Gloria Anzaldúa, Making Face, Making Soul
Francisco Balderrama, In Defense of La Raza
Francisco Balderrama and Raymond Rodríguez, Decade of Betrayal
Mario Barrera, Race and Class in the Southwest
Fran Leeper Buss, Forged Under The Sun: The Life of María Elena Lucas
Ted Conover, Coyotes
Carlos Cortes, ed., Church Views of the Mexican American
Adelaida Del Castillo, Between Borders: Essays on Mexicana/Chicana History
Hector Delgado, New Immigrants, Old Unions
Sarah Deutsch, No Separate Refuge: Culture, Class, and Gender on the Anglo-Hispanic Frontier in the American Southwest, 1880-1940
Nan Elasser, Kyle MacKenzie, and Yvonne Tixier y Vigil, Las Mujeres: Conversations with a Hispanic Community
Raul Fernandez, The Mexican American Border Region
Ernesto Galarza, Barrio Boy
Ernesto Galarza, Merchants of Labor
Manuel Gamio, Life Story of the Mexican Immigrant
Chris García, La Causa Politica: A Chicano Politics Reader
Chris García, Latinos and the Political System
Juan García, Operation Wetback
Mario García, Desert Immigrants: The Mexicans of El Paso
Mario García, Mexican Americans: Leadership, Ideology, and Identity
Richard García, Rise of the Mexican American Middle Class
Juan Gómez-Quiñones, Chicano Politics
Gilbert González, Labor and Community
Juan González, Mexican and Mexican American Farm Workers
Beatrice Griffith, American Me
Richard Griswold del Castillo, Cesar Chávez
Camille Guerin-Gonzales, Mexican Workers, American Dreams
David Gutiérrez, Walls and Mirrors: Mexican Americans, Mexican Immigrants, and the Politics of Ethnicity
María Herrera Sobek, Northward Bound
Abraham Hoffman, Unwanted Mexican Americans
Norris Hundley, ed., The Chicano
Nicolás Kanellos, A History of Hispanic Theatre in the United States
Barbara Kingsolver, Holding The Line
Alan Knight, The Mexican Revolution
Sam Kushner, Long Road to Delano
Louise Lamphere and Patricia Zavella, Sunbelt Working Mothers
James B. Lane and Edward Escobar, eds., Forging A Community: The Latino Experience in Northwest Indiana
Jacques Levy, Cesar Chavez: Autobiography of La Causa

Carey McWilliams, _Factories in the Fields_
Carey McWilliams, _North From Mexico_
Patricia Preciado Martin and Louis C. Bernal, _Images and Conversations: Mexican Americans Recall a Southwestern Past_
Marguerite Marin, _Social Protest in an Urban Barrio_
Mauricio Mazón, _The Zoot Suit Riots: The Psychology of Symbolic Annihilation_
Alfredo Mirandé and Evangelina Enríquez, _La Chicana_
Magdalena Mora and Adelaida Del Castillo, eds., _Mexican Women in the United States: Struggles Past and Present_
Raul Morín, _Among The Valiant_
Thomas J. Noel, _The WPA Guide to 1930s Colorado_
Amado Padilla and Susan Keefe, _Chicano Ethnicity_
Americo Paredes, _A Texas-Mexican Cancionero: Folksongs of the Lower Border_
Americo Paredes, _With Pistol In His Hand_
Mary Helen Ponce, _Hoyt Street_
Dick Reavis, _Without Documents_
Tey Diana Rebolledo, _Women Singing in the Snow: A Cultural Analysis of Chicana Literature_
Mark Reisler, _By The Sweat of their Brow_
Antonio Ríos-Bustamante and Pedro Castillo, _An Illustrated History of Mexican Los Angeles, 1781-1985_
Gregorita Rodríguez, _Singing For My Echo: Memories of a Native Healer of Santa Fe_
Richard Rodriguez, _Hunger of Memory_
Ricardo Romo, _East Los Angeles: history of a barrio_
Vicki L. Ruiz and Susan Tiano, eds., _Women on the U.S. Mexico Border_
George Sánchez, _Becoming Mexican American: Ethnicity, Culture and Identity in Chicano Los Angeles, 1900-1945_
Rosaura Sanchez and Rosa Martínez, _Essays on la Mujer_
Lillian Schlissel, Vicki L. Ruiz, and Janice Monk, eds., _Western Women: Their Land, Their Lives_
John Schockley, _Chicano Revolt in a Texas Town_
John Steinbeck, _Their Blood is Strong_
Chris Strachwitz, _Lydia Mendoza_
Richard Streeter, _Organizing for Our Lives_
Paul Taylor, _Mexican Labor in the United States_
Ruth Tuck, _Not With a Fist_
Armando Valdez, Albert Camarillo, and Tomás Almaguer, eds., _The State of Chicano Research in Family, Labor, and Migration Studies_
Zaragoza Vargas, _Proletarians of the North: A History of Mexican Industrial Workers in Detroit and the Midwest, 1917-1933_
Devra Weber, _Dark Sweat, White Gold_
Emilio Zamora, _The World of the Mexican Workers in Texas_
Patricia Zavella, _Women's Work and Chicano Families_

Professor Vicki L. Ruiz
Office: Women's Studies Program
Office Hours: T 3-5/W 1-3
or by appointment
965-3656
vruiz@asuvm.inre.asu.edu

HISTORY 598

MEXICAN AMERICAN WOMEN

This graduate readings course explores Chicana history from the Spanish Borderlands to the present, focusing on patterns of conquests and migrations. Specific topics to be explored include immigration, folklore, labor, gender roles, community organizations, literature, and politics. It emphasizes Mexican women as historical actors in the economic and cultural development of the southwestern United States as well as an examination of the distinctive regional and generational variations within the nation's second largest group of color. Course requirements involve weekly book precés, in-class oral presentation, ten to twelve page primary research project, and nine page research proposal.

REQUIRED READINGS:

Adela de la Torre and Beatríz Pesquera, eds., Building With Our Hands: New Directions in Chicana Studies

Ramón Gutiérrez, When Jesus Came, the Corn Mothers Went Away: Power and Sexuality in New Mexico, 1500-1846

Sarah Deutsch, No Separate Refuge: Culture, Class, and Gender on an Anglo Hispanic Frontier in the American Southwest, 1880-1940

Patricia Preciado Martin, Songs My Mother Sang to Me: An Oral History of Mexican American Women

Vicki Ruiz, Cannery Women, Cannery Lives

Mary Helen Ponce, Hoyt Street

Fran Leeper Buss, ed. Forged Under the Sun: The Life of María Elena Lucas

Pierette Hondagneu-Sotelo, Gendered Transitions: Mexican Experiences of Immigration

Tey Diana Rebolledo and Eliana Rivero, eds. Infinite Divisions: An Anthology of Chicana Literature

LUISA MORENO CENTER FOR LATINA RESEARCH
DISSERTATION FELLOWSHIP

PROPOSAL GUIDELINES

Application deadline: December 17, 1996

All proposals must contain the following elements:

1. Cover sheet including applicant's name, title of project, and a 200-250 word abstract of the proposal.

2. A description of the proposed study following the guidelines listed below (taken from the **NEH** fellowship application guidelines):

> The proposal is the only demonstration that panelists will have of the substance of the project, the contribution it can make to humanities scholarship, and its general quality. It is essential that the text include enough detail about the ideas, objectives, and methods entailed in the project to enable panelists to assess quality, significance, and feasibility. A simple statement of need or intent is insufficient evidence that a project merits support. Some reviewers will not possess specialized knowledge of the proposed field of study; therefore the description should be free of jargon and, as much as possible, technical terms.

Although no particular form is prescribed, the description of the project should address the questions listed below. The text should not exceed 3,000 words (six normal double spaced pages).

a. What are the basic ideas, problems, works, or questions the study will examine?

b. How does the project relate to the historiographic tradition pertinent to the topic? What new insights can we expect?

c. What relevant background do you have?

d. What sources and what methodologies do you use?

e. What is your timetable for doing the work?

3. Bibliography (2 pp. maximum).

4. Budget (1 p.)

and a myriad of other items. Each student will prepare a ten to twelve page critical analysis along with a brief ten minute talk. The paper will be due on the day scheduled for presentations, November 26th.

Research Proposal

Grant writing is a skill which every historian must develop. Monies do not fall from the sky for research. Whether applying to the National Endowment for the Humanities or the ASU Women's Studies Mini-Grant Program, a scholar must craft a lucid, informative, and often compelling research proposal. Each student will be asked to craft a fictitious grant application to support some facet of study in Mexican American women's history. Instructions are attached. On the last day of class, December 10th, participants will be divided into panels for a blind peer review of their rough drafts (with no names attached). The final proposal will be due on Tuesday, December 17th at 4 p.m. Early submissions are encouraged.

Attendance
Given the time constraints of this course, attendance at every class is mandatory.

Grading

20% Class Participation (includes weekly precís)
15% Monograph Presentation
30% Primary Research Project
35% Research Proposal

Week 10
10/29   Research Day

Week 11
11/5   Feminism, Sexuality, and Mestizaje
           Reading assignment: Infinite Divisions
           Film: The Desert Is No Lady

Week 12
11/12   Women and Work
           Reading assignment: Maid in the USA

Week 13
11/19   Life Cycles
           Reading assignment: Understanding Older Chicanas

Week 14
11/26   Research Project Presentations
           Research Project Due

Week 15
12/3   Claiming Public Space
           Film: Las Mujeres

Week 16
12/10   Mascaras y Muros
           Reading assignment: Cantora
           Bring rough draft of proposal for discussion

COURSE EXPECTATIONS

The Readings

Each student will be expected to give an in-class presentation of
one monograph in which she or he discusses the author's thesis,
narrative line, evidence, and interpretation. The presentation
should not be a rehash of the book, but a thoughtful review of its
contributions to our understanding of the experiences of Mexican
American women. For every monograph, students will prepare a one
page synopsis or precís summarizing the author's major points.
Also, bring to class one scholarly review of the monograph under
discussion.

Primary Research Project

The history of Mexican women in the United States has often
remained in the shadows. As historians, our task is to recover a
past that has been buried, forgotten, and closeted. Drawing on
oral narratives, visual anthropology, folklore, or archival
materials, students will be asked to locate and interpret a primary
source. Such documents include oral histories, photographs, court
cases, corridos, newspaper articles, film representations, memoirs,

Barbara Kingsolver, _Holding The Line: Women in the Great Arizona Mine Strike of 1983_

Mary Romero, _Maid in the USA_

Sylvia López-Medina, _Cantora_

Elisa Facio, _Understanding Older Chicanas_

COURSE OUTLINE

Week 1
8/27   Introduction
             Instructions for Primary Research Project and Proposal
             Film: _Salt of the Earth_

Week 2
9/2   Mosaic of Lived Experiences
             Reading assignment: _Building With Our Hands_
             Potluck Barbecue at Professor Ruiz's home

Week 3
9/10   The Spanish Borderlands
             Reading assignment: _When Jesus Came_

Week 4
9/17   Gender and Village Life
             Reading assignment: _No Separate Refuge_

Week 5
9/24   Narrative Windows
             Reading assignment: _Songs My Mother Sang to Me_

Week 6
10/1   Labor History
             Reading assignment: _Cannery Women, Cannery Lives_

Week 7
10/8   Representation and Remembrance
             Reading assignment: _Hoyt Street_

Week 8
10/15   Migrant Journeys
             Reading assignment: _Forged Under the Sun_

Week 9
10/22   The Public/Private Debate
             Reading assignment: Choose One
             Gendered Transitions or _Holding The Line_

Department of Puerto Rican Studies
Puerto Rican Studies 19
Women in Puerto Rican and Latin American Societies
Professor Virginia Sánchez Korrol

Course Description:

Gender roles in different historical periods. Analysis of race, class, ethnicity and traditional roles prescribed by society and religion. Creative and ethnographic works about women who challenged traditions, social and legal constraints. Current research issues. Cultural affirmations of contemporary women in education, government, politics, the labor force, and the migration experience. Latinas in the U.S.

Readings:

Julia Alvarez. *In the Time of the Butterflies.* (Plume), 1994.

Christine Bose and Edna Acosta Belén, eds. *Women in the Latin American Development Process.* (Temple University Press), 1995.

Elizabeth Burgos-Debray, ed. *I, Rigoberta Menchú: An Indian Woman in Guatemala.* (Verso), 1984.

Marysa Navarro. "Colonial Latin America and the Caribbean," in *Restoring Women to History,* (Organization of American Historians), 1988. Xeroxed selection.

Felix V. Matos Rodríguez. "Women in Economic Roles," in "Mujeres de la Capital: Women and Urban Life in Nineteenth Century San Juan." Columbia University doctoral dissertation. Xeroxed selection.

Altagracia Ortiz, ed. *Puerto Rican Women and Work: Bridges in Transnational Labor.* (Temple University Press), 1996.

Judith Ortiz Cofer. *The Latin Deli.* (University of Georgia), 1993.

Virginia Sánchez Korrol. "Modern Latin America," in *Restoring Women to History.* (Organization of American Historians), 1988. Xeroxed selection.

Videos: (To be viewed in class)

Scraps of Life, (Gayla Jamison, filmaker). Visa for a Dream. (Sonia Fritz, filmaker). Luisa Capetillo, (Sonia Fritz, filmaker). Palante Siempre Palante (Iris Morales, filmaker).

Discussion Topics:

- Introduction to the course. Historical and geographic overview of Latin America and the Hispanic Caribbean.

- The setting and the timeframe. Historical overview of women in pre-colonial and colonial times. Issues of class, color, ethnicity, religion. Land and labor. Non-traditional and traditional roles. Convents. Patriarchy and the family. (Readings: Navarro and Rigoberta Menchú).

- Indigenous communities. Change and continuity. The *testimonio* as a historical/literary text. (Readings: Rigoberta Menchú. Video: *In Women's Hands*).

- Latin American women in the nineteenth and twentieth centuries. Labor and women's economic roles. Socio-political movements. Political and educational reforms. Repression and resistance. (Readings: Bose and Acosta-Belén. Sánchez Korrol).

- Women in nineteenth and twentieth century Puerto Rican society. Socio-cultural and political movements. Worker's organizations. Leadership and economic roles. (Readings: Matos Rodríguez; Sánchez Korrol; A. Ortiz. Video: *Luisa Capetillo*).

- History, memory and literary license. The writer as activist. (Readings: Alvarez).

- Migration, immigration and the formation of diaspora communities. Connections with homeland. Labor. Organization. Intergenerational differences. Change and continuity. (Readings: A. Ortiz; Bose and Acosta-Belén; Ortiz Cofer; Videos: *Visa for a Dream* and *Pa'lante, Siempre Pa'lante*).

Course Goals and Evaluation:

Our goals this semester include the following: (1) to understand the diversity of experience in the history of women in Puerto Rico, Latin American and the Hispanic Caribbean: (2) to facilitate integration of this history into other knowledge bases: (3) to analyze the Puerto Rican woman's experience within the Latin American/Caribbean and United States contexts: (4) to think critically about gender roles in contemporary society.

To achieve these goals we will utilize interdisciplinary texts and material created and/or written by and about U.S. Latinas, Puerto Rican, Dominican, Central and South American women. The class will also avail itself of lectures, symnposia and other events relating to Latin American/Caribbean and U.S. women taking place on campus throughout the semester.

Group discussion and participation at campus functions will form an important part of this course and will be reflected in the final grade. A mid-term exam based on class readings, a final exam and a research paper will comprise the basis for final grade.

268

DATE DUE

Women's Voices on Africa

PATRICIA W. ROMERO, EDITOR

"These personal portraits of Africa are memorable for their lively wit, compassion, and insight."   —*Publishers Weekly*

" . . . Fascinating, maddening, and chilling. . . . These writers had interesting things to say about African women and cross-cultural misunderstanding."
—*New York Times*

Among nineteenth- and early twentieth-century European "discoverers" of the "Dark Continent," women are rarely mentioned. This anthology of Victorian women's writings on Africa provides a fascinating overview of these women's roles as scholars, missionaries, adventurers, spies, and journalists, and gathers outstanding examples of their ground-breaking scholarly treatises, popular accounts, letters, articles, and thrilling adventure stories—all of them firsthand documents of women's and African history.

The writers include Mary Kingsley, famous for her ethnographic studies and travel writings, the intrepid journalists Katherine Fannin and Joan Rosita Torr Forbes, Princess Marie Louise reporting on her diplomatic mission, Jocelyn Murray, witness of the 'Mau Mau' insurrection, and numerous missionaries.

Patricia Romero, Towson State University, is the editor of *Life Histories of African Women*.

ISBN 1-55876-047-4   HARDCOVER, $39.95
ISBN 1-55876-048-2   PAPER, $14.95
298 PP., ILLUSTRATED

A Black Woman's Odyssey Through Russia and Jamaica

THE NARRATIVE OF NANCY PRINCE

Memories of Africa, pre-civil war New England, political turmoil in Russia, the end of slavery in Jamaica, and Caribbean pirates; an intrepid black woman experiences many turning points in world history.

Nancy Prince paints a blunt picture of the struggle of free blacks to make a living in the North. When Boston failed to provide her with a livable wage, she and her husband found employment on a boat bound for Russia. A black household servant was a rare commodity in the land of the czars, and Prince was well compensated in St. Petersburg.

"The author vividly describes local Russian customs, as well as her experiences of the St. Petersburg flood of 1824 and the Decembrist Revolt. She returned to America, and, becoming widowed, went to Jamaica as a missionary to the newly emancipated blacks there. But, disillusioned by the exploitation of the Jamaicans by her fellow missionaries and others, she set sail for home. This adventurous woman offers a singular perspective on the African experience in America."   —*Publishers Weekly*

Ronald Walters, professor of history at Johns Hopkins University, has contributed an introduction providing the historical backdrop to the events described by Nancy Prince.

ISBN 1-55876-028-8   HARDCOVER, $19.95
ISBN 1-55876-019-9   PAPER, $9.95
124 PP., ILLUSTRATED

A Black Woman's Civil War Memoirs
Reminiscences of My Life in Camp
SUSIE KING TAYLOR

"Susie King Taylor's recollections are invaluable for those who wish to understand the civil war from a black woman's point of view. . . . A treasure in the light of today's feminist movement. . . . They are the memoirs of a black woman who was born as a slave and had the good fortune to gain her freedom early in the war, with the education and the ability to observe, and the will to recall it years later." —Willie Lee Rose, Johns Hopkins University

"Taylor's writing is at its strongest and most vivid as she decries the betrayal of the freedom and equality blacks and whites had fought for in the Civil War." —*Publishers Weekly*

"A unique document. . . . Thanks to Willie Lee Rose's instructive introduction, Taylor's work is placed in a deserving historical context." —*Women's Review of Books*

"Quite a life—and book." —*Ms Magazine*

"A book of many surprising rewards and pleasures. It was a delight to read." —C. Vann Woodward, Yale University

Willie Lee Rose, professor emeritus at Johns Hopkins University and author of *Rehearsal for Reconstruction*, has provided a new introduction. **Patricia Romero**, of Towson State University and author of *Sylvia Pankhurst: Portrait of a Radical*, provided the annotations to the text.

ISBN 0-910129-85-1   PAPER, $9.95
160 PP., ILLUSTRATED

Women in Caribbean History

VERENE SHEPHERD, EDITOR

Early historical works portrayed women, especially those of African descent, in a sexist and racist manner. *Women in Caribbean History* embodies the progress of research on Caribbean women. It reveals new historical information on Caribbean women and provides detail on their economic, social, and political roles and activities. This book explains how the use of gender analysis can shape our understanding of Caribbean history.

This introductory reader provides students and the general reader with an accessible overview of the lives of Caribbean women of diverse ethnic origins. Even though this research focuses on enslaved black women, it also describes indigenous European, Chinese, and Indian women who lived in the English-speaking Caribbean. The work represents the desire of the Social History Project of the Department of History, University of the West Indies and Oxfam to link pre-emancipation and post-slavery history, endeavoring to go beyond the Jamaican experience.

Verene Shepherd, University of the West Indies, Jamaica, is co-editor of *Caribbean Freedom.*

ISBN 1-55876-188-8   HARDCOVER, $39.95
ISBN 1-55876-189-6   PAPER, $16.95
204 PP.   AVAILABLE JULY, 1998

About the Editor

Louise L. Stevenson is professor of history and American Studies and chair of the Women's Studies Program at Franklin and Marshall College. Her teaching and research interests center on nineteenth-century cultural and intellectual history, including women's history. Recent articles include "The Home, Books, and Reading in an Age of Commerce," in press for the forthcoming Cambridge University Press, *History of the Book in America*; "Little Women? The Female Mind at Work in Antebellum America," *History Today*, 45 (March 1995), 26–31; "Reading Circles," in *The Oxford Companion to Women's Writing in the United States* (1995), 746–49. Besides numerous articles and reviews on women's history, Stevenson has written *The Victorian Homefront: American Thought and Culture, 1860–1880* (1991) and *Scholarly Means to Evangelical Ends: The New Haven Scholars and the Transformation of Higher Learning in America, 1830–1890* (1986).

She lives with her husband and two daughters in Lancaster, Pennsylvania, where she serves her community as a trustee of the League of Women Voters of Lancaster County and of the Community Economics Foundation, which starts cooperative businesses owned and operated by formerly battered women. She is also a trustee of the James Madison Memorial Foundation.